EXPLORING THE BIBLE

EXPLORING THE BIBLE

By Owen S. Rachleff

Assistant Professor of Humanities, New York University

Abbeville Press · Publishers · New York

TO THE MEMORY OF HARRY N. ABRAMS, FATHER OF THIS BOOK

FRONTISPIECE
Hannah and Samuel by Rembrandt van Rijn
Duke of Sutherland Collection, on loan to the National Gallery of Scotland

The Publisher wishes to acknowledge the valuable assistance of Louis Chapin
in preparing the photographic material for this book.

Library of Congress Cataloging in Publication Data

Rachleff, Owen S.
    Exploring the Bible.

    Bibliography: p. 352
    Includes index.
    1. Bible—Criticism, interpretation, etc.   I.   Title.
BS511.2.R32   220.6   78–15262
ISBN 0–89659–008–9

CONTENTS

Bibles were often the treasured possessions of royalty. Here is a cameo-studded, gold-covered Book of the Gospels that belonged to Theodolinda, a peaceable Lombard queen during the restless period of the 6th and 7th centuries.

EXPLORING THE BIBLE WITH YOUR FAMILY

By the Reverend Dr. Lee A. Belford

Our roots—the way Westerners think, indeed the way we perceive and structure reality, the assumptions we make about life and justice, love and death—are based on the Judeo-Christian heritage. The common denominator of that heritage is the Bible. Our music, painting, sculpture, historical sensibility and literature were all made by people who, when not actively inspired by the Bible, were well versed in it. It has been the most available, familiar and dependable source and arbiter of intellectual, moral and spiritual ideals in the West.

There can be little dispute when it is said that the older generation knows the Bible better than the younger generation and that children soon to reach maturity know even less. Well up into the twentieth century, school texts alluded to Biblical stories and teachings that linked religious virtues with national ideals and literary values. Until recently it was the custom for the Bible to be read as part of the opening exercises in school each day, and many of the psalms were memorized. That is now a part of the past, since the Supreme Court has said that while it is perfectly proper to teach the facts about religion objectively, there are to be no religious practices in the public schools. Consequently, many teachers feel secure in talking about the scriptures of Hinduism, Buddhism and Islam and in teaching something about the myths and religious ceremonies of Africans and Native Americans—Eskimos and Indians—as indeed they must if there is to be an understanding of the peoples of this small world. But unfortunately, virtually nothing is said about the Bible—the single

The Bible has also provided the inspiration for some of the greatest music in Western culture. The great oratorios and chorales were written specifically for use in church. The crucifixion of Jesus inspired Bach's *St. Matthew Passion*. The clash between Elijah and the priests of Baal inspired Mendelssohn's *Elijah*. The encounter between Samson and Delilah and the story of Herod were the basis for operas and dramas. Music was composed so that the psalms might be sung, and anthems were created for ceremonial occasions. America's own spirituals and folk music have found in the Bible the same fountainhead of inspiration.

As for painting and sculpture, simply leaf through this book to see what glorious creations the Bible has inspired. When your children look at the works of

Although United States law is based firmly on separation of church and state, many American ideals of freedom enshrined in the Declaration of Independence derive from the Bible.

most influential book in the development of Western culture.

One of the greatest single documents of which man can boast is the American Declaration of Independence. The idea behind "We hold these truths to be self-evident; that each person has a right to life, liberty and the pursuit of happiness . . ." has its genesis in the Bible. The idea of individual freedom, the freedom of each person to choose his own fate in relation to God, appearing first in the story of the Garden of Eden, permeates the Bible thereafter. The Declaration of Independence was by no means an inevitable historic document, but if Western man had not struggled with the concept of free will in relation to his God, we might not have had our Declaration and liberties.

Johann Sebastian Bach composed *The St. Matthew Passion* in 1728. This page, written in the composer's own hand, shows the Evangel's narration describing the death of Jesus.

Edward Villella and the New York City Ballet dance the frenzy of "riotous living" (see Luke 15:13) in the 1960 premiere of George Balanchine's *Prodigal Son*, based on the Biblical story.

Leonardo da Vinci, Rembrandt, Raphael, Michelangelo and hundreds of other artists they will have a richer and deeper experience if the Bible is part of that knowledge. Indeed, the Bible was so important to the artists of the Renaissance that today we cannot fully appreciate their work without reference to Scripture.

This book also contains many photographs from archaeological findings. Archaeology is so important to contemporary Bible study that a few words need to be said about it.

Mendelssohn's oratorio *Elijah* is directly based on Scripture. The prophet's fiery ascent forms the climax of this famous musical work, composed in 1845-46.

The key to the deciphering of ancient Egyptian was the Rosetta Stone discovered in 1799. It is inscribed in Greek and two versions of Egyptian, hieroglyphic and the everyday demotic script.

Biblical Archaeology

Throughout the Bible there are references to various neighbors of ancient Israel, some friendly but most of them hostile. What were they like, and what were their cultural institutions? How did the people live day by day? What did they consider important, and how did they relate to the Hebrew people? If we could answer questions like that, we would also learn more about our own past. We once thought the questions would never be answered. Then we began to dig up the past and through this interest in archaeology soon learned to decipher inscriptions that we thought would always be a mystery. Since 1822 we have been able to read Egyptian hieroglyphics that are midway between picture and letter/word (alphabet) writing, which means that we know more about ancient Egypt than the Egyptians of 2,500 years ago, for by then they no longer used hieroglyphics and had forgotten how to read them. The Mesopotamians used wedge-shaped (cuneiform) indentations made of soft clay subsequently hardened by baking. We have found so many thousands of them that not all have yet been translated. In 1854 a huge collection of tablets was discovered in the library of the Assyrian king Ashurbanipal. For the first time we were able to read the Gilgamesh epic, which has an account of a great flood that bears some similarities to Noah's flood. In 1887 tablets were found at Tel el Amarna in Egypt that mention the Hebrew people, thereby giving us an extra source of Biblical information. We believe

The Assyrian version of a portion of the Gilgamesh epic, dealing with a flood similar to the one described in Genesis 7, is inscribed in this clay fragment.

we know something of the pharaoh under whom Joseph served and also of the pharaoh who reigned at the time of the exodus from Egypt under Moses. From Mesopotamia we learned of the highly developed legal system, epitomized in the Code of Hammurabi, which bears some relationship to the legal codes of the Hebrew people. We have located the huge ziggurats that are suggestive of the Tower of Babel. We know something of the god Dagon, worshiped by the Philistines, and of Ashtoreth, the widely worshiped fertility goddess. The Hebrew opposition to idolatry was not merely theoretical; it was practical because these gods were actively worshiped, and this worship was the source of political enmity.

Critics of the Bible once thought that the depicted size of Solomon's kingdom was an exaggeration, but archaeological evidence substantiates the Biblical statement. In addition, we now understand that Solomon's huge number of wives and concubines indicates the number of treaties he had with neighboring kingdoms and tribes. It was customary when a king made a treaty with a neighboring ruler for him to marry the ruler's daughter; thus she became more a hostage than a wife, a guarantee that the treaty would not be broken. The daughter of a tribal chieftain or sheik was received as a concubine, again to serve as a hostage. These new discoveries have served to corroborate the facts presented in the Bible and to give us a greater understanding of their meaning.

The Bible has also served as a geological map. The references to King Solomon's copper mines were finally taken seriously, and several decades ago they were located and mined by modern engineers. The references to the fire and brimstone rained

So that his laws would be widely known, Hammurabi had them set up in public places. Carved in this 7-foot slab of diorite are 282 laws. At the top Hammurabi stands before the sun god Shamash, one of the Mesopotamian idols.

Linking the Old and New Testaments, this 13th-century miniature from a luxuriant German Psalter shows Paradise with Jesus seated in the lap of Abraham.

upon the people of Sodom and Gomorrah led to a place where natural gas and oil were discovered. The descriptions of certain mountain passes led to their rediscovery and functional use. Plants and flowers that once flourished in Biblical times give promise as to what will grow in modern Israel. Although the Bible is not about science or anthropology or geology or geography, it contains accurate data in all these fields. What a shame to miss out on these wonderful bits of knowledge through ignorance of the Bible! What a gap in education, culture, even in everyday affairs!

Someone noted that there are almost 500 Biblical quotations or references in one year in *The New York Times*. Surely these and more are sufficient reasons to make sure your child gets to know the Bible. Only you can guarantee this desired end.

There is even more to gather than insight into one's own cultural heritage. The Bible has been significant in the development of other cultures as well. Islam, the newest of the world's major religions, accepts the Bible. Mohammed declared that his followers were descendants of Abraham through Ishmael and listed the great prophets as Adam, Noah, Abraham, Moses and Jesus, with himself as the last, or "seal," of the prophets.

How We Got Our Bible

The Bible is a collection of many documents written by many different persons, in many different centuries and in many different situations. We know something of certain authors, very little about others and absolutely nothing about some.

The Old Testament is the Bible of Judaism and portrays God's relation to Israel. The Apocrypha is also about God's relation to Israel, but because some of the books of the Apocrypha were late in authorship, a council of rabbis, meeting about A.D. 90, decided to exclude them from Holy Scripture. However, when St. Jerome was translating the Bible from Greek into Latin in the fourth century, he included the Apocryphal books as part of the Old Testament. He noted that they should not be the basis for doctrine but should be read as "an example of life and for instruction in manners." Most Protestants put the Apocrypha in a separate section or exclude it altogether.

The New Testament is, of course, the

IMPORTANT DATES IN BIBLE DEVELOPMENT

B.C. 1300–165	Hebrews set down Old Testament on scrolls
250–50	First translation of Hebrew Bible into Greek—the Septuagint
A.D. 50–150	Writing of the New Testament
c. 400	St. Jerome's Latin translation of the entire Bible—the Vulgate
700–900	Old Testament finalized by Jewish scholars called Massoretes (official Hebrew text)
1382	First English Bible by Wycliffe
1455	First version of Vulgate printed by Gutenberg
1525–30	First printed English text revised by Tyndale
1539	First authorized English version—the Great Bible
1582–1610	The Douay Catholic version in English
1560	The Geneva Bible—Protestant version used by Pilgrims in America
1611	The King James Version in England

After this point, new versions and translations were frequently made of all the above. The most famous are:

1881–85	English Revised Standard Version of the King James Bible
1901	U.S. Revised Standard Version of the King James Bible—with amendments in 1952 and 1965
1952	Confraternity Version (based on Douay and on original sources) for U.S. Catholics
1961	The New English Bible (British colloquial)
1976	The Good News Bible (American colloquial)

NOTE: *All early dates are approximate.*

basis of Christianity. It is impossible for the Christian to understand the New Testament without knowledge of the Old Testament, for Jesus and his early followers were all Jews, thoroughly steeped in Jewish thought and tradition. Jews also should be familiar with the New Testament, even though they do not accept Jesus as the Messiah, simply because the New Testament has been so influential in the development of Western culture.

Much of the early material we have in the Bible was transmitted orally before it was written. In ancient days the telling of a tale was considered the most accurate way of presenting what really happened. Even among Bedouin tribes today, men assemble to hear the stories of the past and ancient myths and legends recited. If the teller leaves out a single word or adds one, he is disgraced, because everyone present knows the account and insists on absolute accuracy. The accounts of the Garden of Eden, of Cain and Abel, of the Flood, of the Tower of Babel and of the early fortunes of mankind were transmitted orally, as were the stories of the fathers of Israel—Abraham, Isaac, Jacob and many other important figures. Although the stories were passed on in perfect sequence, the chronology is sometimes askew. For example, it is probable that the Israelites did not settle in Egypt until about 1500 B.C., and yet we are told that Joseph was the great-grandson of Abraham. This discrepancy need not bother us; Joseph is at least a spiritual great-grandson. Beginning about the time of David, court chronicles were written, and around 850 B.C. these were integrated with oral accounts and other materials, eventually forming one of the oldest and greatest histories of a people—the Holy Bible.

After sacred writings have long been used in a religious community, they are often given a seal of approval and are referred to as canonical. The first five books of the Bible, the Pentateuch, also referred to as the Torah or "law," were the first books of the Bible to become canonical. We are told that Ezra and Nehemiah (537–533 B.C.) expounded the "law." We have no reason to assume that anything was added or taken away from the Pentateuch of their time. Of course, the Jews had other books that spoke to them of God, and here we refer specifically to the books of prophets and the narratives that continue the history of Israel. These also eventually achieved canonical status. Jesus refers to "The Law and the Prophets," indicating that they had achieved a stable form by his lifetime. The third collection of Biblical writings includes the Psalms, Proverbs, Job and texts read at annual festivals, such as Lamentations and Esther, as well as additional histories such as Ezra, Nehemiah and Chronicles. Referred to as "the writings," they were not canonized until A.D. 90. However, there is no reason for anyone to question that David was the author of most of the psalms attributed to him and that the tradition of wise sayings or proverbs goes back to Solomon. So although the actual canonization came late, much of the material is quite ancient.

When Jerome in the fourth century translated the Bible from Greek into Latin, a version called the Vulgate because it was in the common (or vulgar) language of the people, his primary source for the Old Testament was the Septuagint, which includes material not found in the Hebrew Bible. The Septuagint gets its name from the ancient legend that King Ptolemy Philadelphus of Egypt, having heard that the

IMPORTANT DATES IN BIBLICAL HISTORY

B.C.

3000–2000	Egyptians pyramids built The Ziggurat of Ur is built
2000–1800	Abraham comes to the Holy Land (Period of Isaac, Jacob and Joseph)
1800–1600	Hebrews enter Egypt
1546–1200	The New Kingdom of Egypt: great prosperity
1370–1353	Ikhenaton is pharaoh of Egypt
1320–1290	Tyrannical pharaohs oppress the Hebrews
c. 1290	Moses leads the Exodus from Egypt
c. 1250	The Hebrews conquer Canaan
1200–1020	Period of the Judges (such as Samson)
1020	King Saul
1000–961	King David
961–925	King Solomon
925	The Divided Kingdom (Israel and Judah)
900–800	Period of corrupt rulers (Ahab in Israel, Athaliah in Judah)
721	Fall of Israel to Assyria
701	Sennacherib invades Judah
c. 630	Good King Josiah in Judah
609	Battle of Megiddo (Armageddon)
c. 600	Nebuchadnezzar invades Judah
586	Fall of Jerusalem
586–538	Jews captive in Babylon
539	Fall of Babylon to Cyrus of Persia
538	Cyrus' edict liberates Jews
520–515	Rebuilding of Jerusalem
515–450	Return of many Jews to the Holy Land
445–440	The Torah (Law) is codified
400–330	Persian rule over Judah (Kings Darius, Artaxerxes, Belshazzar)
330	Alexander of Greece conquers Persia
330–200	Greek rule over Judea
200–167	The Seleucids of Syria control Judea (Palestine)
167	Revolt of the Maccabees
166–63	Jewish self-government in Palestine
63	Romans enter Jerusalem
60–25	Rule of the Herodian kings
20	Herod the Great rebuilds the Temple
c. 5	Jesus of Nazareth is born

A.D.

6–37	Rule of the Roman Procurators (including Pontius Pilate)
30	The Crucifixion of Jesus
47	Paul's missions begin
58–62	The imprisonment of Paul
66–73	Jewish-Roman War
70	The Destruction of Jerusalem by the Romans
73	Fall of Masada—last Jewish stronghold
75	Roman rule entrenched in Judea
132–135	Jewish revolt against Rome
135	Expulsion of Jews from Jerusalem

NOTE: *All early dates are approximate.*

Preserved in a cave by the hot, dry desert climate of Wadi Qumran, the Dead Sea Scrolls were found in 1946.

A section of the Dead Sea Scrolls which deals with the prophetic visions of Isaiah.

greatest book in the world was the Bible and wanting a copy for his library, assembled the seventy-two scholars who knew Hebrew and Greek best and set them to work. After seventy-two days they presented a translation in Greek, the cultivated language of Egypt. The Septuagint version, or "Seventy," is often designated as LXX. The Roman Catholic Church declared in 1546 that all of the books of the Vulgate are canonical.

The letters of St. Paul, which deal with problems that arose in the churches he founded or was associated with, were circulated in his lifetime to form the beginning of the New Testament. Added later were the four Gospels, an early history of the church (the Acts), other letters and an apocalypse called Revelation. Through usage and common acceptance, these books became canonical.

Over many centuries, beginning around 400 B.C., the Old Testament was written down in Hebrew, with the exception of a few chapters in Daniel, Ezra and a verse in Jeremiah that were written in Aramaic, a language akin to Hebrew. The oldest Hebrew manuscript extant until recently was dated about A.D. 900, but the Dead Sea, or Qumran, Scrolls, discovered in 1946, contain a full and a partial scroll of Isaiah, and fragments include verses from almost every book in the Old Testament, going back a thousand years earlier. What is amazing—and what the Dead Sea Scrolls confirm—is how reliably the text was preserved through the centuries.

The earliest known texts of the New Testament are on sheets of papyrus bound together as a book (codex) that were found in Egypt in modern times and date from the second to the eighth centuries. A great many have been found, some merely fragments but others quite extensive. There are also what are called Uncial Codices because they are written in capital, or uncial, letters. Written on parchment, these often include the Old Testament in its Septuagint or Greek form. The Codex Sinaiticus was written a little later in the same century, and others were written in the next several centuries. It should be noted that the early Christians did not have official scribes as the Jews did, and errors and discrepancies occurred in copying the text. The more recent translations of the Bible have used these old texts to clarify the meaning of words that heretofore had been obscure. Modern scholars have also examined the manuscripts of the New Testament from Syrian, Coptic, Armenian, Ethiopian and Georgian translations, as

In present-day Ethiopia, a Coptic priest shares with others his 300-year-old Bible, hand-illustrated on parchment. The subject on these pages appears to be Moses.

Written by hand in Greek, the 4th-century A.D. Codex Sinaiticus is one of the earliest surviving Bible texts. It was discovered in a monastery on Mt. Sinai.

Tyndale's 1553 Bible had woodcut illustrations. Though the Bible was translated into English before 1400, the invention of printing enabled more people to read the Scriptures.

The six days of Creation are illustrated in this 1535 edition of Coverdale's Bible. Like Tyndale's, it went through many printings.

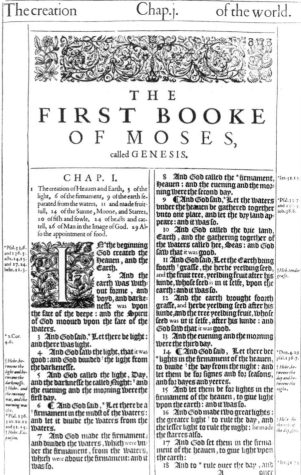

The opening page of the King James Bible (1611), which has been called the most widely read and most influential book ever published.

well as portions of the Bible that were translated into the Latin before Jerome.

Parts of the Bible were translated into Anglo-Saxon quite early. In the ninth century we find the famous King Alfred promoting Biblical translation and study. In the fourteenth century Wycliffe and his disciples translated the complete Bible into English. But it was Renaissance humanism that called for an examination of the original Greek. At the same time, the Reformation urged translation into the spoken language of the day. Luther translated the New Testament into German in 1522, and shortly afterward William Tyndale made an English translation. Because of the opposition of King Henry VIII, Tyndale did most of his work on the Continent. Finally he was kidnapped from Antwerp and was tried and executed for heresy because the Roman Catholic authorities at the time believed that the Bible in the hands of "the people" was bound to breed heresy. The next great translator was Miles Coverdale (1488–1569), who also did his work in Europe. The first printed edition (1535) was dedicated to Henry VIII, who had by now broken with Rome. Other versions of the Bible appeared from then on until finally the great King James version was published in 1611.

Although the Authorized King James version* is used in this text, you, the parent, might well have at hand one of the more modern versions of the Bible. There are a number of excellent translations, among them the Revised Standard Version and the New English Bible. Choose the one you are most comfortable with, remembering that the King James is the one most often quoted in the English-speaking world and is also a Bible that includes the Apocrypha. The same text, revised for Americans around 1901, was called the American Revised Edition (ARE). In the 1950s further revisions were made in what became the Revised Standard Version (RSV).

Some Weighty Questions

The Bible declares that behind all creation is a personal and purposeful God. God is personal—that is, like a person—a simplified way of saying that just as people can love and care for others and make promises and forgive, so too can God. In

*The Holy Bible King James Standard Version; "The Authorized," 1611, is published by the Syndics of the Cambridge University Press, London and New York.

some parts of the Bible God is described quite literally as a man. We read of his walking in the Garden of Eden in the cool of the day and of his calling Adam by name. Some people have been embarrassed by this humanlike description, which is called anthropomorphism. They have preferred speaking of God in highly abstract terms, such as absolute Truth, pure Being and that sort of thing. Of course, these terms might be helpful for a philosopher, but most people—especially children—do not think that way; we make images in our minds. Indeed, not all philosophers are satisfied with abstractions. The great seventeenth-century philosopher and scientist Blaise Pascal, for example, said that he did not care for the God of the philosophers but for the God of Abraham, Isaac and Jacob. What he meant is that regardless of what else we may say about God, we must remember that he is indeed a very personal being who loves and cares for all people.

The very first chapter of Genesis begins with an act of God—the Creation. Soon after, God calls Abraham away from his native home to found a new people and promises this people—the Hebrews—care and protection. He delivers them from slavery in Egypt and leads them into a promised land. In return for all that God did, his people owe him love and obedience. The Ten Commandments are the essential laws that bind this relationship of love between God, who cares, and the people who want to keep their relationship with God and one another. God's people often made mistakes. They rebelled, as children often rebel. They repented and they were forgiven. They were punished when they deserved punishment in order that they might change their ways. Yet through the whole story runs the shining thread of God's love for them and their love for God.

The New Testament also starts with God's action, with his sending his only begotten son into human life, a being born as a man but as one who bears the sins of mankind and through whom man, although sinful, is made one with God. The Gospels, or four accounts of the life of Jesus, announce the "good news." The rest of the New Testament shows how people, in love and gratitude to God, spread the message of Christianity.

How to Use This Book

The Bible is like a library that contains different stories, and, as with any library, one can begin reading with almost any book. Some children might be interested in adventure stories at first. But you, knowing your child and where he is in his emotional, spiritual and intellectual development, should comprehend the entire sequence of the Bible so that the most appropriate selections will be made.

It is assumed that many of the people who use this book will, like the Bible writers, see God at work in history and in the hearts of men, but some may not quite agree. For them, as well as for the adult not familiar with the Bible from childhood, Biblical reading can be a difficult literary experience. For one thing, it is awesome to meet for the first time people who are truly and thoroughly God-obsessed. For another, the ethical, moral and philosophical questions raised by the Bible are enormous, and the Bible's answers may seem at first unclear or even contradictory.

Exploring the Bible presents the Biblical stories and events from the same point of view taken by the Bible writers themselves, retaining the flavor of Biblical prose and adding generous portions of the original, clearly annotated by chapter and verse. This book does not attempt to dictate how you should relate to the Bible or what you should tell your children about miracles, God or religion. What it does superbly is to demystify the Bible for the modern reader, old or young. *Exploring the Bible* makes the Bible easily approachable by providing an overview of the whole story; it puts the Biblical writings in the context of their time and place by providing historical continuity and archaeological background, when and where they are known. In short, it provides a map with which to search for treasure.

To begin to read and study the Bible is an exciting quest. Your child, like everyone else, can enjoy a story well told, and in the Bible there are marvelous stories of adventure and romance, war and intrigue, struggle, defeat and achievement. The clarity with which the characters are drawn, and their inner motivations, show us human nature at its most constant. The eternal beauty of the psalms is a sheer delight. There are words of wisdom we ought to remember throughout our lives, and the Bible speaks so powerfully of God's actions and of man and his needs and wants—and what should be his concerns —that it continues to be the most widely read book in the entire world. As your family is a part of that world, let them now share in its riches.

—Rev. Dr. Lee A. Belford

EXPLORING THE BIBLE

God points majestically to the newly created sun with his right hand and to the moon with his left. The painting by the Italian Renaissance artist Michelangelo is one of a series of frescoes (paint applied to wet plaster) on the ceiling of the Sistine Chapel in the Vatican. This monumental 16th-century work has done much to define modern man's visual conception of God.

CHAPTER ONE

IN THE BEGINNING

(Genesis)

"IN THE BEGINNING GOD created the heaven and the earth . . ." are the very first words of Genesis. "But who created God?" the inquisitive reader, echoing centuries of theological debate, may ask. It is a pertinent as well as provocative question. God, or Yahweh (or Jehovah, which is the Latinized form of Yahweh), is the leading figure of the entire Bible. In effect the Bible is his biography, and its theme is God's interaction with man and the revelation of his law.

We can probably best begin to explain God as he appears in the Bible by assuming that God existed in his own right long before the events of Genesis; that no one knows anything more about him than we may derive from the evidence of our own lives and from the Bible. Because life and the universe exist we have every reason to believe that he exists, and, for this subtle lesson, the old adage about the clock proving the existence of the clockmaker may come in handy.

God is the first cause, many philosophers say; he is without beginning as he is without end. In Psalm 90:2 we read: "Before the mountains were brought forth, or ever thou hadst formed the earth and the world, even from everlasting to everlasting, thou art God." From beginning to end and before the beginning and after the end, God will be. This is the Bible's answer to "But who created God?"

Along with this question there inevita-

The abundance and variety of God's handiwork are depicted on the painting *God Creates the Animals* by the Flemish artist Paul Brill (1554-1626). Prominent is the unicorn, the mythical one-horned animal which symbolizes Christ in Christian allegory.

bly arises the "anthropomorphic" problem, namely: What does God look like? Artists—as we see in these pages—tend to make God look like man.

The Bible also provides humanlike glimpses of God and poetic references to him as a king, as a father, as a glorious sovereign on his throne and in his heaven. This view is strengthened by God's own statement in Genesis 1:26: "Let us make man in our image, after our likeness." Besides, Moses in Exodus 33:18–23 was allowed to see a fleeting rear glimpse of God, further implying a physical form to the Almighty.

But is this the whole story?

Many Biblical scholars believe that because God may at certain points in Scripture appear to have human form, it does not follow that this is his entire or exclusive form. According to the Bible, God is omnipresent and omnipotent (everywhere and all-powerful), "the first . . . and the last" (Isaiah 44:6) and, above all, the one and only God of all that is. "Hear, O Israel: The Lord our God is one only Lord" (Deuteronomy 6:4). Thus he may appear as a king, if he chooses, or as a spirit (Genesis 1:2), or he may be beyond knowing: "Touching the Almighty, we cannot find him out" (Job 37:23).

Many adults favor this more mystical, nonspecific view of God. However, most young people will respond with more empathy when God is viewed as a quasi-human figure—a great creator, a glorious king, an active, thinking, articulate entity with whom they can identify.

The Hymn of Creation in Genesis offers just this sort of image by its use of active verbs and everyday descriptions, even concerning the most awesome event of all time: the creation of the universe.

The Creation

Starting in Chapter 1, we read that God "*moved* upon the face of the waters" (1:2), that he "*said*, Let there be light" (1:3), that he "*saw* the light, that it was good" (1:4), that he "*divided* the waters" (1:7) and, finally, after having created light, space, heaven and earth and all living things, "God ended his work which he had made; and he *rested* on the seventh day . . ." (2:2).

A natural question at this point may be: "Was God so tired that he needed to rest? And if it took only seven days to make the universe and all that's in it, why should he have been tired at all?"

This line of inquiry leads us gradually on to the major theme of the Bible: God's interaction with man. At the same time it touches on the literary technique generally employed in the Bible, the poetic allegory, or allusion, that is intended to reduce cosmic wonders to a satisfactory and understandable form. The Bible tells us that God created the universe in seven days simply as a poetic means of indicating the element of time in creation. Each day may have been a million years in duration, or a twenty-four-hour period. The point to convey here is that the Bible is written within the framework of what man knows. Just as a man requires time, so does God require time.

In a similar way, what better way to signify the importance of a day of rest for man than to show that even God rested from his labors? Thus was born the Sabbath (Day of Rest) and the commandment to keep it holy (Exodus 20:11).

As a result of its style, Genesis 1, with its powerful imagery, portrays the deity not only as an awesome creative force but as a personality as well. God, in a very human way, saw that what he had done was

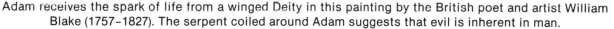

Adam receives the spark of life from a winged Deity in this painting by the British poet and artist William Blake (1757–1827). The serpent coiled around Adam suggests that evil is inherent in man.

"good." In a compassionate manner, he allowed the creatures of the earth to possess a small part of his own great creative powers: "Be fruitful, and multiply," he tells them (1:22). Above all, like a loving father, he established his special concern for the human race by creating it in his own image, endowing it with creative powers of its own and allowing it mastery "over every living thing that moveth upon the earth" (1:28). God gives man (Adam) not only food and shelter but, as we soon shall see, an earthly paradise in which to flourish.

Adam and Eve in Eden

God creates the human race in Verse 27 of Chapter 1 of Genesis; he then apparently specially forms one man to stand symbolically for the rest and to be the keeper of a wonderful garden established eastward in a place called Eden. This man is Adam, whose name means "from the earth" (out of which he was formed, 2:7). His paradise garden was located somewhere near the Tigris and Euphrates rivers in the area we presently call Iraq. It was supposed to provide him with all manner of food and shelter, and there he would live eternally, never knowing toil, suffering or death.

One day, as Adam slept, God provided a female companion for him in Eden. She was Eve (Mother) and was created out of Adam's rib (2:21–22). (*Note*: An ancient legend said that the rib was the one closest to Adam's heart.) Does this mean that woman is secondary to man, since she was formed from a minor part of his anatomy? Women of all ages—especially today—may very well want to know. The Bible does not mean to diminish woman by this reference, as the very next verse reveals, for here Eve is shown to be what Adam calls "bone of my bones, and flesh of my flesh . . . ." In other words, she is an indispensable part of life, second to Adam only in time but not in value.

The Fall

Adam and Eve are to live a blissful, innocent life in their garden, so long as they choose to be obedient to God and leave in his hands their fate and well-being. To test this trust, God plants a certain tree in the middle of the garden and forbids Adam and Eve to eat of its fruit, "for in the day that thou eatest thereof thou shalt surely die" (2:17).

This tree represents "the knowledge of good and evil"—that is, the knowledge of everything. Many scholars interpret it to be a symbol of man's commitment to God, for should he choose to eat of this tree, he would in a sense be saying: "I do not really trust God with my destiny. I want to con-

Lucas Cranach the Elder (1472–1553) painted *The Garden of Eden* with a humanlike Deity instructing Adam and Eve, who hear him with gestures of obedience. In the background are scenes of Eve's creation (center), the Temptation (right), Adam and Eve hiding from the all-seeing God (left) and their expulsion from Paradise (far left).

In *The Fall of Man*, Michelangelo condensed the story into one tragic image of transgression and punishment. Both Satan, who emerges from the serpent's coils, and the angel, with a sword, grow like branches from the forbidden Tree of Knowledge.

trol my own fate. I want to know as much as God knows and thus be like a god."

Whether Adam and Eve will eat of this tree is suspensefully related beginning with Chapter 3. First a serpent is sent into the garden by God to tempt Eve into eating the forbidden fruit (which is not necessarily an apple). He convinces her to do so by assuring her that neither she nor Adam will die if they do (3:4). He means, of course, that they will not *immediately* die, but Eve ap-

parently thinks he speaks of continued immortality, and so she plucks the fruit, eats of it and persuades Adam to do the same. As soon as they have tasted the fruit, the two become ashamed of their nakedness, which was up to then an innocent part of their existence. So confused are they that they hide from God, who comes "walking in the garden" at sunset (3:8). Already they feel cut off from his intimacy.

The Lord obliges Adam and Eve to confess their disobedience, the so-called Original Sin, and institutes a series of punishments that fall on all the guilty parties: serpent, woman and man. The serpent is forced to crawl on its belly for all time and be hated by mankind (3:14–15). Adam and his descendants will earn their bread by "the sweat of thy face" (3:19) in toil; women henceforth will bear children "in sorrow" or pain (3:16). Most fearful, death comes into the world as God had warned;

In this bone handle from Palestine (8th century B.C.), the Tree of Life is a very stylized date palm, whose branches look like a hand.

"for dust thou art, and unto dust shalt thou return" (3:19). Accordingly, "lest [Adam] put forth his hand and take also of the tree of life and eat and live forever" (note the two trees: one is the tree of knowledge of good and evil; the other is the tree of life), he and his wife must be expelled from the garden of Eden. Think of the implication of this story. Because of their mistrust in God, their disobedience and impetuosity, Adam and Eve have passed on to their descendants—to every man and woman, girl and boy—the pain and toil of mortal existence.

One of the most perplexing questions that may arise at this point is the one that asks: "Didn't God know in advance that Adam and Eve would disobey? Why did he need to test them?"

In attempting to answer this, we get to the core of the foregoing story and the Biblical view of man's relationship to God. It has to do with "free will"—man's choice to obey or disobey, to live righteously or wickedly. As vividly shown in Genesis, man chose to put himself above God's law and thus he cut himself off from intimacy with his Creator, walking instead on an uncertain, painful path. From this point on, the Bible concerns itself with man's troubled journey through history, with his frequent transgressions and with his continual attempts to rediscover Paradise—and God.

Despite this less than optimistic unfolding, the theme of Genesis 1–3 remains hopeful. God created the world for man and gave him mastery over it and the choice to live for good or ill. Though man seems to have chosen the negative way—for which he has paid with suffering and death—there is implied an eventual redemption for the human race, a victory over the original disobedience and a return to an intimacy with God and to the glory of Paradise. We gather this because God does not destroy Adam and Eve but allows them to live and try to redeem themselves by toil and prayer.

Flemish artist Pieter Bruegel The Elder (1525–1569) portrayed the effects of Adam's transgression in *The Triumph of Death*, in which violence, torture and murder appear to be the fate of mankind.

The story of Cain and Abel appealed to artists from earliest times. In this 4th-century Roman painting, Abel offers a young lamb; Cain, his sheaves of wheat.

Cain and Abel

Man's disobedience not only led to physical hardship but eventually to greater sin. In Chapter 4 of Genesis the first murder is presented in a dramatic short-story form comprising less than 500 words.

Adam and Eve have two sons. The eldest, Cain, is a farmer (4:2) and his brother, Abel, a herdsman. Possibly in hopes of atoning for his sins, Adam has instituted the ceremony of holy sacrifice, and both sons are expected to make burnt offerings to God. Abel dutifully sacrifices the firstborn of his flock (4:4) and wins God's respect, probably signified by the fact that the smoke of his fire rises upward. Cain's offering of grains does not fare as well, for he has not brought forth the *first* of his harvest. The smoke probably blows back in his face and as a result he becomes bitter.

Cain—like his parents before him—chooses to take matters into his own hands. He murders Abel while the two are conversing in the field (4:8). God attempts to redeem Cain by making him freely confess his crime. "Where is Abel thy brother?" he asks (4:9). But Cain, avoiding responsibility (as had Adam and Eve by hiding from God after the fall), pretends not to know: "Am I my brother's keeper?" he responds.

Of course, God knows all about the murder. However, he does not punish Cain with death but rather sentences him to roam the earth as "a fugitive and a vagabond." Hearing this, Cain becomes alarmed. Suppose that someone finds me, he asks, and, taking me for an enemy, he slays me? In the hope that even Cain will repent his crime before he dies, God sets a mark upon him so that all finding him shall be warned away from killing him. Miserable, cut off from family and, more important, from God, Cain wanders off east of Eden, where he marries, has a son and apparently dies a natural death.

"But if Adam and Eve have only two sons, Cain and Abel, then who else is there in the world who might slay Cain—and

Though the Bible does not specify the murder weapon, Cain bludgeons his brother with the jawbone of an animal in this 14th-century painting by the German artist Master Bertram. In this manner Samson later attacked and slew an army of Philistines (Judges 15:15).

whom does Cain marry?" These logical questions have been asked by generations of Scripture readers. Some students point out Genesis 1:27, which says: "So God created man . . . male and female created he them." This event, which is reported before the creation of Adam (2:7), implies, they say, that other people coexisted with the special family. These are the potential enemies of Cain and from this population comes his wife.

Proving that even in those terrible days there were worthy believers, there is a

third son of Adam and Eve. His name is Seth (4:25–26), and he is the ancestor of a man named Enoch: a righteous man who "walked with God" (5:22).

The Story of Noah

Beginning with Chapter 5 of Genesis, the Bible enumerates the many other descendants of Adam and Eve. The longest lived of these is Methuselah, whose age is given as 969 years (Genesis 5:27). How do you convey the reality of this man's age to the modern mind? For an explanation you must fall back on ancient concepts of the calendar. The Mesopotamians (who dominated the area in question) often measured the year by moons (moon-th or month). There were approximately twelve such moons per year. By this reckoning you will note that Methuselah's age reduces to a mere eighty or so years (12 divided into 969). But whether in moons or years, this great age implied special sanctity to the people of the early Biblical period. But part of Methuselah's sanctity rests also in the fact that he was the grandfather of Noah, who is the first full-fledged hero of Genesis.

Noah's Character

Noah's story begins with Chapter 6, when God becomes angered over the corruption of the earth and the violence of men (6:11–13). Accordingly, he decides to destroy the world, all except Noah and his family (including his daughters-in-law), because "Noah was a just man. . . ." (6:9).

The oldest known Mideastern genealogy is this inscribed clay prism listing Sumerian kings. The blank area, lower left, shows the gap in royal descent, caused by a flood that devastated the region.

A skin-covered boat with oars is depicted on a Mesopotamian wall carving. Such boats are still in use on the Tigris and Euphrates rivers.

The Ark

Noah is told to build a very specific sort of ship, an ark, the description of which is precise and detailed (beginning at 6:14). According to modern equivalents of ancient measurements, this bulky vessel would have been about 450 feet long, 75 feet wide and 45 feet high—a virtual luxury liner.

Ark-shaped watercraft existed in Mesopotamian times, mostly made of skins tightly wrapped around wooden frames. The Babylonians called such boats "couffas," or baskets. Noah's ark must have resembled a huge basket intended for floating, not for navigating. You can confirm this deduction by referring to Genesis 7:17. Apparently the ark was not built by the sea but was moored on dry land in readiness for the time when the water would rise up to its hull.

The purpose of this huge vessel was to contain "every living thing of all flesh . . . ." The description of the animal occupants of the ark is very touching. Each species shall go in twos, "every creeping thing of the earth" (6:20). Cattle necessary for food are an exception; seven each of these are to be allowed (7:2). Birds, insects—"creeping things"—and mammals all have a place inside the three stories of the ark (while apparently all aquatic life remains where it is, in the water). Some scholars estimate that 7,000 species could have been accommodated in the huge vessel, making it a veritable floating zoo.

The Flood Begins

Perhaps the most startling language in Genesis is that describing the onset of the flood (7:10–12 and 7:18–24). Early concepts of the universe viewed the earth as a flat surface supported by columns. Beneath the floating disk great fountains of water continually surged; above, the heavens held back torrents of rain. By "breaking up the fountains of the deep" and opening "the windows of heaven," God released the full fury of the inundation. At its worst it rose 15 cubits upward—nearly 300 feet. Everything was caught in this torrent and drowned.

The American artist Edward Hicks (1780–1849) showed the animals docilely entering the Ark in pairs while birds escape storm clouds.

According to the Bible, only Noah and his family survived and finally came to rest, in the ark, high up in the mountains of Ararat (presumably in modern-day Armenia). The ark had floated some 500 miles from the Mesopotamian basin over the period of nearly five months. Seven additional months were spent in the ark on the mountain before dry land appeared (8:4–14). To test that the flood had ended, Noah sent out from the ark first a raven, then a dove (8:7–8). The dove finally found a roost, and Noah knew that the worst was over. You should note that because of this story, the dove to this day has come to represent hope and peace, particularly because when she first returned to Noah "in her mouth was an olive leaf plucked off " (8:11). Seeing this leaf, Noah took heart, for he knew that trees were once again appearing above the waterline.

The Symbols of Noah

The dove and the olive leaf, or branch, are only two of the many undying symbols that have continued in Western thought as a result of this famous story. The threat of rain for forty days and forty nights (7:12) is another Biblical reference from Noah, and the world-recognized image of a rainbow representing peace and harmony comes directly from Genesis. God establishes a covenant, or peace pact, with Noah proclaiming that no such destructive flood will ever again menace the earth (9:11), nor will God ever again separate the righteous from the wicked. The token of this promise is God's "bow in the cloud" (9:13–14).

Style of the Story

The happy ending of this tumultuous story is couched in beautiful prose, highlighted by the Biblical use of repetitive phrases. Note how many references to the rainbow, or the "token," are made between Verses 13 and 17. The scribes of this section wanted to impress this positive symbol on all who heard about it. They probably realized that it was something frequently seen in nature, usually following rain and always of an extraordinary quality.

Charming phrases such as "but the dove found no rest for the sole of her foot" (8:9)

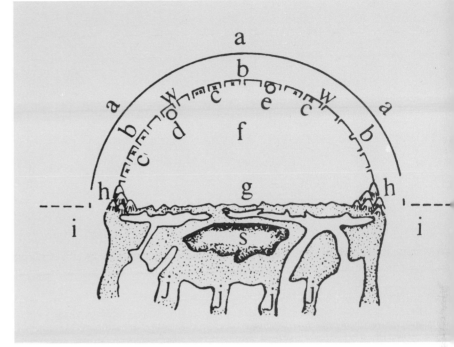

No pictures survive from ancient times showing how the Hebrews viewed the physical universe. But this modern drawing, based upon various Biblical references, attempts to illustrate the Hebraic concept of the universe. At the top was Heaven (a) where God dwelt. Below Heaven was the firmament (f) or sky, the vault that supported Heaven. Between Heaven and the firmament were the waters (b) which fell from time to time through windows (w) to the flat earth (g) below. Also fixed in the firmament were the stars (c), sun (d) and moon (e). Like an island, the earth was surrounded completely by waters (i), an unknown and frightening place called Tehom—the watery abyss. At the far ends of the earth were the mountains (h) that held up the firmament, and deep below the earth were the pillars (j) supporting the terrestrial world. Beneath the surface was Sheol (s), the abode of the dead or the departed spirits.

A dove painted in a Roman catacomb bears an olive branch. This image became a symbol of peace in many lands.

fill the text like brilliant colors. The unusual portrayal of God as a very human figure is another striking literary device in this story. In 6:6, for instance, God repents that he made man. No wonder in folklore the story of Noah always strikes a homey note. A good example is Marc Connelly's Biblical play *Green Pastures* (1930), in which God and Noah engage in a little debate. Along with the animals, two by

In *The Flood*, Michelangelo shows a rocky world and its people about to be engulfed by the rising waters. Some clamber to the highest

places, some try vainly to enter the ark (notice the dove at the window), and a few continue to affront God and their fellow man.

A scene from Marc Connelly's 1930 play *Green Pastures*, which is based on the Bible as interpreted by ordinary people.

two, old Noah wants to take "two kegs of likker" aboard the ark. God insists on only one—and that to be used solely for snakebite. Noah, of course, obeys. Now, as in his prediluvian days, Noah is "a just man and perfect in his generations."

The Other Flood Story

From the early Mesopotamian *Epic of Gilgamesh* (a series of tablets written in cuneiform characters) comes the story of Utna-pish-tim and the great flood which the gods caused to inundate the Mesopotamian world in ancient times. *(Note: Mesopotamia is the generic term for the kingdoms of Assyria—north—and Babylonia—south—which occupied the area of modern Iraq and Syria.)*

In the ancient *Epic*, Utna-pish-tim is spared by his gods and told to "build a ship. . . ." Furthermore, he is instructed to take aboard the ship "the seed of all living things." This is precisely what Noah was told to do by God: build an ark, or a ship, and save all living things from the forthcoming flood.

Most scholars believe that the similarity of these two ancient stories, that of Noah and of Utna-pish-tim, as well as other legends of the area point to the reality of a great flood stretching throughout the Tigris and Euphrates valley and possibly affecting the Mediterranean. Archaeologists, in fact, have shown evidence in soil stratum of flood deposits in modern Iraq going back to 5000 B.C. Since the local residents of Biblical times took their area to be the entire world, they no doubt believed that the frequent and widespread flooding they endured was a universal experience.

The Tower of Babel

After the flood the sons and daughters-in-law of Noah gave rise to a whole new population in the world. Chapter 10 names these generations, supplying not only the names of new families but of major new cities and nations as well. The most prominent of the new men is Nimrod (10:8), a great-grandson of Noah, an unfailing hunter (hence today hunters are popularly known as "Nimrods") and one who "began to be a mighty one in the earth."

Within only fifty or so years after the flood, people began all over again to forget God and to consider their own ambitions first and foremost in the world. The building of a great city and a tower, at a place called Shinnar, symbolized this attitude. Some archaeological experts believe Shinnar to have been ancient Babylon and that Nimrod was the force behind this ambitious building plan (Babylonia was long known as "the Land of Nimrod"), a plan essentially motivated by arrogant desires. "Let us build a city, and a tower, whose top may reach unto heaven; and let us make us a name . . ." (11:4) said the builders of Shinnar. In other words, let us flaunt our greatness and try to reach heaven itself and come face to face even with God.

Rudimentary building techniques had been perfected in the days of early Babylon. No doubt men felt confident that they could indeed construct a "stairway to heaven." They also took encouragement from the fact—mentioned at the outset of Chapter 11—that all people spoke a single language and could therefore easily communicate. Both the dream of confronting God in heaven and the efficiency of speaking a single language were to be undone by God's own intervention (11:5–8), for he, angered by the apparent affront of the builders and also desirous of scattering people more widely over the globe, confounds man's language, causing confusion and dissension. The great city and tower of Shinnar are accordingly abandoned and henceforth come to be known as Babel, or place of confusion, from which we get the English word "babble."

Archaeological Note: The ancient Babylonians built "ziggurats," huge buildings that rose up many feet in stepped levels. In the 1870s, at the site of ancient Babylon, a huge pit believed to be the foundation of a ziggurat tower and temple dedicated to the Babylonian god, Marduk, was uncovered. Nearby, an archaeologist found a tablet reading: "The building of this great tower offended the gods and they threw it down

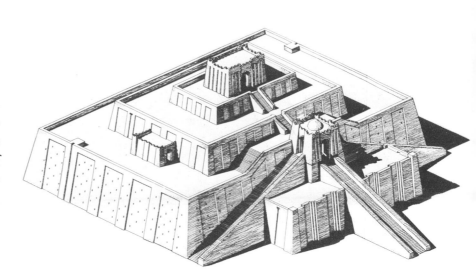

Above is a model of the ziggurat of Ur. The temple at the top was covered with silver and the terraces decorated with trees. Could this have been a model for the Tower of Babel?

An aerial view shows clearly the steps leading to the top of the ruins of the ziggurat built in the city of Ur, the home of the patriarch Abraham. Like other Assyrian structures, ziggurats were built of dried brick, which eventually crumbled.

in a single night and scattered [the builders] abroad and made strange their speech"— practically a word-for-word account of Genesis 11, indicating a historical basis for this story of overweening ambition.

Abram, the Idol Breaker

By the time we get to Genesis 12, some 400 years have passed since Noah's ark came to rest after the flood. Generation upon generation has come into the world. Cities have flourished, kingdoms have grown and with the passing of time there has come also the thing we call religion: man's attempt by organized ritual and communal worship to communicate with his gods. A strange development in religion of this period encouraged the worship of many gods, and it seemed that except in the memories of a handful of people, Jehovah, the Creator—the one true God—had been all but forgotten. In place of the Lord Almighty, one could now find gods and goddesses dedicated to the sun, the moon, the stars, even to animals.

In the flourishing kingdom of Egypt, people venerated gods with lion's heads or with the heads of hawks. In Mesopotamia, particularly in the great city of Ur, the favorite was Ningal, goddess of the moon. Statues or idols of her adorned the city, and people would bow before these images of clay and lay sacrifices at her feet.

One resident of Ur, Abram, son of Terah, is said to have despised these super-

A 13th-century Biblical picture book shows the Tower of Babel being ingeniously built. The book itself became a thing of many languages; commissioned by the Pope from Parisian artists, it was carried as a gift to a Persian ruler, and acquired marginal inscriptions in Persian and Hebrew before passing successively into Arabic, Greek, English and American hands.

This figure of Ningal, wife of the Sumerian moon god Namma, sits upon a throne, hands clasped before her. It was excavated in Ur, Abraham's home.

The Egyptian god of death, Anubis, is represented as a wooden jackal with gold decorations. Found in Tutankhamun's tomb, it is typical of the pagan idols Abraham despised.

45

Meandering through the valley, the River Jordan irrigates the ground and makes it fertile, as it did in Biblical times. This view is near Beth-el, one of the first of Abraham's settlements.

stitions from boyhood. There is a story in folklore that tells how he once smashed the idols in his father's house, saying, "How can one worship these figures of clay when they were fashioned by a man, baked in an oven, some of them not yet one year old?"

Chapter 12 of Genesis begins the story of this remarkable and righteous man, Abram (later to become Abraham), who believed in Yahweh and who, at God's command, left his father's house in Ur so that he might found a new nation of believers in the land of Canaan (12:1–3).

The Bible tells us that Abram was around seventy-five years old when he started on his pilgrimage to the promised land, in the company of his wife, Sarai, and a nephew named Lot. We can judge his dedication to God by the fact that he halted his journey soon after arriving in Canaan so that he might erect not an idol but an altar to God. He built this symbol of respect at a place near the city of Beth-el (which means "house of God") in the land now called Israel, and by this act he claimed the place for his God.

Unfortunately, famine soon drove Abram and his caravan southward to Egypt, where he was obliged to contend with a tyrannical pharaoh who wanted to purchase Sarai, thinking her to be Abram's sister. The Bible reports this peculiar story (12:11–20) in order to establish the reason why Abram could not possibly remain in Egypt and why, despite famine, he soon returned to Canaan, back to Beth-el, where he had erected the altar to God.

The Hebrew Nation

Abram eventually becomes a wealthy prince, leader of a growing nation known as the Hebrews (from a word thought to mean "wanderers," or nomads). His nephew Lot was also a man of means and like his uncle had many flocks. Inevitably trouble began between the herdsmen of Abram and those of Lot, so uncle and nephew decided to separate for the sake of peace (13:8–9). Lot took his people and belongings southward toward the Canaanite city of Sodom.

The promised land, then as now, was a place of great beauty, so beautiful, in fact, that the Bible compares it to Eden (13:10), a land filled with lush valleys and verdant hills that might truly inspire men to the love of God. From his earliest days in

A long view across the land of Canaan, from near Bethlehem toward the Dead Sea.

Beth-el, Abram knew this inspiration and frequently communed with God, as God communed with him, promising the Hebrews all the land for as far as the eye could see (13:14–15) unto eternity. In order to measure this promised territory, Abram moved his dwelling place from Beth-el southward to Hebron, a place not far from the present city of Jerusalem. But once settled in Hebron, Abram heard news that his beloved nephew, Lot, had been captured in warfare by the aggressive kings of Sodom and nearby Gomorrah. Because he loved Lot and considered him to be his heir, Abram was obliged to rescue the captive

and did so at great risk, considering he had only 318 troops at his command (14:15–16).

Lot was saved, Abram recognized as a great warrior and the local kings forced to pay over huge ransoms to him. Only one of these, Melchizedek, king of Salem (Jerusalem), welcomed Abram's victory as a sign of God's intervention in Canaan. Melchizedek was, like Abram, a believer in Jehovah, whom he called "most high God" (14:18–20).

Soon after the battle, God appeared again to Abram (15:1) and in stirring language renewed his promise about Canaan,

47

saying, "I am thy shield, and thy exceeding great reward." Part of this reward is to be the land of Canaan, but Abram wonders: How can I inherit this land, he asks God, "seeing I go childless?" (15:2). God assures Abram that he shall indeed one day have a son and that a great nation shall rise from his seed, a nation serving God, one that will be sorely afflicted but which, in the end, will greatly triumph (15:13–14), its descendants as numerous as the stars.

A stunning poetic phrase follows the promise, describing the setting of the sun and implying a rare and wonderful natural event meant to inspire Abram beyond all doubt. "And it came to pass, that, when the sun went down, and it was dark, behold a smoking furnace, and a burning lamp that passed between those pieces." Could this smoking furnace have been a volcano, the burning lamp a firestorm?

Hagar and Ishmael

Though Sarai was barren, Abram was nevertheless able to have a son by a second wife, an Egyptian handmaiden of Sarai's named Hagar. According to the custom of those days, she might bear children for her mistress. When Hagar became pregnant, however, Sarai grew jealous and implored Abram to send Hagar away. Two versions of this episode appear in the Bible. In Chapter 16, before Hagar has given birth, she is driven away by Sarai but saved by an angel in the desert (16:5–7). In Chapter 21 the same thing happens to Hagar, this time after the birth of her son, Ishmael. The boy is about fifteen years old when Sarai again causes Hagar to flee to the desert, now with Ishmael. Again the two are rescued by an angel, and because Ishmael is the son of Abram, God promises him leadership over a mighty nation (the Arabs) and establishes him in the desert of Arabia as a chieftain and a hunter (21:20).

Frequently, the Bible emphasizes a story or an incident by repeating it in slightly different forms. Some scholars believe that this indicates two sets of authors responsible for the early Biblical texts (especially in Genesis). Others explain the parallel stories as demonstrations of Biblical accuracy. There are two accounts, they say, because two similar events are being faithfully described. We had an example of this in the first chapter of Genesis when God

Biblical marriage customs as revealed in the Genesis story of Abraham, Sarah and Hagar, prevailed throughout much of the ancient Near East. This cuneiform tablet, found in the city of Nunzu, east of the Tigris River, describes the marriage of a man named Shennima. If his wife bears him sons, Shennima may not take other wives; but if she does not, she must provide her husband with a handmaid to bear her children, just as Sarah provided Hagar to Abraham.

Rembrandt's drawings always touch the heart of Biblical events. Here, Hagar's heavy sadness at being expelled with Ishmael is shown through just a few lines of movement.

created "male and female" (1:27) and then in Chapter 2 when he specifically created Adam (2:7). Note also the several instances where God's promise to Abram is repeated (12:2, 13:15, 15:7 and in Chapter 17). Clearly, the scribes of the Bible wish to impress us with the importance and validity of these repeated episodes. In the case of Hagar, the fact that Ishmael was an heir of Abram is considered likewise significant, and today in light of the tensions between Israel and Arab countries it is interesting to remember this most ancient connection and the fact that Jews and Muslims share a patriarch in Abram.

The Covenant

In the ancient world, men were bound to certain responsibilities by covenants or contracts, usually concluded with some symbolic ritual (remember God's covenant with Noah). The Bible wishes to show that Abram was in this fashion committed to God—and God to Abram—by a physical act. Beginning with Chapter 17, this sacred contract is carefully described and solemnized. First, the promise of a great and sacred nation is reiterated by God (17:4). In token of this pledge, God commands Abram to modify his name so that it becomes Ab*ra*ham ("great father" of the nations). Then the ritual of circumcision is established for all Hebrew males—an unalterable and sacred ceremony performed by the Jewish people even to this day (17:11 and 13). Finally, God announces that Sarai—now to be called Sarah (princess) —will become a mother so that Abraham may have an heir of his beloved wife. At the same time, God remembers Ishmael (17:20) as noted before.

Chapter 17 is one of the most important in Genesis, for it establishes the unbroken commitment between God and the people he has chosen to carry his word throughout the world: the Hebrews, of whom Abraham is the founder and patriarch.

Note: The word "Hebrew" stands for both a language and a people. This same people in later days came to be called Jews (from Judea, the name given to Canaan by its Roman conquerors). Technically, the religion of this people is Judaism, although some refer to the Hebrew religion in the same way. Racially, the tribe of Abraham is called Semitic, from Shem, the son of Noah. This group includes both Hebrews (Jews) and Arabs. In Exodus we will see that the Hebrews take on still another name, Israelites (Children of Israel). Hebrew, Jew and Israelite are therefore interchangeable when describing the descendants of Abraham.

The Three Visitors

At the opening of Chapter 18 we read that the Lord appeared to Abraham as he sat resting near his tent in the plains of Mamre. But how did God make this appearance? The surprising answer is given in the next verse: "and lo, three men stood by him . . ." three men whom Abraham nevertheless addresses as "My Lord," adding, "rest *yourselves* under the tree." In a mysterious way, God seems to be changing before Abraham's eyes from three separate figures back to one. Of course, it may also be assumed that God is the chief spokesman of the three and the other two are merely his companions.

In any case, Abraham is obviously aware from the first that he is in the company of sacred visitors, and, being a most reverent and hospitable man, he calls on Sarah to prepare three measures of refreshment for the guests. The three visitors eat (18:8) and when finished they inform Abraham and Sarah that a child will soon be born to them. Because she is very old (as is Abraham), Sarah cannot believe the prophecy and she laughs despite herself (18:12). God gently rebukes the aged lady: "Is any thing too hard for the Lord?" he asks (18:14). Later, in remembrance of this incident, when the child is born, Sarah names him Isaac, meaning "laughter" (21:3 and 6).

Sodom and Gomorrah

The announcement of a forthcoming birth is not the only reason for God's mysterious visit to Abraham. The cities of Sodom and Gomorrah have grown so wicked that the Lord has decided to pay a personal visit to each place so that he may determine whether he will destroy them. He does not wish to hide this terrible news from Abraham, "seeing that Abraham shall surely become a great and mighty nation, and all the nations of the earth shall be blessed in him" (18:18).

Abraham is the gracious host and Sarah the astonished eavesdropper in Antonio Guardi's portrayal of the three angels visiting Abraham.

Remembering his nephew Lot, who lives in Sodom—and because he is a compassionate man—Abraham intercedes and asks the Lord: "Peradventure [perhaps] there be fifty righteous within the city: wilt thou also destroy and not spare the place for the fifty righteous that are therein?" (18:24).

God agrees to spare the cities if fifty righteous people can be found, and, at Abraham's insistence, he even agrees to spare them should only ten decent people inhabit each place.

Sodom and Gomorrah were Biblical cities that existed not far from Jerusalem on the southern shores of the vast Dead Sea. In 1924 an eminent archaeologist, Dr.

William F. Albright, discovered evidence of city life in mounds at the southeast corner of the sea. Life in these cities, he believed, came to an abrupt end around 2000 B. C. Apparently the sudden cataclysm of "brimstone and fire" that rained down on these cities of the plain (19:24) is a historical fact. Sulphuric pits once capable of exploding are still evident in the region, as are the peaks of Mount Sodom, which resemble ruins of buildings after an explosion.

The Angels

The three visitors who came to Abraham's tent are now transformed into two specific angels (19:1). This is not the first

Lot and his daughters flee the city in Corot's *Destruction of Sodom*. But Lot's wife has turned back (right).

reference in Genesis to angels, and we would do well at this point to pause and consider who or what these creatures were. According to the Bible, angels are spiritual beings slightly exalted above man (see Psalm 8:5) but greatly inferior to God. Most often they function as messengers, some of whom are airborne. The concept of winged angels predates the Bible and derives from the images of Assyrian gods, who are frequently winged. From Persia —as well as from Assyria—comes the concept of winged groupings, ranging from the lowest or most common seraphim and cherubim to the exalted archangels who in Hebrew tradition stand by the throne of God. As we have seen in Chapter 18, God himself may sometimes

assume the form of an angel, or angels may appear as heroic, handsome men. In any event, the Bible wishes us to conceive of these beings as forces for good who serve God and in some cases, as with Hagar (16:9), aid and rescue human beings.

The two angels who visit Abraham go to Sodom and are convinced of the city's wickedness. Among all the inhabitants, only Lot and his family are worth saving. So the angels instruct Abraham's nephew, his wife and daughters to flee the city in advance of the destruction, warning them "look not behind" while doing so (19:17).

Altered by earthquakes, the area of Mt. Sodom today is no longer the "well-watered" land where Lot's flocks grazed.

At sunrise, the terrible rain of fire and brimstone begins which utterly destroys Sodom and Gomorrah. Unfortunately, Lot's wife is possessed by curiosity, and as she turns to look back on the holocaust, she is turned into a pillar of salt (19:26). Many jagged pillars of salt, formed by natural erosion, crowd the ridges of Mount Sodom even to this day. Is one of them Lot's wife caught forever in disobedience?

The end of Chapter 19 and all of Chapter 20 tell how Lot and Abraham survived the disaster just related and tell how Abraham had to contend with a local chieftain, Abimelech, regarding equal use of the wells in the arid Negev, or desert, of Canaan.

Isaac

The birth of Isaac is probably the most joyous event in Abraham's life (21:1–3), but in time the lad comes to represent the

A 9th-century B.C. Assyrian carving of a winged figure defines an ancient Mideastern concept, from which the idea of angels may have developed.

greatest challenge as well. Chapter 22 deals with the unusual, heartbreaking sacrifice God demands of Abraham—the sacrifice of Isaac!

From the first, as we read this gripping story, we must believe that God merely intended to tempt, or test, Abraham's faith by his command: "Take now thy son, thine only son Isaac, whom thou lovest, . . . and offer him . . . for a burnt offering . . ." (22:2). At the same time, we may imagine another lesson embedded in the tale. In the period under discussion, child sacrifice by fire to the pagan gods was common, especially in Canaan. God wanted the Hebrew people to reject such barbarisms and knew that only a dramatic event could break the tradition. That event would be the last-minute intervention by an angel of God as Abraham readied the knife to kill his son. Two servants accompany Abraham and Isaac to Mount Moriah (in Jerusalem), where the sacrifice is supposed to be done (22:3). These men will serve as witnesses of the miraculous intervention and thus be able to broadcast God's rejection of human sacrifice to all the people of the land.

They will also tell of Abraham's unquestioning faith, which is so magnificently demonstrated by this episode. To reward this faith, God again promises the old patriarch a great blessing for the Hebrew people, through whom "all the nations of the earth be blessed; because thou hast obeyed my voice" (22:18).

What of Isaac throughout this tragic ordeal? By most reckonings he was at that time a boy of about thirteen or fourteen years old, the apple of his father's eye and the joy of his mother. He is clearly puzzled by the three-day journey to Mount Moriah and innocently observes that Abraham has brought wood, fire and a knife for the sacrifice but no lamb. "God will provide himself a lamb . . ." Abraham grimly remarks (22:7–8). Does Isaac suspect the worst and, if so, does he not also demonstrate great courage and faith in the Almighty— befitting the son of Abraham?

It is interesting to note that Abraham does indeed carry through a sacrifice before descending the mount; it is not of Isaac, of course, but of a ram caught in a nearby thicket (22:13). From this ram comes the sacred *shofar*, or ram's-horn trumpet, used by Jews to this day in religious ceremonies, a trumpet that summons them to faith as God summoned Abraham in this dramatic story.

The Death of Sarah

Sarah was a very old lady when she died (about 127), and Abraham mourned her grievously. The main point of Chapter 23, which begins with Sarah's passing, concerns Abraham's purchase of a burial plot at a place called Machpelah. Though he is at first offered the plot free, in respect of his patriarchal position, he nevertheless insists on paying a large quantity of silver for the land. His decision is of great political significance, for by buying Machpelah, Abraham legalizes his claims in Canaan and establishes the right to make it an eventual home for his people.

Isaac and Rebekah

Not long after Sarah's death, Abraham fell ill (Chapter 24). Fearing he would soon

In Rembrandt's painting *The Sacrifice of Isaac*, the angel appears at the crucial moment to stay Abraham's hand and allow his knife to fall harmlessly to the ground.

Excavated from a royal tomb at Ur, this gold and lapis lazuli figure of a goat suggests the "ram caught in a thicket" sacrificed by Abraham in place of his only son, Isaac.

die, he solemnly instructed his faithful servant Eliezer to seek out a suitable wife for Isaac, his son. According to the customs of the time, this wife was to be chosen from Abraham's own family. In this way, the patriarch hoped to keep his people free of idolatrous influence, for Abraham's

family—even those who had stayed behind in Mesopotamia—were apparently believers in the one true God.

Abraham insists on two conditions concerning the bride for Isaac: One, she must come freely with Eliezer to the land of Canaan, and two, Isaac must not go out of Canaan in order to seek her (24:8). Abraham's servant works out the following "game of chance": He leads his camels to a well in the city of Abraham's brother, Nahor. There he awaits the girls of the town who come to draw water for their household needs. He will select the one who favorably responds to his request for a drink for him *and* his camels (24:14).

Happily for Eliezer—and for Abraham and Isaac—a beautiful maiden soon comes to the well and eagerly offers drink to Eliezer and his camels. She is a niece of Abraham's; she is furthermore unwed, and she also is willing to follow Eliezer back to Hebron. The girl in question is Rebekah. Her brother Laban (who seems to be her guardian) gratefully accepts the dowry offered him and commends Rebekah to Eliezer's care. When she arrives in Canaan, Isaac is at once smitten with his bride-to-be—as she is with him—and the story ends happily with their marriage.

This chapter is one of the longest so far in Genesis and seems intent on emphasizing the worthiness of Rebekah and the customs surrounding betrothal in Abraham's time. Another interesting theme of the story concerns the servant, Eliezer. His name does not appear in this chapter, but he is earlier identified (15:2) as the steward or overseer of Abraham's house (see 24:2). Apparently Eliezer is not a Hebrew, for he prays to the Lord not as *his* God but as "God of my master" (24:12). By the end of the story (24:52) Eliezer seems ready for conversion, no doubt deeply impressed by God's help in making his plan work out.

Isaac the Patriarch

Abraham, though old and stricken, marries again and produces sons (25:1–2), but Isaac, as his first-born, is his heir and successor. The great patriarch's death is described with typical Biblical brevity and impact. It is one of the most impressive "obituaries" in literature (25:7–8). Abraham was buried near Sarah at Machpelah, and Ishmael came to mourn him. (The sacred burial place of Machpelah is still intact and is today a Muslim shrine.) The Bible delineates Ishmael's genealogy—or family tree (25:12–18)—then turns back to Isaac and Rebekah.

The couple are to be blessed by the birth of twins. Rebekah learns this from God (25:23) and furthermore discovers that the younger twin is to be "stronger than the other," both as a man and as a patriarch. Because of this prophecy, Rebekah is to instigate a plan which causes a great deal of family anguish (as we soon shall see).

The twins are Jacob and Esau; their names tell of their temperaments. Jacob means "he who takes hold," for he tried to take hold of his brother's heel as the two were being born. This desire to supplant his brother will become a dominant factor in Jacob's life. Esau simply means "ruddy and hairy."

Rebekah favors Jacob mainly because of the prophecy concerning his greatness and she no doubt convinces him, as a boy, that his brother's birthright as first-born and successor to Isaac rightfully belongs to him. Thus influenced, Jacob sets about to

In Veronese's elegantly composed painting, Eliezer's meeting with Rebekah at the well becomes a gracious Renaissance ceremony, the camels (upper left) notwithstanding.

purchase this right and finds his opportunity one day when Esau, famished from hunting, comes upon his younger brother, who is cooking a thick red-bean soup, called pottage (25:29–34). This remarkable short story, in which Esau sells his birthright for a "mess of pottage," is one of the most famous in the Bible.

Note: There is a cunning play on words at Verse 30. Esau (ruddy) was to become leader of Edom (ruddy clay). Because he craves the *red* bean pottage, his national name seems all the more appropriate.

The following chapter (26) in Genesis almost seems to be a word-for-word repetition of an earlier story, the one concerning Abraham and a local chieftain called Abimelech (Chapter 20 and Chapter 21:22–34). In this case, it is Isaac who comes up against Abimelech—probably the son of the first man so named. Most of the key incidents in this story are the same as the earlier tale: Isaac, in order to safeguard Rebekah from abduction, says that she is his sister (throughout that world a man's unmarried sister was untouchable). Abimelech is angered by this deceit and grows aggressive. Isaac disputes with local tribesmen about the digging of wells but finally comes to terms with Abimelech —as had Abraham—and peace is restored. All this discussion about wells and property, about wives and sisters, is presented in order to demonstrate the legalistic tangles with which even the patriarchs had to contend. But of greatest importance in this chapter is Verse 24, in which God reaffirms his covenant with Isaac concerning the growth of the Hebrew nation.

Although no one knows who posed for Rembrandt's *The Jewish Bride*, it has come to be called *Isaac and Rebekah* because it depicts the mutual devotion of the Biblical lovers.

Jacob—the Supplanter

The fascinating character of Jacob returns center stage with Chapter 27, where the birthright again becomes the main concern. Now Isaac is old and blind; he feels compelled to dispense his legacies to his sons and appropriately calls forth Esau so that the 'blessings of the firstborn' may be bestowed on him. Before attending to the business at hand, Isaac instructs the hairy hunter to kill a deer and prepare him a savory dish of venison. In the interim, while Esau is out hunting, Rebekah approaches Jacob with the news of Isaac's plan. Eager for her younger son to fulfill his destiny, she suggests that he deceive Isaac by pretending to be Esau. For this ruse she has obtained her older son's garments as well as the skins of young goats to tie around Jacob's arms, thus making it appear that he is the hairy Esau (27:15–16). She also cooks up a dish of savory venison to fulfill Isaac's request. No stone has been left unturned in her plot.

Jacob agrees to this deception without much protest, and, dressed as Esau, his arms covered with hair, he comes before his father with a bowl of venison in hand, saying, "I am Esau, thy firstborn" (27:19).

Isaac is surprised that the hunter has returned so quickly and asks to touch the man who stands before him. We can sense the father's suspicions in his famous remark, "The voice is Jacob's voice, but the hands are the hands of Esau" (27:22). Jacob unflinchingly insists that he is Esau and presents his father with the venison. After Isaac has eaten, he again appears doubtful. This time he tries to determine if the man before him is really Esau by smelling his clothing. Because Esau is a hunter, his garments no doubt smell of the outdoors.

Rebekah was wily enough to foresee this

Abraham and his wife Sarah were buried in the cave of Machpelah, now topped by a mosque.

possibility when she made Jacob don his brother's robes. As a result, Isaac is convinced and he proceeds to dispense the blessing or inheritance of his wealth and patriarchy to Jacob. "Let people serve thee, and nations bow down to thee: be lord over thy brethren . . ." (27:29).

Jacob leaves his father's side in the nick of time, as Esau returns with the venison. You can imagine Isaac's dismay and Esau's rage when the ruse is discovered. One must feel pity for the hunter as he laments his fate and begs for even a small part of Isaac's inheritance: "Hast thou not reserved a blessing for me?" (27:36).

But Isaac cannot renounce his earlier dispensation, which is a sacred oath. To Esau goes the minor legacy of the second-born, including the bitter fact that "thou . . . shalt serve thy brother . . ." (27:40).

Rebekah is rightfully worried by Esau's anger toward Jacob; she urges her younger son to flee and take refuge with her brother Laban "until thy brother's fury turn away." The last verse of this chapter further implies that Rebekah is concerned lest Jacob marry outside his faith, as he might were he to remain in Canaan. Very often the Bible gives two reasons for an action, both of them logical and realistic.

This dramatic and distressing story, in which Rebekah and Jacob conspire to fulfill Jacob's destiny, provokes many questions of morality. How may a future patriarch like Jacob ever be forgiven such a crime? Or, did God really condone Rebekah's plot? These problems imply the power of the Bible as a book that appeals to true emotions and to the reality of life. Jacob, who is to become one of the greatest of all Hebrew leaders, is a complicated individual. This the Bible wishes to show without evasion. He is, furthermore, a man who must be tested and who must learn full obedience to God. Like a diamond in the rough, he must be polished and faceted in order to shine, and the following chapters tell of the painful and long-term process in which Jacob passes from an ambitious, even reckless, youth to a tempered, thoughtful patriarch. Besides, had not God promised Rebekah that Jacob "shall be stronger" than his brother and the "elder shall serve the younger"? (See 25:23.)

In no way do the Biblical scribes condone Jacob's deception of his father and brother, but they were obliged to report the truth, and in this case the truth concerned a very real and unalterable deceit.

The Ordeal of Jacob

Alone and afraid, the fugitive Jacob comes to the very place where his grandfather, Abraham, had earlier erected an altar to God—the place near Beth-el. As night descends, the guilty man lies down on the ground to sleep, with only some stones for his pillows (28:11); his blanket,

Blind Isaac blesses Jacob, disguised as Esau, while Rebekah watches. The real Esau enters at left in van den Eeckhout's Dutch painting.

The custom of erecting sacred pillars, as Jacob did, was widespread throughout patriarchal societies of the Mideast. These were found in a temple at Hazor.

the open sky. In his troubled dreams, Jacob sees a vision of God that is both a justification of his deceptive acts and a sort of prophecy of things to come. On the one hand, God seems to exonerate Jacob by telling him that he will indeed inherit the land of Abraham and Isaac and that his seed will be blessed as was theirs. But along with his vision of God, Jacob dreams of a group of angels ascending and descending a ladder that reaches to heaven (28:12), advising him of the "ups and downs" that are yet in store for him before the day of his deliverance. For all its comforting promise, we know that Jacob's dream disturbs him: "How dreadful is this place," he cries upon waking (28:17).

In the morning, already chastened, Jacob takes the stone he had used for a "pillow" and sanctifies it as an altar to God (repeating Abraham's devotion of 12:7). Furthermore, Jacob vows penance to the Lord for his deception and a tithe, or 10

percent payment, of all he acquires as sacrifice.

Jacob's actual penance is worked out by twenty years of servile labor to his uncle, Laban, to whose house he now journeys. Only one bright spot gleams through this ordeal, the person of Rachel, "the beautiful and well-favoured" daughter of Laban. From the moment he sees her at the well (the same well where Eliezer saw Rebekah), Jacob is smitten with love. The Bible tells us that he kissed the young woman there and then wept with joy (29:11).

Laban is a shrewd and calculating herdsman who agrees that if Jacob tend his flocks for seven years, he may marry Rachel. At the end of the time—which passes quickly for the anxious suitor (29:20)—Jacob comes to claim his bride. Now retribution begins to be felt, for Laban, who wishes to marry off his older, weak-eyed daughter, Leah, substitutes her for Rachel at the wedding. This he may easily do because brides of the time were obscured by veils and awaited their new husbands in darkened tents. And so the man who once disguised himself as Esau now wakes in the morning, after his wedding night, to find that he has consummated an unwanted marriage with Leah disguised as Rachel.

Laban justifies his deception, saying that it is the custom of his country to marry the elder daughter before any other. Jacob may have Rachel, he adds, and have her at the end of that very week, *if* he serves another seven years as Laban's hand. Jacob agrees. Possibly in his heart he realizes that God's punishment for his own deceits is being meted out and that he must accept his fate like a man.

Rachel, whom Jacob loves best, is barren and cannot produce children, a condition that was true of Sarah and Rebekah as well until God intervened. The Bible thus wishes to show that the Hebrew patriarchs are born of the Lord's own will. Leah and two lesser wives provide a total of eight sons and one daughter (Dinah) over the years. Then after more than a decade "God remembered Rachel" (30:22), and she gives birth to a son named Joseph.

The names of Jacob's sons, in order of

Raphael paints Jacob high on a Vatican wall, dreaming of angels who ascend and descend a staircase above which God hovers.

The French painter Eugène Delacroix (1798–1863) depicted Jacob wrestling with the Angel while Esau and his band approach at right. The spear on the ground points straight to Jacob's leg, injured in the fight.

birth, were Reuben, Simeon, Levi, Judah, Dan, Naphtali, Gad, Asher, Issachar, Zebulun, Joseph and, later, Benjamin.

Jacob on His Own

Something seems to have stirred Jacob to a sense of independence after Joseph's birth, and he tries to break away from his demanding father-in-law, requesting that he be allowed to leave with his entire family. Laban is anxious to keep Jacob and his daughters nearby and so concedes to pay his son-in-law a wage in the form of cattle if he will serve him another several years. Jacob accepts the offer but contrives a complicated means of obtaining the

stronger of Laban's flocks while leaving the feeble animals for his father-in-law (30:32–42).

By his clever methods, Jacob grows rich, so much so that Laban's sons resent him and inspire a similar bitterness in their father. Sensing trouble and having served now six more years, Jacob decides to shorten his servitude to Laban. Secretly at night, with his wives' consent, he packs up children, servants, cattle and belongings and journeys out of Laban's land at God's behest (31:13–18).

All is well until Laban discovers that his good-luck idols are missing (for Rachel has taken them, unbeknownst even to Jacob).

Furious, the older man sets off with his sons to track down the runaways. It is interesting to note that Laban—an idol worshiper—respects the God of Abraham, Isaac and Jacob, who has warned him, in a dream, to be peaceful when he finally catches up with his son-in-law. Accordingly, Laban does not physically attack Jacob's caravan, but accuses him of having stolen the idols (31:30). Knowing nothing of the idols, Jacob insists that Laban search his tents and kill anyone caught with the goods. The older man and his servants ransack everything in sight, all the while denouncing Jacob as a thief.

The precious idols are hidden under Rachel's saddle, which doubles as a chair. On the pretext of being unwell, Rachel remains seated, and Laban, not wishing to disturb her, returns to his son-in-law empty-handed.

Now the once guilt-ridden Jacob feels justified in ending his days of servitude, and he chides Laban as though to say: "I have had enough of your tyranny and accusations; I'm my own man now and it's time I faced the future unburdened by past guilts and fears. You cannot hinder me any longer."

Properly cowed, Laban begs forgiveness and concludes a peace covenant with Jacob by erecting a pillar, or boundary marker, beyond which neither man will pass to attack the other.

Jacob Wrestles a "Man"

Though Jacob has reconciled his relationship with Laban and struck out on his own, he still faces another major emotional event: he must meet Esau, his angry brother, who rules the nearby territory. Remembering the deceit of years past, Jacob is naturally afraid of what Esau might do to him and separates his family into fortified groups. Then he prays that God will strengthen him because the news is rather frightening: Esau is headed toward his caravan with four hundred men (32:6).

Several unusual things occur that fateful night as Jacob attempts to reconcile his past. For one, a band of angels brings him comfort (32:1). For another, he selects a large drove of animals as a peace offering for his brother (32:13). But of most significance is the mysterious wrestling match that Jacob fights with someone simply called "a man" (32:24). This is one of the most perplexing and yet psychologically revealing moments in all the Bible. Here Jacob, guilt-ridden and yet on the verge of a new life, seems to be wrestling with his inner self as well as with God so that he might finally atone for all his past deceits. This purge, this stripping away of immaturity, is so effective that in the morning, when he has triumphed over the mysterious man, Jacob is informed by God that he must change his name, becoming Israel—"he who has prevailed" (32:28)—a name that will echo through the ages.

Though he now limps from his forceful encounter with this angelic wrestler, Jacob-Israel finally emerges as a patriarch worthy of God's covenant. When Esau arrives he recognizes his brother's new-won stature and lovingly accepts his atonement. The two men are reconciled and join together for a heartfelt reunion (33:3–4).

The Rise of Joseph

Ironically, after Jacob's transforming crisis, his career seems to take second place to the activities of his sons. In Chapter 34, two of them, Simeon and Levi, become

An Egyptian painting of Canaanites shows them wearing the kind of coat Jacob may have made for Joseph. It was probably of this style, though more colorful.

The Tomb of Rachel, near Bethlehem, a relatively modern edifice, built in 1841. Today it is sacred to Jewish women.

entangled in a rather dishonorable war, vindicating the honor of their sister, Dinah. The outcome of this episode, in which treachery plays a leading part (34:24–25), is that Jacob's reputation is tarnished among his neighbors. As a result, he must move his tribe and rededicate himself to God. This he does at Beth-el (35:3), where God repeats his covenant and blesses the patriarch with the birth of a new son, Benjamin. Tragedy accompanies this joyful event, for Rachel dies in giving birth to Benjamin (35:18–19). Jacob-Israel buries his beloved wife near the tiny town of Bethlehem, and to this day her tomb stands in that place as a shrine to motherhood and the devoted wife.

A long genealogy follows in Chapter 36 describing the descendants of Esau. Many such lists of names fill Genesis, serving to mark the legal rights of families. This fairly uninteresting chapter leads to the fascinating character of Joseph, the eleventh son of Jacob, first-born of Rachel, who at seventeen has already begun to emerge as his father's favorite (37:2–3). Joseph's famous "coat of many colours," a gift from Jacob, signifies this paternal admiration; it also causes jealousy among Joseph's older brothers, who fear the loss of their own inheritance to the younger man.

Joseph does not calm his brothers' fears but on the contrary implies his own ascendancy. This is revealed to him in a series of dreams in which sheaves of wheat and the very stars in heaven bow down to Joseph, signifying eventual glory (37:7–10).

One day, when the young dreamer is alone with his brothers in the field, they

Joseph Thrown into the Pit by Murillo (1617–1682) depicts one of Joseph's brothers (right) holding the coat.

conspire to rid themselves of their competitor by slaying him and leaving him for dead in a pit (37:20). The eldest, Reuben, tempers this evil plan for his father's sake, persuading his brothers merely to throw Joseph alive into a pit and not actually to murder him. (It is Reuben's hope to return later and rescue the lad.) The other brothers agree. Before they dispose of Joseph they strip him of his coat.

God is keeping watch over the boy, for while he languishes in the pit a group of Bedouins, called Ishmeelites (descendants of Ishmael), come by looking for slaves. Judah convinces his brothers to sell the boy to them and thus be rid of him forever. At this point in the story there is a moment of minor textual confusion. Do the Ishmeelites actually take Joseph as a slave or does a group of merchants called Midianites carry out the deal? Only by examining 37:28 very carefully can we come to some conclusion. This is worth doing since it will accustom the reader to the problem of pronouns that constantly crops up in the Biblical text. In this case the pronoun "they" is the word that causes confusion. "Then there passed by Midianites merchantmen; and they drew and lifted up Joseph out of the pit and sold Joseph to the Ishmeelites for twenty pieces of silver: and they brought Joseph into Egypt." Who are all these *theys*?

The verse makes sense if we substitute "his brothers" for the first "they" (who draw him out of the pit) and then add the unspoken part of the text after "twenty pieces of silver"—namely: "The Ishmeelites then sold Joseph to the Midianites and *they* (the Midianites) brought him

Joseph's brothers tell Jacob that he has been killed by a lion—a frequent mishap, as seen in this Assyrian ivory relief from the 8th century B.C.

into Egypt." This seems accurate because the Midianites traveled often to Egypt on business, while the Ishmeelites tended to stay close to their tents. Our conclusion is also substantiated by Verse 36.

Once they are rid of Joseph, the brothers contrive to make it appear as though a wild beast has devoured the boy. They dip his colorful coat in goat's blood and with it convince the stricken Jacob that his son is dead. As the Bible concisely reveals, the father's grief is enormous (37:34–35).

The fate of Judah, who is probably the most powerful of Jacob's sons, is told in Chapter 38. It is not a pretty story and is noteworthy only to reveal how God loses trust in the older brothers and comes to look on only Joseph and Benjamin as worthy of his covenant. The thread of Joseph's story resumes with the following chapter.

Joseph in Egypt

At the time Joseph was sold as a slave, around 1500 B.C., Egypt was the great-est civilization in the world, complete with magnificent architecture, a well-established nobility and an artistic culture that impresses us to this day. Joseph is brought to the household of a minor aristocrat called Potiphar, and there he rises to become chief overseer of the house (39:4). By God's will, both Joseph and his master prosper for a period of more than a dozen years.

The story of Joseph, however, is one of ups and downs, and to accomplish the next turn of his fate a troublesome woman, Potiphar's wife, causes the young man's temporary downfall. In a story reminiscent of a popular Egyptian tale of the time, Joseph is set upon by this woman, who falsely accuses him of seducing her. Potiphar, believing his wife, has Joseph arrested and cast into a royal prison.

But God has not abandoned Joseph, for in this prison the young man befriends two high court officials of the pharaoh, both accused of unspecified crimes. They are the wine steward and the chief baker, or cook. Worried about their fates, each man has a disturbing dream, which Joseph cleverly interprets. The butler's dream is filled with positive omens: blossoming vines and ripened grapes. This Joseph reveals to mean that he shall soon be released from prison (40:9–13). But the baker has dreamed of birds pecking at his head and this, says Joseph, bodes ill.

The young prisoner's prophecies are fulfilled. The baker is hanged, while the butler returns to his position at court. "Think on me when it shall be well with thee," Joseph implores the butler. The official promises to do so (40:14), but two full years will pass before he remembers.

Then the pharaoh himself has a series of troubling dreams and none of his court magicians can properly interpret them. At this moment the butler recalls Joseph and recommends him to the pharaoh. Cleanly dressed and shaven (for the Egyptians despised facial hair), Joseph appears before the mighty Egyptian king (41:14). Reminding the pharaoh that God alone is the source of his interpretation—for he is not a magician—Joseph listens to the dreams and renders the following prophecy: Because the pharaoh has dreamed of seven well-fed cattle coming out of the Nile River (the chief river of Egypt), this means seven prosperous years of harvest will follow in which the Nile will nourish the land. But in the same dream the seven lean cows who come up out of the river and devour the fat ones represent seven years of famine, brought about by drought. This Joseph knows because the lean cows do not grow fat even after having eaten the others

(41:17–21). The pharaoh dreams the same dream again and again with different images representing prosperity and drought. God clearly means to bring famine on Egypt within seven years—so Joseph reveals.

The pharaoh is naturally alarmed and wonders what to do. Then Joseph speaks the words that will ensure his success. He suggests that the king appoint a "man discreet and wise" to garner the prosperous harvests in preparation for the famine (41:33–36). Pharaoh immediately appoints Joseph as that man: "Only I will be greater than you," he tells the former slave and decks him with official insignias, including a ring and a gold chain. What a turn of events! In a day, Joseph rises from the dungeon to the highest estates in the land. He was but thirty years old and yet before long he masterfully enacted his antifamine plan,

A modern sound-and-light show at the Pyramids of Gizeh—a new way of dramatizing the great civilization of ancient Egypt, to which Joseph came as a slave.

A soldier is barbered in accord with Egyptian hygienic custom, as was Joseph when Pharaoh summoned him.

married into the nobility, had two sons and became a mighty ruler, just as his boyhood dreams had prophesied.

There is much archaeological evidence to support the reality of details in this story of Joseph. From Egyptian scrolls and wall carvings we know of the wide dependence on dreams and omens as a guide to daily life. We can see, as well, how the pharaoh often endowed foreign and local commoners with the insignias of high office, and as regards Joseph specifically, we learn from the eminent Egyptologist Sir Flinders Petrie that the ruins of a palace near Thebes

bears an inscription that reads: "I collected corn . . . and when a famine arose, lasting many years, I distributed corn to the city, each year of the famine." Compare this to 41:53–56 to see the striking parallel.

Joseph and His Brothers

The drought afflicting Egypt spread to Canaan, where Jacob assembled his sons and instructed them to seek out the governor of Egypt and buy foodstuffs for the hungry people. Ten of the brothers make the journey, leaving the youngest, Benjamin, behind.

An Egyptian general receives gold chains symbolizing his office,
as Joseph received them from Pharaoh.

Cattle carved in an Egyptian tomb are as sleek and well-fed as the fat variety described in Pharaoh's dream.

Egyptian officials used seals with their names and ranks inscribed in hieroglyphics. These seals bear Semitic names.

One of the most dramatic scenes in Genesis depicts the weary Israelites bowing before the great "Egyptian" governor —in reality their own brother, Joseph, whom they had sold into slavery some twenty-five years before. Joseph recognizes his brothers at once, "but they knew not him" (42:8).

Now begins a series of suspenseful incidents in which Joseph chastises his brothers and makes them "sweat out" the good fortune he is to bestow on them, for he wishes to have them repent of their crime. First he accuses them of being spies (42:9) and imprisons them. Then, because he knows his father may be starving, he releases all but one, telling them to prove their innocent intentions by bringing their youngest brother—whom they have described—when next they return. In a moving scene, Joseph overhears his bro-

This dagger handle belonged to a high Egyptian official called Nahman, who was, like Joseph, a Semite. The carving depicts a hunting scene.

Periodic droughts still plague the Mideast, creating famines such as the one that sent Joseph's brothers to Egypt.

Semitic envoys pictured on an Egyptian tomb humble themselves as did Joseph's brothers when they came to Egypt.

thers lamenting their earlier crime against him and saying, "This is now our punishment." Touched by their new understanding and their pain, Joseph weeps secret tears (42:21–24).

Arriving back in Canaan, the brothers, after much persuasion, convince Jacob to release Benjamin to their care, for the father is loath to lose this son as he lost Joseph (42:38). In due time, they return to Egypt,

worried indeed because when they had gotten home from their last trip they had found money scattered in their sacks, along with their foodstuffs, money they fear they will be accused of stealing.

With Benjamin in hand and laden with presents for Joseph, the brothers arrive again at Joseph's palace. To their surprise, they are invited to dine with the noble Egyptian, whom they find most cordially disposed. When he sees Benjamin, however, Joseph's emotions overflow and he rushes from the scene to weep in private (43:29–30).

Again the brothers hasten to leave Egypt with their purchases, but unknown to them Joseph has had a silver goblet of great value placed in Benjamin's sack. When their caravan is a little way off, he sends soldiers to arrest the youngest brother for theft. Remembering Jacob, the others insist on returning with Benjamin and sharing his fate. In fact, Judah, the very brother who schemed to sell Joseph as a slave, now offers his life in Benjamin's place after pleading a lengthy appeal for mercy (44:18–34).

Overwhelmed by his brothers' obvious atonement and unwilling to agonize them further, Joseph stands before them and declares: "I am Joseph your brother, whom ye sold into Egypt" (45:4). At first the brothers are terrified of what vengeance Joseph might wreak on them. But he assures them that he has forgiven their crime, for God has willed that he suffer slavery and rise to glory for some greater end.

The Children of Israel

The greater end is indeed also the end of Genesis—namely, the arrival in Egypt of Joseph's entire family, led by Jacob (Israel) and now called the Children of Israel (45:21). God apparently wished this growing nation of believers to experience the values of the world's greatest civilization, the Egyptian civilization, with its elaborate laws, customs, artistry and folklore. And so the joyous Jacob is reunited with his beloved son, Joseph, and is presented to the pharaoh, who establishes the land of Goshen in the fertile delta of Egypt as a territory for the Hebrews. Here they may herd cattle and sheep, an occupation apparently not favored by Egyptians of the time.

The Children of Israel were well treated by the pharaoh of Joseph's day, who some scholars think may have been Akhenaton, founder of monotheism in Egypt. So long as Joseph lives they will thrive. Chapter 47 tells of his continuing rulership over the pharaoh's kingdom and the sensible taxes he imposed to offset the famine.

The story of Joseph and his brothers to this point is perhaps the most literary in the Bible. No wonder it inspired the great contemporary writer Thomas Mann to create his three-part masterpiece *Joseph and His Brothers, Young Joseph* and *Joseph in Egypt*. The Bible has appealed to many authors (as well as painters) in this way. John Milton's *Paradise Lost* is a retelling of the Adam and Eve story and it is perhaps the greatest of all Biblically inspired poems.

The Finale

In Goshen, Jacob, now nearing death, elevates Joseph's sons to the rank of his first-born, blessing the youngest before the eldest (48:19).

In Chapter 49, the dying patriarch utters a great hymn of blessing which establishes the twelve tribes of Israel and reminds them of God's special covenant (49:25). Then extracting the promise that his sons will bury him in his homeland, at Machpelah—where Abraham and Isaac lie—Jacob departs the world, or, as the Bible says, he "yielded up the ghost, and was gathered unto his people" (49:33). Joseph carries out his father's last request and with permission of the pharaoh escorts his remains to Canaan in "a very great company" (50:9).

The remainder of Genesis, a few short verses, tells of Joseph's final days, how he

secured the prosperity of his brothers and how, before he died—at the age of 110—he made his children swear an oath that in time his bones would be brought to the land of his fathers, for he somehow knew that the children of Israel would not dwell for long in Egypt (50:25).

With this hint of things to come, the book of Genesis ends. It began at the beginning of all things in the world and told how a great nation of believers in God, the nation of Israel, came to be through the efforts of Abraham, Isaac, Jacob and Joseph. Many wicked happenings preceded the founding of the nation and many punishments were levied at man, first in the fall of Adam and then in the flood, the dispersion of the people at Babel and the testing of Abraham. In fifty chapters the Bible has established a whole history of mankind.

Summary of the Book of Genesis

1. Creation (1:1–2:3)
2. Adam and Eve (2:4–3:24)
3. Cain and Abel (4:1–4:24)
4. The Generations of Adam (4:25–6:7)
5. Noah and the Flood (6:8–10:32)
6. The Tower of Babel (11:1–11:9)
7. The Descendants of Noah (11:10–11:32)
8. Abraham (12:1–25:10)
9. Isaac (25:11–26:35)
10. Jacob and Esau (27:1–35:29)
11. The Descendants of Esau (36:1–36:43)
12. The Children of Jacob (37:1–38:30)
13. Joseph in Egypt (39:1–45:28)
14. Israel in Egypt (46:1–50:26)

It is now Jacob's turn to pass on the blessing he received from Isaac. In Rembrandt's painting *Jacob Blesses the Sons of Joseph*, the artist shows how the patriarch, near death, thinks of the future of his people.

Guarding the pyramids at Gizeh is the Great Sphinx, combining a lion's body with the head of the Pharaoh Chephren; the pyramid seen here was Chephren's tomb. Both are symbols of Egypt's ancient grandeur.

CHAPTER TWO

THE GOING OUT

Exodus · Leviticus · Numbers · Deuteronomy

The next four books of the Bible concern two events central to the Old Testament: the flight of the Hebrew slaves from Egypt and the giving of the Law by God at Mount Sinai. The dominant figure of these books—indeed he is considered their author—is Moses, probably the most dynamic and influential man of the Old Testament. His personal story as well as the establishment of the Hebrew nation under law is told mainly in the book of Exodus but is amplified in Leviticus, Numbers and Deuteronomy. One seventh of the whole Bible, in fact, concerns this inspired leader and his works. But it is important to note that the miracles, struggles and world-shaking events beginning in Exodus actually go back, for their roots, to Genesis and the coming of Jacob-Israel to Egypt at Joseph's request.

Some 300 years have passed since Joseph's death. The tribes of Israel living in Goshen have increased from a mere seventy adults upon arrival to more than half a million persons (some say twice as many, since Biblical population figures never included women and children). Such a large group of "foreigners" could not long enjoy peaceful treatment in Egypt, especially when—as the Bible tells us—"there arose a new king over Egypt, which knew not Joseph" (Exodus 1:8). We can be sure that the new pharaoh—more specifically, the new dynasty or family of pharaohs—remembered who Joseph was: he had been a very important figure in Egyptian history. What probably happened was that now they chose to ignore his accomplishments so that the Hebrew people might be enslaved.

The Bible implies that the pharaoh was afraid of the large numbers of Hebrews because in case of a war they might "join also unto our enemies, and fight against

Many scholars believe that Ramesses II was the pharaoh who enslaved the Hebrews. He is seen here, at left, paying homage to the god Amon-Re.

us" in order to escape their slavery (Exodus 1:10). Accordingly, a devious plan begins forming in the pharaoh's mind. Not only would the Hebrew slaves be forced to harder and more rigorous labors, but also the population would be reduced by the slaughter of all Hebrew baby boys (Exodus 1:22).

Who was this pharaoh of the Exodus and what was he like? Many Bible scholars believe there were two kings of Egypt who figure in this section of Scripture: the one who initiated Israel's slavery and the other who confronted Moses and at first forbade the Exodus. The pharaoh of 1:8 was thus Ramesses II, whose rule began around 1300 B.C. His name appears on bricks in the ruins of Pithom (see picture), one of the granary cities that the Hebrew slaves were forced to build (Exodus 1:11). Another city mentioned in the Bible is called Raamses, probably in honor of the pharaoh himself. His successor, Merneptah (whose rule began in 1235 B.C.), was thus likely the second pharaoh whom we meet in Chapter 5. The Egyptologist Sir Flinders Petrie in 1906 uncovered a slab recording Merneptah's victories, which at one point reads: "Israel is desolated." This may imply the sufferings of the Hebrews immediately after their exodus.

Of course, there are other opinions about the identity of the oppressive pharaoh, but the reigns of Ramesses II and Merneptah fit with the usual dates of the Exodus—namely, around 1200 B.C. Sigmund Freud, in his book *Moses and Monotheism,* believes the Exodus occurred

You can see the straw in this mud brick as well as the seal of Ramesses II, the pharaoh who is believed to have kept back the straw as a punishment for the Hebrews.

A carved head of Merneptah, who may have been the pharaoh of the Exodus.

The victory stele of Pharaoh Merneptah includes an ironic reference: "Israel is laid waste, it has no seed."

between 1358 and 1350 B.C., placing it directly in the reign of Ramesses II. The Bible commentator Henry Halley sets the period back a hundred years before. Unfortunately, the Egyptians in their records never mention the Exodus, and the Bible does not date it specifically. Nevertheless, it forms the nucleus of Jewish historical experience.

The Man Called Moses

When the slaughter of Hebrew male babies began, a Jewish woman called Jochebed, wife of Amram of the Levi tribe (see Exodus 6:20), was pregnant. When she delivered and saw that the baby was a boy, she initiated a desperate plan to save him. With the aid of the baby's sister, Miriam, she built a small cradle, or ark, out of bulrushes (a reed plant used for matting), made it watertight and set it into the Nile River (Exodus 2:3). Her plan was not to abandon the baby but rather to keep it

This line of hieroglyphs includes the word *isr'l* and is from Merneptah's stele, which proclaims the pharaoh's conquests in Canaan.

This fresco, painted in the plaster of a 3rd-century Syrian synagogue, shows both the moment when Moses is lifted from the bulrushes and when he is placed in the arms of Pharaoh's daughter.

alive in a quiet part of the river with Miriam standing by at all times.

Now as God would have it, the daughter of the pharaoh comes to this very bank of the river. She sees the ark, takes pity on the child and has him drawn from "the flags [or papyrus reeds] by the river's brink" (Exodus 2:3). The pharaoh's daughter knows at once that "this is one of the Hebrews' children," but she appears compassionate. Perhaps she herself was childless and craved a son. Miriam, the baby's sister, is quick to act and suggests to the princess that a Hebrew woman be called to nurse the baby. Naturally, Miriam fetches her own mother, who is thus able to rear the baby in the safety of the pharaoh's palace.

The pharaoh's daughter names her adopted son Moses. In Egyptian, Moses means "child" or "son" and appears in the pharaoh's own name—Ra-moses: Ramesses, or child of the god Ra. In Exodus, the explanation is that Moses was named from the Hebrew word *Mashah*, meaning "to draw out," because as the pharaoh's daughter says, "I drew him out of the water" (2:10). It is indeed a symbolic name, since Moses is to live as part Hebrew, part Egyptian for almost forty years.

All we know of Moses' childhood is told in ten verses (Chapter 2), yet from this brief account we can deduce that Jochebed, his mother, influenced the boy as he grew up in the royal Egyptian household. From her he learned about the Hebrew people, their heritage, God's promise and the land of Canaan. Thus it happened that when Moses, now grown to manhood, beheld a Hebrew slave being mistreated by an Egyptian soldier (2:11), he flew into a rage and killed the Egyptian on the spot. Spies in the Hebrew village where this killing occurred reported what they saw and in a short time Moses became a hunted man, sought by the pharaoh himself. To escape punishment, he flees to the land of Midian, to the east of Egypt.

What an ironic life Moses has lived thus far! As a baby he is condemned to die by the pharaoh for being a Hebrew but is rescued by the pharaoh's own daughter and raised as an Egyptian. Then as a man, by staying loyal to the people of his birth, he is once again condemned by the pharaoh and his life is placed in jeopardy. Does God plan a momentous life for this troubled man? Clearly, the theme of Exodus so far is that God has very definite plans for Moses and also for the Hebrew people, for God did

not forget them in their bondage (2:24–25), nor did he forget Moses, who, though now a fugitive, finds a home with a Midianite chieftain called Reuel (later Jethro), marries this man's daughter, Zipporah, has a son and settles down in the rugged mountains to the simple life of a shepherd (2:21).

The Burning Bush

Imagine being settled into the humble routine of a shepherd, cut off from the hurly-burly of daily affairs, and then, one day, while tending your flocks, God himself confronts you and reveals a world-shaking plan which he wants you to enact! What would be your response? In Chapter 3 of Exodus, Moses is faced by such a situation when he sees a bush burning in the wilderness, and yet "the bush was not consumed" (3:2). As he draws closer, Moses hears a thunderous voice from within the fire commanding him to remove his shoes, for he stands on holy ground. Then the voice reveals: "I am the God of thy father, the God of Abraham, the God of Isaac, and the God of Jacob" (3:6).

What will be Moses' response? At first, awe-struck and amazed, he says not a word and listens respectfully as God announces his plan: "I am come down to deliver [the Children of Israel] out of the hand of the Egyptians, and to bring them up out of that land unto a good land . . . flowing with milk and honey . . . therefore . . . I will send thee unto pharaoh that thou mayest bring forth my people, the Children of Israel, out of Egypt" (3:8 and 10).

Haltingly, Moses speaks and his reaction is a very human one, for in so many words he asks: "Why me? Why have you chosen *me*, such a humble man?"

There follows one of the most amazing dialogues in all the Bible—indeed, in all literature—God trying to convince Moses that he will stand by him in this monumental effort and Moses perplexed, questioning and unsure. For nearly two full chapters the conversation ensues—a back-and-forth duet that sometimes resembles an argument and at other times a bargaining session.

MOSES: Oh my Lord, I am not eloquent. . . . I am slow of speech and of a slow tongue.

GOD: Who hath made man's mouth . . . have not I the Lord. . . . I will be with thy mouth, and teach thee what thou shalt say (4:10–12).

To convince Moses, God reveals that he shall afflict Egypt "with all my wonders" until the pharaoh frees the Hebrew slaves. The Lord even demonstrates his magical powers to the reluctant shepherd by transforming his rod into a serpent (4:2–4) and then back into a rod.

Finally, Moses, still worried and reluctant, agrees to be the liberator of the Hebrews, so long as his older brother, Aaron, may do all the speaking (Moses convinces God on the point of his eloquence (4:14–16), causing the Lord to appoint Aaron as "spokesman" for the forthcoming encounters with the pharaoh). One other revelation is made in Chapter 3 that is of great theological importance. It concerns the perplexing nature of God—in fact, it provides him with a specific name, therefore enriching his reality. When Moses, still bewildered by his great experience at

In the multicolored stone mosaic at San Vitale, in Ravenna, a bush burns with stylized spurts of flame as Moses removes his sandals in reverence.

the burning bush, asks: "Who shall I say sent me [to free the Hebrews]?" the Lord replies: "I am that I am . . . thus shalt thou say unto the Children of Israel, I AM hath sent me to you."

The Hebrew words spoken at this point have been formed into what is called an anagram, or a transposition, based on the verb "to be" (I am) and appearing as the letters YHWH in English. Thus the name of God is given in some places as Yahweh and in others as Jehovah (its Latin form, as earlier noted). But in fact, this is not a name at all. It is rather an idea, a characterization: "I am, I will always be. I am all that is and all that will come." In short, the Lord, by this thrilling revelation, is saying to the world that God is a verb, not a noun, and the verb is the very essence of existence; it is *being* in and of itself.

The Contest

For ten chapters (5 to 15) a suspenseful, active battle ensues between the pharaoh (with his magicians) and Moses (with Aaron) on one level and between the Egyptian gods of Egypt and Yahweh on the other. One dominant theme emerges from this epochal contest of wills, a theme earlier revealed in the story of Adam and Eve—namely, that while God participates actively in human affairs, he leaves to men the freedom to choose between righteousness and wickedness. In this case, it is the pharaoh who has the choice and who repeatedly vacillates between allowing the Hebrews their liberty and withdrawing his promise at the critical moment. God had warned Moses that this would happen when he appeared in the burning bush. "I am sure that the king of Egypt will not let you go . . ." he told him (3:19), not until

A plague of locusts, like the one that assaulted Egypt during Moses' time, settles in recent years over the Moroccan countryside, as a cow glumly watches its food supply being devoured.

God has visited ten miraculous plagues on Egypt as proof of both his power and his protection of Israel.

Only a careful reading of these ten famous chapters can convey the tension of battle that culminates in the great exodus, or going out. The weapons of this battle are steeped in magic and miracle as well as in the resources of human will. On the one hand, the pharaoh resorts to the hocus-pocus of his court magicians, who must invoke their animal-headed gods. On the other side stands Moses (and God), bringing down the ten plagues on the gods and people of Egypt, striking at the very foundation of Egyptian religion and culture.

The first plague transforms the sacred Nile and all its tributaries into a mess of bloody mire (7:19–25). The next sends a swarm of frogs into Egyptian streets and homes, even into the "kneadingtroughs" where the bread is prepared (8:3). Frogs, creatures of the Nile, were sacred in Egypt, but with this plague they become loathsome and offensive. So it is with lice made from the sacred dust of the land (8:17) and flies, which were gods in Canaan (Beelzebub is the Lord of the Flies); now they become a "grievous swarm" (8:24), reaching even into the pharaoh's house and corrupting the land with disease (8:24). Throughout these horrible visitations, the

Children of Israel are entirely spared. But even seeing this, the pharaoh's heart is hardened. Each time a plague runs its course, he reneges on his promise to free the Hebrews (8:15, 19:32), for the choice is his despite the suffering of his people and the justification of the Israelites to be free.

In wake of the flies, a rare disease afflicts the cattle of the Egyptians. It is called murrain (9:3). There follows an increasing crescendo of ruin: boils and blains (or sores) break out on man and beast alike—except for the Hebrews—and the magicians of Egypt are powerless to counteract the disaster. Then a hailstorm strikes, ruining every animal, house, even "every herb of the field . . ." (9:22). Locusts, who devour everything in sight and "cover the face of the earth, that one cannot be able to see the earth" (10:5), are the next affliction, and when the pharaoh refuses to be moved by this scourge, Moses "stretched forth his hand toward heaven" and there was a thick darkness in all the land of Egypt (10:22); three days of darkness hung over Egypt even at noon, and the sun god, Ra, was obliterated and made ridiculous. Only in Goshen was there light. Frightened but still contemptuous, the pharaoh relents and promises to let the Hebrews go. But again when the darkness is lifted he changes his mind (10:27).

The Passover

Now the climax is approached in this long and bitter contest between God and the pharaoh. Repeatedly the king has reneged. In addition, he had earlier increased the bondage of Israel by forcing the slaves to provide their own straw for the making of bricks—a costly and difficult task (5:10–19). He had resorted to trickery and threats, promising liberation on the one hand, withdrawing it on the other. Moses and Aaron had trekked to his palace countless times, demanding release of all the Hebrew slaves so that they might worship Yahweh in the desert free from Egyptian idolatry. Numerous times had Moses raised his rod at God's command to bring terror upon Egypt so that forever after the people—Hebrew and Egyptian alike—would remember the power of God. And now the final plague was to be enacted: the

". . . tomorrow will I bring the locusts into thy coast: And they shall cover the face of the earth. . . ."
(Exodus 10:4-5)

In this tomb painting from Thebes, the ceremonial sound of mourning is emphasized through the rhythm of the lifted arms and upturned heads. Perhaps Pharaoh and his people mourned in this fashion at the slaying of the first born.

smiting of the first-born of each Egyptian man and beast.

"And it came to pass, that at midnight the Lord smote all the firstborn in the land of Egypt, from the firstborn of the pharaoh that sat on his throne unto the firstborn of the captive that was in the dungeon . . ." (12:29). Only the Hebrews were spared, for God had instructed Moses to command each head of household in Goshen to sacrifice a lamb in memorial of this awesome night when the angel of death passed over all Hebrew houses. Forever after, the holiday of Passover was to be celebrated by Jews, as outlined in 12:21–22. Today, the Jewish people no longer sacrifice a lamb at Passover, but instead attend a symbolic feast called a *seder*, in which a lamb's shank is eaten along with edible representations of the mortar used for making the bricks of Pithom and Raamses, bitter herbs to recall

the agonies of slavery, and a cup of wine from which ten drops are extracted in remembrance of the ten plagues.

Also on the table of every *seder* is a plate of *matzohs*, or unleavened flat bread, which God commanded be made in remembrance of the time when the Children of Israel fled Egypt in such haste that the bread could not be leavened so that it might rise when baked (12:34).

The Going Out

Even the mighty pharaoh cannot resist the final plague. He summons Moses and Aaron and cries out: "Rise up, get you forth from among my people . . . be gone!" (12:31–32). Hastily organized and laden with their own belongings as well as restitution paid by the Egyptians (12:35), the Hebrews at last begin their going out, or exodus, from the land of bondage, taking with them, as pledged in Genesis 50:25, the bones of Joseph (13:19). According to the Bible, six hundred and three thousand men (Numbers 1:46), plus women and children, depart from Egypt. The people, headed by Moses and Aaron, first cross from Goshen in the delta toward the wilderness of Shur along the Mediterranean coast of the Sinai Peninsula, an area reached by crossing the Red (or Reed) Sea, which was thought to have been at the location of present-day Suez. Before they go God informs Moses of several laws and rituals (including the Passover) that must be observed and which relate to the maintenance of order among the tribes (12:43–51, 13:1–19). In this section the Lord also reminds the people of his promise regarding Canaan (13:11) and calls on them to remember forever, by ritual, prayer and reverence, the fact that "with a strong hand hath the Lord brought thee out of Egypt" (13:9). In token of his protection over Israel, God "went before them by day in a pillar of a cloud . . . and by night in a pillar of fire, to give them light" (13:21–22).

While camped before the Red Sea on the threshold of their escape, the Hebrews hear the approaching armies of the pharaoh, who has once again changed his mind and now comes after the fugitives with every intention of recapturing them. It is God's plan at this point to demonstrate his ultimate power over Egyptian idolatry by a fearful destruction of the pharaoh's army. This event takes place in the miraculous parting of the Red Sea, for Moses is able to lead the Children of Israel safely through

the parted waters "on dry ground" (14:16); but when the pharaoh's pursuing chariots charge through the cleavage, the Lord instructs Moses to raise his hand over the area "and the sea returned to his [its] strength . . . and the Lord overthrew the Egyptians in the midst of the sea" (14:27), drowning the pride of the pharaoh's army. God had sworn that even the Egyptians "shall know that I am the Lord, when I have gotten me honour upon pharaoh" (14:18), and that moment is now at hand.

Note: The pharaoh himself does not drown in this catastrophe; only his army is destroyed. Apparently he returns, a beaten man, to oversee the eventual decay of Egypt's glory, which historically dates

A family in Jerusalem, reading from the Haggadah, celebrates the Passover holiday, the first of which took place in Moses' time.

A NASA space photo of the Sinai peninsula, over which the Children of Israel roamed after leaving Egypt (left—center).

from a period around 1100 B.C. The mummies of both Ramesses II and Merneptah may be seen in the Cairo Museum today.

The Sojourn

Safely arriving in the desolate Sinai Peninsula, Moses and his sister, Miriam, raise their voices in joyous songs of deliverance—two impressive poetic utterances found in Chapter 15. Moses sings: "The Lord is a man of war . . . pharaoh's chariots and his host hath he cast into the sea . . . they sank into the bottom as a stone. . . . Who is like unto thee, O Lord . . . glorious in holiness, fearful in praises, doing wonders?" (15:3–5,11).

Likewise Miriam rejoices: "Sing ye to the Lord, for he hath triumphed gloriously; the horse and his rider hath he thrown into the sea" (15:21).

But no sooner are the Hebrews established in the wilderness when the hardships of their sojourn begin, for they are stranded, so it seems, without water. Starting with Chapter 15, Verse 24, the "murmuring" or complaining of the people becomes an unpleasant theme of the rest of Exodus (and the following books). How soon they have forgotten God's promise and deliverance. To be sure, their murmurings are quieted when water is discovered at the end of Chapter 15. But by Verse 2 of Chapter 16 they are murmuring again, even yearning to return to Egypt, where their hardships were familiar ones. To answer their complaints and their hunger, God sends down "bread from heaven," the substance called manna, which according to our best knowledge was like a sort of coriander seed, or sweet-tasting flake (16:31), useful as a grain in the making of dough. The miraculous nature of this substance—and of the quails, or game birds, that later appear—is demonstrated by the fact that equal portions of each were available to the head of every household no matter how greedy or lazy he might be. On the sabbath—the day of rest—no manna fell, but an adequate surplus was provided in advance (16:16–31).

The discomforts of hunger, tribal strife and the constant threat of war with nomadic groups plagued the hard, long trek of the Israelites as they made their way toward the sacred mountain of Yahweh, Mount Sinai (or Horeb), believed to have been located at the narrow southern tip of the Sinai Peninsula. The rugged and towering twin peaks of Jebel Musa (Moses' Mount) can be seen today rising from the

The waters of the Red Sea have just closed over the pharaoh's pursuing army in this eventful painting by Bernardino Luini. Note Moses with his rod and his sister Miriam, at right.

desert floor. Many believe this is the very same Mount Sinai of the Bible.

Three months have passed since the Exodus from Goshen (19:1). The Israelites have now arrived at the place designated for the most important historical and religious aspect of Exodus: the giving of the Law and the Covenant with Yahweh (Chapter 19 to the end of the book—Chapter 40). Two narrative accounts (Chapters 17 and 18) precede this event and tell of a war with the Amalekites, in which a young general named Joshua distinguishes himself under God's protection (17:9–13) and of the reunion between Moses and his father-in-law Jethro. This is a most significant reunion, since Jethro helps the great liberator organize his sprawling nation into workable groups or governments of "ordinances and laws" (18:20).

It is law that will thereafter govern Israel—not the law of Jethro but the laws of God as handed down to Moses on Sinai. The first ten of these laws are the immortal Ten Commandments (Chapter 20:1–17), but these are only the most famous of the more than 600 regulations and ordinances eventually issued by God through Moses to the Children of Israel and through them to the rest of the world. These laws concern all manner of daily conduct, ethics, diet, warfare, ritual, agriculture and cattle raising. As important as they are, they form only the details—the fleshing out—of the basic covenant, or pact, that God establishes between the people through Moses at Sinai. This event occurs amid great rumblings of thunder, during which a wondrous thick cloud appears on the mount "because the Lord descended upon it in fire" (19:18). At first the people are mightily fearful of this awesome visita-tion, but Moses calms them by going on before, up the mount, to receive the Ten Commandments as directly spoken by God (20:21). This is followed by a reverent ceremony, enacted by the people, in which the covenant is sealed (20:24–26, also 24:3–8).

Moses on the Mount

Moses receives the numerous commandments from God during his forty-day sojourn on the mountain (Chapter 24). But while he is gone, the restless people begin again their murmuring and their yearning, not only for the relative security of Egypt but also for the idols of the pharaoh's land.

"And when the people saw that Moses delayed to come down out of the mount [they] gathered themselves together unto Aaron, and said unto him, Up, make us gods . . . and he . . . made it a molten calf" (32:1, 4). The people's idolatry is distressing in light of their miraculous salvation and especially in view of the thunderous covenant made at Mount Sinai, specifically forbidding the worship of idols or images. The fact that Aaron, Moses' own brother, soon to be high priest of Israel, willingly participated in this desecration implies that it was done mainly to keep the peace until Moses could return and rectify the wickedness. This he does dramatically (32:15), smashing the tablets on which God had himself written the Ten Commandments, destroying the golden calf and grinding it into powder and then commanding the tribe of Levi to go through the camp with

This air view of Mt. Sinai suggests the loneliness surrounding the Hebrew sojourn in the wilderness.

drawn swords so that all the guilty will perish in one fell swoop. As a result, three thousand of the chief idolaters die that day.

Though enraged with what he calls this "stiff-necked people" (32:9), the Lord is nevertheless willing to forgive them their grievous sin for Moses' sake. Moses offers his own life as penance for the people (32:32) and the Lord is moved. He goes so far as to repeat his bountiful promise regarding Canaan (33:2–3) causing the people to "mourn" for their wickedness. Even Aaron is forgiven by dint of Moses' virtue, and God calls Moses once again to the mount so that the law may be finally inscribed in stone (34:1–2).

A Summary of the Law

Among the many commandments Moses receives on Sinai, the ones concerning the building of a tabernacle are most extensive, detailing size, furnishings, fixtures and materials (Chapters 25 to 31 and 35 to 40). *Highlights*: The entire sacred building is to be forty-five feet long, fifteen feet wide and fifteen feet high. Its opening will face east; ten curtains made of the finest linen and decorated with golden designs (of cherubs) will cover the walls of the inner structure. These walls are to be made of acacia wood. The entire building is to be covered over by a huge tent of goat's-hair cloth. Within the tabernacle, at its core, is to be the Holy of Holies, a perfect cubical room intended only for Moses, the high priest and God himself. Here too the Ark of the Covenant—a

Tintoretto, in this detail of a larger painting, places the worship of the golden calf on a kind of inner stage (above). Aaron, the high priest, supervises the collection of gold, while others sit idly by.

wooden chest, three and three quarters feet long by two and one quarter feet high, overlaid with gold—will stand and in it will rest the tablets of the Ten Commandments. Two carved cherubs with golden wings shall sit opposite each other on the lid of this ark, for it is intended as a throne for God.

A courtyard surrounds the temple, 150 feet long by 75 feet wide. In it shall stand a laver, or font, for bathing the feet (a ceremony required of all those who will enter the sacred building). Nearby is an outside altar for burnt offerings. A candelabrum, or menorah, beaten of pure gold (the same gold taken from Egypt as restitution) will light the inner chamber and altar room of the tabernacle. Amazingly, this entire complicated structure and all its fixtures are to be entirely portable. In its precincts, the Children of Israel shall see God descend as a cloud, filling the tabernacle and the surrounding desert with glory (40:35).

Along with the building of a sacred place for worship and sacrifice, God commands the institution of the priesthood, led by Aaron and his sons (Chapters 28 to 29). Again hundreds of details concerning the rituals, garments, ornaments and functions of the priests are outlined. Of particular interest is the gem-laden breastplate representing the twelve tribes of Israel to be worn by the high priest (28:13–25) at official ceremonies.

Other details of the law are given in Exodus, including the well-known concept of retaliation: "Eye for eye, tooth for tooth . . ." (21:24), which marks a great advance over unrestrained retaliation by

Rembrandt's Moses, returning from thunderous Mt. Sinai, holds high the tablets of the Law, which he will soon throw to the ground in anger.

limiting the punishment to fit the crime; the prohibitions against incitement: "Thou shalt not follow a multitude to do evil . . ." (23:2) and many other meaningful laws and rules of conduct, such as "Ye shall not afflict any widow, or fatherless child" (22:22); "If thou lend money to any of my people that is poor by thee, thou shalt not be to him as a usurer . . ." (22:25); in short, "Ye shall be holy men unto me . . ." (22:31).

The Impact of Exodus

This last commandment may be called the summing up of Exodus—that Israel should be a holy nation chosen by God to spread his law into the uncivilized and pagan world. This they would do in remembrance of their own benighted days as slaves and not out of pride or aggression. The total law of Israel, which is recorded in the first five books of the Bible (but especially in Exodus and Deuteronomy), is called in Hebrew the *Torah* (Law) and in Greek *Pentateuch* (the five books). It forms the basis of the Jewish religion and, in turn, of Christianity, and its influence may be found in all the greatest legal and political documents of the Western world, including the Constitution of the United States.

Though it took the Children of Israel only about a year to reach the borders of the Promised Land, they were obliged, as we shall see, to remain in the wilderness for a total of forty years until they had acclimated themselves fully to this challenging law. The following books tell of this adjustment, of battles fought in advance of the crossing over, of numerous other regulations, of the people's incessant murmurings, of Moses' troubles, of miracles, rebellion, holidays and the overall power of

Flanking the Commandments on this Torah breastplate of silver are Moses and Aaron (who wears his own breastplate).

God. Now follow the highlights of each of these books of the exodus.

Leviticus

This book, named for the priestly tribe of Levi (the tribe of Moses), concerns the theocracy or government of the priests, from whom came ordinances concerning taxation, administration of the temple (and religion) and of the law courts. Priests also decided on the proper nature of sacrifices to be made at the temple altar. Burnt offerings· of bullocks, rams, doves and goats were intended as dedications to God; peace offerings of cattle and sheep in hopes of tranquility; sin offerings when restitution was sought (Chapters 1 to 5) and so forth. The manner of sacrifice is also described as

well as the frequency of offerings and the observation of special holidays set aside for atonement.

Chapters 8 and 9 of Leviticus go into great detail concerning the consecration of Aaron and his sons. Once again, the specifications of the priestly garments and regalia are carefully delineated. In Chapter 10 the story of Aaron's rebellious sons is briefly told. Because they disobey the rituals, they are devoured by fire and their functions are assumed by younger, more pious brothers.

From Chapter 11 to 15 we read of health regulations, including the laws of *kashruth* —dietary cleanliness; what makes something *kosher* (permissible food) or unkosher, such as pork and shellfish. Purification after childbirth, tests for leprosy (a very contagious disease of that period) and general physical purity are further detailed. Chapter 16 outlines the Day of Atonement (Yom Kippur), a somber holiday of fasting and personal prayer in search of penance. The ancient ritual of the scapegoat, upon whom Aaron lays the sins of the community, is given at 16:7–10.

Details of conduct in all possible areas —marriage, commerce, the treatment of the aged, of the trespasser; prohibitions against witchcraft, lewdness and injustice —fill the verses. At 19:18 one of the most powerful commandments of all is offered for the world: "Thou shalt love thy neighbor as thyself: I am the Lord."

The special holidays of Israel, including the Jubilee Year (every fiftieth year, when slaves could be freed and debts cleared), are

An Israeli scribe devotes himself painstakingly to the traditionally prescribed hand-lettering of a Torah, the first five Books of Moses.

listed. Starting with Chapter 23 we read of real-estate requirements, taxation (or tithing), and then in Chapter 26 there is presented a reiteration of the prohibitions against idols, false gods and impiety. Leviticus ends with a discussion of cattle related to tithing.

Numbers

Long lists of families and the numbering of the people according to tribe begins this book, clarifying the makeup of the nation. The position of each tribe in terms of the temple (where each may stand during services) and a repetition of laws from Exodus and Leviticus follow.

Beginning with Chapter 10, the narrative portion of the text resumes when Moses declares that it is time at last for the people to cross over into the Promised Land. All the tents and livestock, the tabernacle and holy ark, all the women and children are gathered up by the tribal leaders and the march northward begins; so does the murmuring and the complaining as before (11:1–3). To satisfy the people's hunger, manna once again falls from heaven and edible birds appear in great flocks. But still the people complain and vent their bitterness on Moses. Even his sister, Miriam, turns on the great liberator and begins to stir up trouble in the camp—sadly for her, because the Lord afflicts Miriam grievously with a punishing illness. Only the prayers of Moses himself eventually save her life (12:11–13).

Encamped at a place called Kadesh, the Israelites can practically see the Promised Land. But Moses, as a sensible leader, exerts caution. He decides to reconnoiter Canaan before leading more than half a million people any farther. Twelve men are chosen, one from each tribe, headed by his commander Joshua, and are told to spy in the Promised Land and to report back as to its fortifications, prosperity and general terrain. After forty days the spies return laden with thick juicy grapes, figs and other luscious fruits as proof of the bounty in Canaan. But along with this positive evidence, ten of the spies—unsophisticated from living as slaves so long—tell frightening stories of walled-in cities and of gigantic men (probably guards standing on parapets) so tall that "we were in our own sight as grasshoppers . . ." (13:33).

Hearing such tales, the timorous people "lifted up their voice, and cried; and . . . wept that night" (14:1). So terrified are they, in fact, that plans are secretly drawn by some of them to return to Egypt. Joshua and another spy named Caleb insist that Canaan is peaceful and that it contains no giants. But the people answer this news by flinging stones at its bearers.

Now God is sorely vexed and enraged. Once again he is ready to destroy the people at one fell swoop, but Moses, as ever, intervenes. "Pardon, I beseech thee," he cries, "the iniquity of this people according unto the greatness of thy mercy" (14:19). God is persuaded but decides on a drastic plan by which he hopes to improve the quality of people he has chosen to dwell in the holy land. He commands Moses to turn back from the borders of Canaan and resume the wandering in the desert.

For thirty-nine years the people are to remain encamped in the arid regions of Sinai until every complaining person over the age of twenty has died. Only Joshua and Caleb, among the men, would be entitled to enter Canaan along with a new breed of Israelites—a breed tempered by the desert sun and freed of the inhibiting memories of slavery (and of Egypt). A nation of true fighters and true believers will thus emerge, for by means of disease and natural attrition the old stock shall "be consumed" (14:35) and a brave new generation prepared for greatness.

In the wake of this discouraging news, the people mourn greatly and rebellion fills the camp. One man, named Korah, is more outspoken than the rest. He plots to usurp the leadership of Moses (Chapter 16) and assume the holy priesthood of Aaron. With several other malcontents, Korah approaches the tabernacle with holy vessels and censers (for the burning of incense). God, angered at this rebellion—which is

One of the Biblical subjects on this panel of 18th-century Dutch tiles shows two of Joshua's reconnaissance team (upper right) carrying a load of grapes. Other scenes include Moses' burning bush.

In Joachim Uytewael's canvas, the Israelites and their animals scurry for drink, as Moses strikes impulsively at the rock (right) and water gushes out.

based purely on the lust for power—brings it quickly to an end. Korah and his cohorts and everything they own are swallowed up by the earth and they "went down alive into the pit, and the earth closed upon them . . ." (16:33).

Unfortunately, Moses' troubles were not ended with this decisive act. War broke out with the aggressive Amalekites, then with the Edomites and Moabites. On top of this, and probably because of his woes, Moses offended God—and this is one of the most perplexing of all Biblical incidents. As we read in 20:8, God told Moses to bring forth water for the thirsty people by calling upon a certain rock "to give forth his water" as proof of God's abiding miraculous powers. But Moses, exasper-

ated—or confused—by the constant murmuring of the people, inadvertently struck the rock with his rod (the same "magical" rod he had used to bring about many of the plagues in Egypt). Thus for a moment Moses forgot the true source of miracle; for a split second he had forgotten God. His punishment was grave indeed (and it likewise fell on Aaron). "Because ye believed me not . . ." said the Lord, "therefore ye shall not bring this congregation into the land which I have given them."

To be sure, Moses was allowed to glimpse the holy land from a mountain peak nearby (Deuteronomy 34:1), but he himself would never set foot on the land he had sought so long. Why? Was his misconduct at the rock so grievous to merit this hard punishment? Or was there another reason behind this seemingly tragic turn of events? Perhaps the answer lies again in Deuteronomy 34, where the death of Moses is related. Note that his passing is perfectly blissful in the company of God and that God himself "buried him in a valley . . . but no man knoweth of his sepulchre [or tomb] unto this day" (Deuteronomy 34:6). The implication here is that God wished to prevent any undue idolatry arising around Moses. Had he entered Canaan, the people might have insisted that he be their king. Had he died there, they would surely have erected an elaborate tomb to honor their greatest prophet (and king), and this tomb might have become a shrine, an idol, like the golden calf. Moses was the liberator, the lawgiver, the man of miracles. But his day had passed. Younger men, more in tune with the coming generations, were now required to lead the people in Canaan. And so the man called "meek, above all the men which were upon the face of the earth" (Numbers 12:3) continues as leader in the wilderness, knowing he shall never journey hence.

A gap of over thirty-five years takes place between Chapters 19 and 20 in Numbers, for we read at 20:22 that the journey begins again from Kadesh northward toward Canaan. Apparently the "waiting period" has ended. Two miraculous stories follow as the Children of Israel trek onward. First, because of their in-

The American painter Benjamin West (1738–1820) shows a classical Moses looking from the top of Mount Nebo toward a Promised Land he will never reach, as angels gather to lift him away from earth.

cessant complaining—obviously all the complainers were not yet dead—God sends fiery, or venomous, serpents into the camp (21:6), and many are bitten and die. Again Moses prays and he is told by God to "make thee a fiery serpent [out of brass] and set it upon a pole: and it shall come to pass, that every one that is bitten, when he looketh upon it, shall live" (21:8). This story seems to imply a form of sympathetic magic or faith healing taking place between the object and the people. Impressed by its powers, the Israelites preserved this brazen serpent and centuries later they even worshiped it when they lapsed back to idolatry (II Kings, 18:4).

The next most interesting episode in Numbers concerns a magician named Balaam (Chapters 22 to 24), who is hired by Israel's enemies to curse Israel with his magic. He finds he cannot, because, unknown to him, an angel is altering his speech. When Balaam invokes a curse, a blessing issues from his lips! Only the magician's little donkey sees the angel and in amazement "thrust herself unto the wall" (22:25), jostling Balaam and causing him to grow exceedingly wrathful. So wrathful does he become that he begins to beat the little animal. "What have I done unto thee?" the donkey asks, like any creature in an Aesop fable. Fortunately, Balaam soon becomes aware of the angel and learns to regret his wrongdoings regarding Israel. (The talking donkey is never heard from again.)

Living up to its name, the book of Numbers undertakes a census, or counting, of Israel at Chapter 26, and we gather from this that the old generations have now been weeded out, so that the people are once again deemed ready to enter Canaan. Before this occurs, a series of laws

and commandments are issued (27 to 35) describing feasts, sacrifices, the continuing problems of warfare and statutes involving marriage, widowhood and chastity. The record of Israel's wanderings in the desert is given special mention (Chapter 33), and the book closes with a discussion of inheritance rights.

Deuteronomy

In Greek, Deuteronomy means "second law." It is an eloquent recounting of the basic commandments handed down at Sinai, and its is interwoven with certain dramatic episodes that occur just before the Children of Israel begin the conquest of Canaan. Few Biblical books are as lofty and significant. Indeed, when the book of Deuteronomy was discovered many years after the Exodus in the recesses of the temple in Jerusalem, it served to inspire the people, then fallen to idolatry, to a new sense of religious dedication (see II Kings 22:8–13 and 23:2).

Several noble themes emerge from its verses:

1. The grandeur of God as the universal spirit and power whom man must love "with all thine heart, and with all thy soul" (6:5). The section in which this commandment is announced is known in the Hebrew religion as the *Sh'ma* ("Hear O Israel, the Lord our God is one Lord," meaning the one and only God of the world). This *Sh'ma* is the nucleus of the Jewish faith and its clearest proclamation of monotheism. The unique concept of a universal loving God who has given man

Rembrandt, in this early painting, shows Balaam on his way to curse the Israelites, frustrated both by the ass he is riding and by an intervening angel.

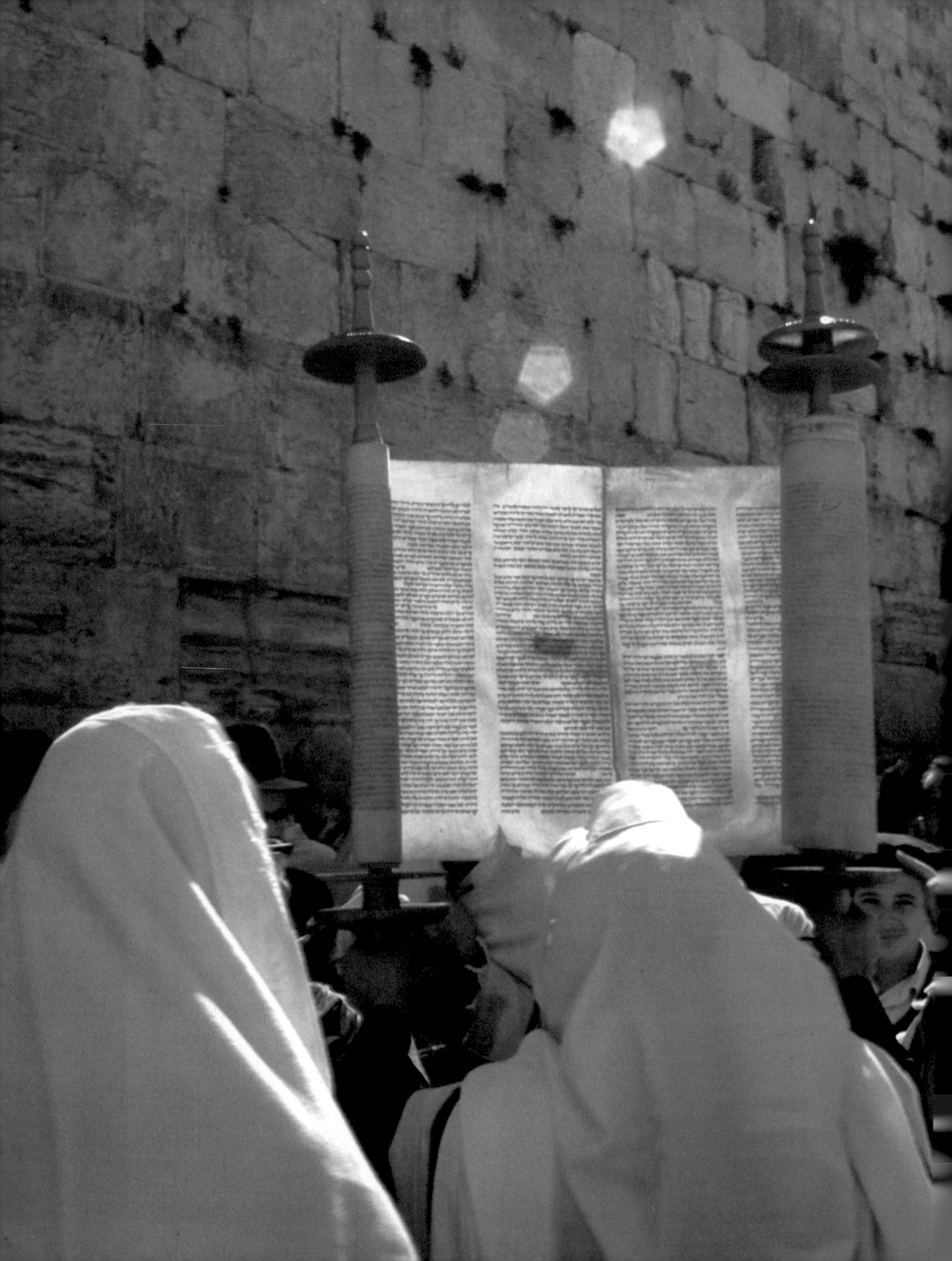

the law as his guide is one of the most profound themes in all the Bible. It inspired Jesus to call this section of Deuteronomy "the first of all the commandments" (Mark 12:29) and to repeat it faithfully word for word.

2. Deuteronomy establishes a central and formal religious system for Israel. No longer were the people to worship scattered shrines and altars. These were to be utterly destroyed lest they lead to idolatry. All sacrifices and worship were to be centered in the temple (12:5–6), the principal focus of which is the Lord. The details of religious observance are spelled out in this book not just as a repetition of earlier pronouncements but as the rules and regulations of a specific religious ideal.

3. In Deuteronomy, the basic laws and commandments are somewhat revised and humanized, emphasizing care of the poor, the downtrodden and the stranger. A series of blessings and curses is furthermore established. According to the degree of reverence each man shall show the statutes of the law, some will be blessed in the law and others disgraced (Chapter 28:1–19).

The emergence of a truly poetic, vital literary style dominates this book, as evidenced in such passages as the *Sh'ma*, just mentioned, in the blessings and curses and in Moses' thrilling farewell hymn (32:1–41): "Give ear, O ye heavens, and I will speak; and hear, O earth, the words of my mouth. . . . Because I will publish the name of the Lord: ascribe ye greatness unto our God. He is the Rock, his work is perfect. . . ." Similarly, Moses' blessing on Israel rings with a fervor so far unheard in the Biblical text. "Happy art thou, O Israel: who is like unto thee, O people saved by the Lord, the shield of thy help . . . thine enemies shall be found liars unto thee; and thou shalt tread upon their high places" (33:29).

With the passing of Moses and his burial by God (34:5–6), Deuteronomy comes to an end and with it the first five books of the Bible, the books of Moses, called *Torah* in Hebrew and universally regarded as the foundation of all Judeo-Christian ethics and morality.

Summary of the Exodus Books

1. Exodus: the bondage of Israel in Egypt; the birth of Moses; the burning bush; the confrontation with the pharaoh; the ten plagues; the liberation; the Passover; the crossing of the Red Sea; the wanderings; the law given at Sinai; the covenant; the golden calf; the tabernacle.

2. Leviticus: the nature of sacrifice and temple worship; the priesthood of Aaron; laws of diet and daily life; festivals; taxation.

3. Numbers: the census of Israel; rebellion in the camp; the spies go to Canaan; the turning back; Moses' disobedience; Balaam the magician; the miracles in the desert; various rules and regulations.

4. Deuteronomy: approaching Canaan; the great commandments; laws of every sort (repetitions of the above in detail); Moses' final blessing and death.

A Torah scroll, held high in the light during a service at the Wailing Wall in Jerusalem, dramatizes Jewish reverence for the Law, which God gave Moses at Mt. Sinai.

The Jordan River valley: "The Lord hath given you the land. . . ."(Joshua 2:9)

CHAPTER THREE

THE GROWTH OF THE SACRED NATION

Joshua · Judges · Ruth · I and II Samuel ·
I and II Kings · I and II Chronicles

The Book of Joshua is sometimes called "the sixth book of Moses" because it continues the story of the Israelites, which we have just read in the Exodus books. Joshua, as you will remember, was the courageous general appointed by Moses as his successor (Deuteronomy 31:23) and one of the few men to survive the cleansing of the people after they refused to enter Canaan some forty years before. Although he greatly contributed to the religious and moral values of Israel, Joshua was primarily a warrior, and his story is, by and large, a record of conquests interspersed with amplifications of the law and narratives of intrigue. Two important ideas are highlighted in his book: the conquest of Canaan and the establishment of the Hebrew nation in the Promised Land.

Crossing the Jordan

The book begins with an emphatic pronouncement by Joshua of his succession to Moses' leadership. Of prime importance is his message to the people: "Be strong and of a good courage; be not afraid, neither be thou dismayed: for the Lord thy God is with thee whithersoever thou goest" (1:9).

It is Joshua's intention to lead the Children of Israel across the narrow Jordan River at a place midway between present-day Jerusalem and Jericho. Before attempting such a difficult trek, in view of the fact that hostile Canaanites await him in the walled cities beyond, Joshua dispatches two spies to gather information in Canaan. We are reminded of his own reconnaissance mission years before (Numbers 13:8, 16). In the course of their adventure, the

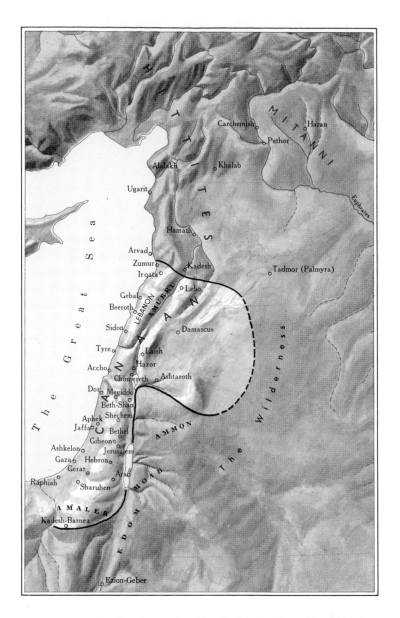

The land promised by God to the Israelites (Joshua 1:3, 4) is outlined in this map, its boundary bulging uncertainly into the wilderness.

The spies take heart from Rahab's attitude, and when they safely return to Joshua they tell him: "Truly the Lord hath delivered into our hands all the land; for even all the inhabitants of the country do faint because of us" (2:24). Emboldened by this report, Joshua begins the memorable crossing over, from the east, into the Promised Land (Chapters 3 to 4). With the sacred Ark of the Covenant in hand, the priests approach the river's bank, now swollen with spring rains. As soon as the ark is brought in contact with the waters, the floodtide abates and the people pass over "on dry ground in the midst of Jordan" (3:17) in a miraculous manner reminiscent of the Red Sea crossing in Exodus.

To celebrate the wonderful event, Joshua has memorial altars erected at nearby Gilgal; the stones of these altars are drawn from the dry bed of the Jordan, which stays dry until the priests and the ark pass up onto the land (4:11). Four days after the crossing, the joyous people rededicate themselves to God and celebrate the Passover, this time—at last—in the Holy Land.

The Battle of Jericho

Not far from the site of the crossing looms the great walled city of Jericho. Joshua knows that he will be obliged to conquer this fortress if ever Canaan is to be taken. His hopes are raised by the visitation of someone called "captain of the host of the Lord" (5:14), possibly an angel, who implies divine guidance for the coming battle.

The vivid and famous description of the fall of Jericho, particularly of its massive walls, begins at Chapter 6. No formal attack was launched by Joshua but rather, in

spies narrowly escape capture by taking refuge with a local woman named Rahab, who hides them in her house. Of greatest interest in this story is Rahab's conviction that the Israelites will someday conquer her own people: "I know that the Lord hath given you the land . . . for we have heard how the Lord dried up the water of the Red Sea for you . . ." (2:9–10). Rahab thus extracts a promise from her guests that when the conquest finally takes place, she and her family will be spared. The spies agree and tell her to display a scarlet thread in her window as a signal of her friendliness (2:18).

The site of ancient Jericho, whose walls were circled by Israel's trumpeters.

obedience to God's word, he merely marched his army around the fortress for six days (6:3), while the priest bore the ark and others blew on trumpets. On the seventh day the trumpeters were instructed to blow "a long blast" and all the people were told to "shout with a great shout," whereupon the walls of Jericho fell down flat (6:20). It was then an easy matter for the Hebrew army to overrun the city, confiscate its treasuries—avoiding its idols—and generally annihilate all resisters (except for Rahab and her family).

Archaeological evidence in recent years has revealed what seems to be some startling corroborations of this miraculous conquest of Jericho by the Israelites. Collapsed walls of heights reaching thirty feet have been excavated in the area, and they appear to have indeed fallen down *flat*, like

A man about to blow a ram's horn illustrates the means of Joshua's victory at Jericho in this relief carving from Carchemich, an ancient Hittite city.

Jean Fouquet depicts Joshua and his army in the costumes of France in the 15th century. The gabled houses and rolling countryside are also typically French.

This segment from the Dead Sea Scrolls describes the blowing of trumpets and horns in "a great battle fanfare to melt the heart of the enemy."

both slightly northwest of Jericho. Unfortunately, the Israelites taste defeat at Ai, because a Hebrew named Achan trespasses and loots the idols of Jericho, violating God's prohibitions (6:18). This defeat is clearly intended to discipline the people now grown arrogant in victory. God's plan is entirely effective, for "the hearts of the people melted, and became as water" (7:5) in the face of defeat. Joshua, intervening with God as had Moses before him, (7:7–8), brings about a change of fortunes, and the people, now rededicated to the Lord, ambush the armies of Ai, utterly destroy-

dominoes. But are they the walls of Joshua's time, or earlier fortifications? Dr. Kathleen Kenyon, who excavated modern Jericho, believes them to be earlier. Others point to the evidence of charring and conflagration, such as that described at 6:24—"and they burnt the city with fire . . . ." According to this school of thought, the burned debris dates back to around 1400 B.C. Accepting the date of the Exodus as between 1200 and 1350 B.C., we can see how Joshua's conquest of Jericho may relate to the archaeological evidence recently found. The question of the walls, however, stills remains. If they are earlier specimens, does it mean that Jericho was attacked even before Joshua's time? Or are the archaeologists mistaken?

An excavation at Jericho, considered the oldest inhabited city in the world. The circular wall (lower left) is even older than those which Joshua destroyed.

The Various Campaigns

After Jericho is razed, the word of Joshua's power reaches far into the various kingdom cities of Canaan (small independent monarchies sharing religious ties and territorial boundaries). Two of these cities marked for conquest are Ai and Bethel,

Detail from a painted chest found in Tutankhamun's tomb. The king, leading his orderly troops into a chaotic thicket of Nubians and their chariots, is experiencing the kind of fighting that Joshua faced in Canaan.

ing the kingdom, including its "accursed things," the idols.

One must read Chapter 8 in detail to sense the terror of conquest and comprehend the agonizing battles between the peoples of the promised land. Though brutal and perhaps unsettling for sensitive minds, the descriptions of this and subsequent battles convey a pious message, for these campaigns were undertaken in the belief that the monotheistic fervor of Israel could not be spread by mere conversion or persuasion.

The intensity of these battles is corroborated by archaeological findings. W. F. Albright, the dean of Palestinian excavators, uncovered in the 1930s, in the region of Bethel, a five-foot-thick mass of burned debris indicative of warfare and conflagra-

tion. Nowhere in the Holy Land, said Albright, had he seen remains of such fierce destruction.

In face of the conquest of Ai and Bethel, Joshua gathered the people on nearby Mount Ebal and rededicated them to the Law. The event took place not far from the site where Abraham had erected his first memorial altar to God over 600 years before.

A succession of fearsome battles ensued, the most famous at Gibeon, where Joshua commanded the sun to stand still (10:12–13) so that the Hebrew armies could defeat the onslaught of five united kingdoms who had hoped to take advantage of nightfall and escape. "And there was no day like that before it or after it" (10:14). At the end of this miraculous battle, Joshua and his

Joshua's stopping of the sun and moon as it appeared in this 16th-century French tapestry. The immediate reference is to Petrarch's poem *The Triumph of Time*; Joshua, in the ceremonial chariot, is one of several characters (including Noah and Methuselah) who in some way stood up to time's ravages.

The presumed tomb of Joshua at Khirbet Timna, traditionally identified as the Biblical Timnath Serah—the site of his inheritance.

armies stood conquerors of at least seven major Canaanite cities. More were to fall, even as far north as Galilee, including the sacred pagan city of Hazor. Again, archaeological evidence at that site reveals undeniable clues of warfare, of burning and destruction as the Bible reports. An Egyptian tablet dating from about this same time (1400 B.C.) further elucidates Biblical descriptions, for it reads: "Let my Lord the king [pharaoh] recall what Hazor and its king have already had to endure" (at the hands of the Israelites).

The end of Chapter 11 brings a promise of peace, for it seems that now Joshua had finally conquered Canaan "and the land rested from war" (11:23). There follows in Chapter 12 a list of those kings and kingdoms defeated by Israel in what seems to have been a fairly brief—though intensive —period of battle. The strain of it all may have weakened Joshua, for by the beginning of Chapter 13 we find him "old and stricken in years" and preparing to establish his legacy.

The Nation Is Formed

Following the lead of Jacob, who outlined the tribal structure of the Hebrews centuries before, Joshua now divides the conquered land among the twelve tribes, except for Levi, which was to be a priestly tribe without specific territory (13:14). *Note*: The added tribe of Joseph (i.e., Manasseh-Ephraim) rounded out the number to twelve.

Primarily Joshua bases his concept of government and law on the ideas of Moses and warns the people that enclaves of pagan worship are still among them and that warfare will therefore probably continue from time to time, especially with people bordering on Canaan (such as the Philistines and Hittites). The detailed establishment of the nation of Israel in ancient times is given in Chapters 13 to 22 and includes references to the tabernacle (Chapter 18), to the concept of cities of refuge—where murderers and other criminals might await trials and judgments unmolested (Chapter 20)—and to various rules of conduct and government. In short, we read at 21:45, "there failed not ought of any good thing which the Lord had spoken unto the house of Israel; all came to pass."

Joshua's Farewell

Approaching death, Joshua calls together many of the tribal leaders (Chapter 22) and repeats to them the commandments of Moses and blesses them for riches and prosperity. The old warrior also settles disputes and gives advice about rituals and territories. Then at a place called Shechem he holds a final congregation of the tribal league and reminds the people of their sacred history and miraculous triumphs. Warning, as ever, against

A gold-finished bronze statue of the Canaanite goddess Ashtoreth, worshiped by many of the backsliding Israelites.

known as judges (in Hebrew the word means chieftains), tribal representatives who combined—in some cases—military skill, legal knowledge and piety to the advantage of the nation. The Lord God was supposed to be the real ruler of the tribes in Canaan at the time, but the people often forgot this fact. The Bible makes it quite clear that their resultant sinfulness was paid for by the general disruption of peace. About a dozen judges ruled in the time between Joshua and the First Book of Samuel. Their stories are told in twenty-one chapters, which are dominated by one theme: Idolatry leads to suffering and redemption is possible only through reverence for God.

The list of the Judges is as follows, with an approximation of the length of time each ruled and the chapters in which their stories may be found. We will focus on only four of them (Deborah, Gideon, Jephthah and Samson)—the four who best exemplify the drama and grandeur of Biblical narrative.

idolatry, Joshua sets a great stone beneath a sacred oak (24:26), carved with the words: "The Lord our God will we serve, and his voice will we obey" (24:24), for the people have so declared that day.

In his 110th year, Joshua dies and is buried midway in the land that he had conquered for God.

The Judges

The next 300 years or so of Israel's history are a complicated matter of warfare, internal strife and regression to idolatry. This is the period when the twelve loosely federated tribes were governed by leaders

Othniel—forty years (Chapters 1–3)
Ehud—eighty years (Chapter 3)
Shamgar—indefinite reign
   (Chapter 3:31)
Deborah—forty years
   (Chapters 4–5)
Gideon—forty years (Chapters 6–8)
Abimelech—three years (Chapter 9)
Tola—twenty-three years
   (Chapter 10)
Jair—twenty-two years (Chapter 10)
Jephthah—six years (Chapters 11–12)
Ibzan—seven years (Chapter 12)
Elon—ten years (Chapter 12)
Abdon—eight years (Chapter 12)
Samson—twenty years
   (Chapters 13–16)

Note: After Samson (Chapters 17–21) there seems to have been a long period of civil strife resulting from a series of idolatrous and sensuous crimes committed by the tribes of Dan and Benjamin. The period is best summed up by the very last phrase of Judges (21:25): "In those days . . . every man did that which was right in his own eyes."

Deborah—the Woman Who Ruled

How it is that a woman became one of the most celebrated leaders in Hebrew history we do not know. But the tradition among the Israelites shows a respect and admiration for women such as Sarah, Rebekah and Rachel. Possibly Deborah was of a priestly family, for she is called a prophetess (4:4), and she seems to have also been an arbiter—a true judge—of daily problems for the people (4:5). Deborah did not rely on her own knowledge when it came to military matters but appointed a soldier named Barak as her general. A good soldier was needed, because the land was menaced at that time by foreign armies, particularly one led by a captain named Sisera.

Both Deborah and Barak join in battle against the foe at a place called Kadesh. But it was left to another woman, not a Hebrew but an ally of the Israelites, actually to rid the world of Sisera. She was Jael, and her story is of extraordinary dramatic quality, reminiscent of the story of Judith, which we will read in the Apocrypha (see page 243). Sisera, fleeing from battle, takes refuge in Jael's tent, at her invitation. There she apparently drugs him so that he falls quickly asleep. When she is sure the warrior is in her power, Jael takes one of the long pegs, or nails, that holds the tent ropes to the ground and with a hammer "smote the nail into his temples . . ." (4:21). When the armies of Barak learn of this assassination, they are greatly encouraged and soundly defeat the Canaanite troops.

The most impressive part of Deborah's story (which really seems to be the story of

The rich, embroidered clothing of this Canaanite woman was carved into an ivory inlay during the 13th or 12th centuries B.C., and was found at Megiddo. Did Rahab possibly look like this?

Barak and Jael) is the song she and her general offer up to the Lord in Chapter 5. This section is believed to be among the earliest of the Bible committed to record. It pulsates with triumph and with an uncanny sense of eyewitness reality. "I Deborah arose . . . a mother in Israel" (5:7), the woman sings. "My heart is toward the governors of Israel, that offered themselves willingly among the people. . . ." Deborah now names and describes the various roles in the battle of each tribe. Some she extols, others she seems to criticize (see 5:17–18). She praises Jael (5:24) and recites her story, adding a poignant note about Sisera—namely, that his mother awaited him after the battle and wondered why he tarried (5:28).

Deborah ends her exultation in praise of God, and we are told "the land had rest forty years" (5:31).

Gideon—the Reluctant Savior

The glorious triumph of Deborah and Barak soon fades from memory as the people return to their evil ways (6:1), and the Midianites and Amalekites sweep down on Israel and practically enslave the nation, forcing many people to flee to the mountains and hills in escape. Gideon (also called Jerubbaal—7:1) was a farmer, the son of an idolater. Because of his passion for Yahweh, the God of Israel, Gideon one day smashes the altars of the pagan god Baal (6:28). He has no doubt been inspired to do this by the visit of an angel (6:11) who

Gideon and two of his soldiers surprise the sleepy Midianites with lanterns and trumpets in this page from the much-traveled 13th-century picture book of the Bible given to the Persian ruler (see p. 44).

(see p. 44).

Rubens sets up a match of strength in his tensely composed painting of young Samson wrestling the lion.

comes to persuade the reluctant farmer to take up Israel's cause and be a judge over the land. Gideon's confrontation with the Lord (in the form of the angel—6:11–18) is reminiscent of the events concerning Moses at the burning bush. Like Moses, Gideon must be convinced of his mission, and only after he beholds certain wondrous signs in nature, such as the heavy falling of dew (6:21 and 6:36–40), does he assume the leadership that God requires.

It is military skill that enables Gideon to repel the Canaanite foe, for he chooses only the best soldiers in Israel for his attack, though they number a mere three hundred men. At night he assembles these three hundred above the enemy camp.

Each man carries a trumpet and a covered lantern. Three groups of one hundred troops so armed encircle the enemy and at a signal from Gideon, "the sword of the Lord and of Gideon," each man blows his trumpet and uncovers his lantern. The Midianites, startled out of their sleep by the din, assume that a great horde is about to descend on them. "And all the [enemy] host ran, and cried, and fled" (7:21).

Gideon's victory reestablishes Israelite rule in Canaan, and the people clamor to make him a king. Valiantly, the pious farmer resists this offer. "The Lord shall rule over you," he tells his friends (8:23). However, Gideon does extract a large quantity of gold in payment for his services. His lust for gold, in fact, backfires against him (8:27), and by the time of his death the people "neither shewed they kindness to the house of Jerubbaal, namely, Gideon, according to all the goodness which he had shewed unto Israel" (8:35). Gideon's son, Abimelech, rules briefly as a "king" (actually a warlord) in one province of the land, but he is overthrown after three short and difficult years.

The Fatal Oath

In Chapter 11 the story of the judge named Jephthah is told, and it is a weighty tragedy that demonstrates the rashness of ambition and the fact that a righteous man may misinterpret God's intention.

On the eve of a decisive battle with the Ammonites—who now menace Israel —Jephthah, the general and judge, vows to sacrifice "whatsoever cometh forth of the doors of my house to meet me, when I return in peace . . ." (11:31). God wishes no such oath, but Jephthah, possibly influenced by local pagan ideas, is determined to win at any cost. To his horror, on returning home in victory, the general beholds his daughter, his only child, rushing to meet him from his house. Compulsively, the tragic leader carries out his pledge and offers his daughter as a living sacrifice to God, even though such an act was strictly forbidden in Israel.

As we see from Verses 36–37, Jephthah's daughter is extremely brave about her impending death and asks only to be allowed two months' time in prayer with her companions so that she may bewail her fate. After her death, "the daughters of Israel went yearly to lament the daughter of Jephthah . . ." (11:40).

Samson—the Strongman of Israel

Biblical scholars have interpreted the fascinating story of Samson in various ways. To some it is a straightforward chronicle of history and of God's intent. To others, it is a legend derived from the Babylonian *Epic of Gilgamesh*, which tells of a similar lion-killing hero. Some say that Samson's encounter with the seductive Delilah is an allegory, or symbol, of the struggle between light (Shimson—that is, Samson—in Hebrew means "man of the sun") and darkness (De-lay-lah means "of the night"). Whatever it is, the story of Samson serves two distinct functions unique in the Bible—the first, to absorb our interests in the daring exploits of a colorful character, for Samson is, as we shall see, both a brawny strongman and a sensitive leader, a foolish swain blinded by love and a tragic figure, literally blinded by his enemies. In addition to the fascinating figure of Samson, the story affords us a novel message, well worth remembering —namely, that God can forgive and redeem even the most lusty, bombastic and sinful of men. This has been a theme of great appeal and comfort to generations of Bible readers.

Samson's birth is ordained by God (13:3), and his parents are told, by an angel, that he will be a man of unusual strength and power, one who shall deliver the Israelites from the yoke of the Philistines so long as he does not consume strong drink, eat forbidden food and—as we later learn (16:17)—shave or cut the hair of his head.

From early manhood Samson demonstrates both physical strength and reckless temperament. At one point he boldly wrestles a lion to its death (14:5,8). He also demands of his parents that they allow him to marry a foreign woman, because he is

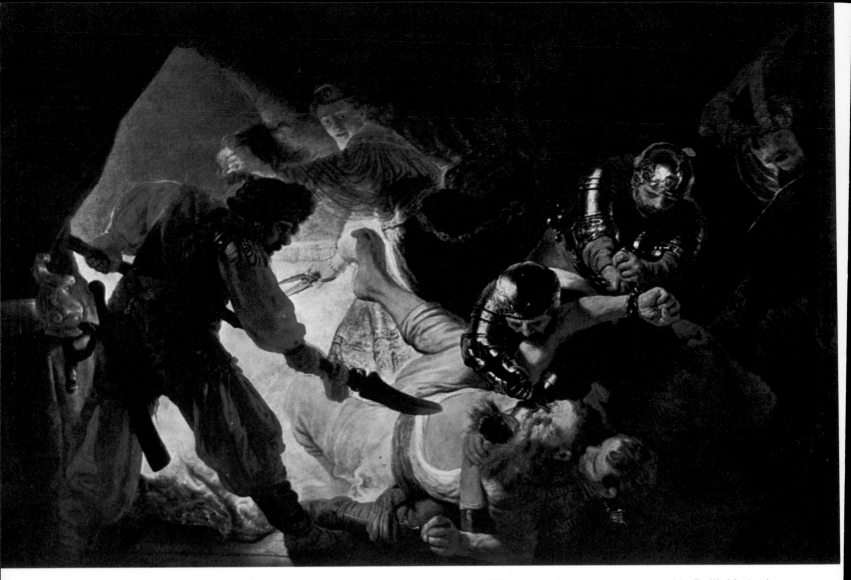

In an early, dramatic painting Rembrandt shows the savage blinding of Samson when he was betrayed in Delilah's tent.

smitten with her beauty (14:1–3). Later he is to regret this action when his wife proves unfaithful and leads him into a series of reckless brawls and wildness, including the vengeful burning down of cornfields, vineyards and olive groves (15:5).

When angered by Philistine aggression, Samson turns his prowess to Israel's advantage and in several pitched battles defeats large hordes of the enemy. Indeed, at one point, we are asked to believe that he slays a thousand men merely by wielding the dried-out jawbone of an ass (15:14–16); "heaps upon heaps" of Philistines did he kill by this means!

Noting his lusty appetites and bravura, the Philistines plot to capture Samson and commission the beautiful Delilah for this purpose. "See wherein his great strength lieth," they tell her, "and we will give thee

. . . eleven hundred pieces of silver" (16:5). Delilah preys on Samson night after night, and he, being susceptible to womanly wiles, does not defend himself and thus falls in love with her. Repeatedly, she asks him the source of his strength, and playfully he repeatedly invents some fiction as an answer. Finally Delilah threatens to withhold her love from him and Samson can resist no more. He reveals the sacred secret: "If I am shaven; then my strength will go from me, and I shall become weak, and be like any other man" (16:17). Delilah at once acts on this information, and when Samson is asleep in her tent she has his hair cut off by a barber so that the Philistines may easily capture and blind their foe.

Samson's disgrace and captivity is a grievous blow to the people of Israel. But, at the same time, it is a victory for the idolaters of Philistia. They bind the blinded strongman and cause a little boy to lead him, like a dray horse, into the midst of their pagan temple, so that they may make sport with him (16:25). Humiliated but repentant, the fallen leader of Israel stands before his enemies—some three thousand men and women—and once again turns his thoughts to God.

"O Lord God, remember me, I pray thee, and strengthen me, I pray thee, only this once, O God, that I may be at once avenged of the Philistines for my two eyes" (16:28).

The intensity of Samson's prayer redeems him in the sight of God; strength and power return to his body. Feeling this new surge of life, Samson braces himself between the two main columns that support the roof of the temple and, crying out "Let me die with the Philistines . . . he bowed himself with all his might; and the house fell . . . upon all the people that were therein . . ." (16:30). Thus was Samson mightily avenged through God's forgiveness and Israel temporarily relieved of the foreign yoke.

The Story of Ruth

Like a welcome interlude of spring in a wintry climate, there comes at this point in the Bible the idyllic Book of Ruth, four brief chapters that have the impact of a romantic novel and a message of far-reaching significance. Here is the story of a non-Jewish woman who converts to the Hebrew faith and eventually becomes the great-grandmother of Israel's glorious king, David. From the Book of Ruth we learn not only the universality of pious love but also countless details of agricultural life in the eleventh century before

This helmet from Ur was finely crafted, 45 centuries ago, from a single piece of gold. It depicts an ornate male hairdo such as Samson may have boasted.

Christ. In addition to these valuable elements, the story is written in exquisitely simple prose that rises to the heights of poetry.

The action begins in tragedy with the death of a father and two sons, the husbands of Naomi and her daughters-in-law, Ruth and Orpah. Naomi is a Hebrew woman living in Moab, a country bordering Israel near the Dead Sea. Having become a widow, she decides to return to her native land and bids her daughters-in-law farewell (1:8–9). Orpah kisses her mother-in-law and reluctantly prepares to return to her home, perhaps to find a new husband. But Ruth, inspired by love and possibly by a sense of destiny, refuses to part from Naomi and utters one of the most beautiful and noble passages in all the Bible, in which she commits herself to the Jewish people and their God: "Intreat me not to leave thee, or to return from following after thee: for whither thou goest, I will go; and where thou lodgest, I will lodge: thy people shall be my people, and thy God my God . . ." (1:16).

Ruth and Naomi journey to Bethlehem in time to partake of the barley harvest. They are able to do so because Naomi has a

Members of a present-day family harvest barley together in the Valley of Jezreel, similar to the way Ruth worked in the fields of Boaz.

relative, a wealthy farmer, named Boaz, and according to the law of the Hebrews, he must allow strangers and the poor to glean, or gather, what the reapers have left of the grain after their work is done. Boaz sees Ruth gleaning one day and is struck by her dignity. He soon learns that she is the daughter-in-law of Naomi, his kinswoman, and because of her devotion to Naomi, he promises to protect Ruth and favor her so long as she stays close to his fields (2:8–9).

Possibly Boaz has another idea in mind, for he is unmarried and seeks a wife. The watchful Naomi is no doubt aware of this fact, and, anxious to see Ruth remarried and blessed with motherhood, she instructs the younger woman to present herself to Boaz as a prospective wife. "Wash thyself therefore, and anoint thee, and put thy raiment upon thee, and get thee down to the floor [of Boaz's barn] . . ." (3:3). Once there, Naomi continues, Ruth is to wait until Boaz has finished dining and retires to his barn for a nap. "And it shall be, when he lieth down, that thou . . . shalt go in, and uncover his feet, and lay thee down; and he will tell thee what thou shalt do" (3:4). In other words, by placing herself under Boaz's blanket at his feet, Ruth will signal her willingness to be wed.

Boaz is overjoyed when he realizes Ruth's intentions but advises her that there is in Bethlehem a nearer kinsman than himself and this man, who is also unmarried, has prior claim by law to the widow of Naomi's son and to the purchase of all his land. The course of true love apparently does not run any more smoothly here than in all romantic literature. But there is always the possibility that this nearer kinsman may publicly refuse his claim. If he does, then Boaz and Ruth will be free to wed.

In a formal ceremony held at the city gates, where legal matters were decided, Boaz confronts his rival and happily learns that he is willing to relinquish his claims both to the land and to Ruth (we never learn the reason why). To signal his decision, the kinsman removes one shoe and hands it to Boaz, for as the Bible tells us, "this was the manner in former times in Israel concerning redeeming and concerning changing" (4:7).

And so Boaz and Ruth are wed, and in due time a son is born. Naomi, who thought her life had ended with widowhood, is now redeemed and joyous. A great family is thus founded, a family that is to produce Israel's greatest kings and in time the child called Jesus.

The Man Called Samuel

Ruth and Boaz lived in that hazy period following Samson's death when "every man did that which was right in his own eyes" (Judges 21:25). Possibly because of the corruption and confusion of this period, a new sort of judge was required, one who might assume not only political power but religious authority as well. Samuel was to be such a man: a spiritual leader of great religious fervor and a priest of uncanny political ability.

As is the case with so many important Biblical figures, Samuel's birth is presented as a divinely ordered event. He—like Isaac and Jacob and Joseph—is the

Essentially the same scene of harvesting appears in a 13th-century B.C. tomb from Egypt: the husband reaps while the wife gathers fallen ears into a reed basket.

child of a woman believed to be barren, a woman named Hannah, no longer young, who comes to the tabernacle at Shiloh, where the holy ark resides, to pray for a son. So fervently does she pray that Eli, the high priest, observing her, believes that she is drunk! (I Samuel 1:13–14) He is quickly convinced of his error and is moved to pray for Hannah, so that in time her great desire comes true. She bears her husband a baby boy, calling him Samuel "because I have asked him of the Lord" (1:20). (Samu-el means "asked of God.")

Hannah's gratitude to the Lord is boundless (2:1–10), and when Samuel is old enough she brings him to Eli so that he may be devoted to the priesthood for the remainder of his life. Clearly, it is God's plan that Samuel shall replace the older man, for Eli's sons and heirs are evildoers (2:12–17), not fit for their exalted positions—in fact, they are idolaters. Nor is Eli himself competent any more for his task, being old and weighed down by the wickedness of his sons.

One night, as he tries to sleep, Eli is visited by the young Samuel, who says he thought he heard the old priest calling him (3:5)—but Eli had not called. Twice more, Samuel hears a voice calling his name, and twice more he comes to Eli. Finally, the old man understands: "And Eli perceived that the Lord had called the child" (3:8). So it was, for now the Lord speaks directly to Samuel and tells him that the priesthood of Eli is ended and that Samuel himself shall soon be the holiest man in the land and the foremost leader of Israel.

Eli is reconciled to his fate, but in one last effort to assert himself he allows the sacred Ark of the Covenant to be taken from its sanctuary by the leaders of the army, who wish to employ it as a charm for a miracu-lous victory over the hated Philistines (4:4). God does not sanction magical uses of his power. Besides, the Israelites do not deserve any victory, owing to their continued wickedness, and so that day the Philistines triumph and capture the holy ark. In that same battle, Eli's sons are slain, and when the old priest hears of this and of what happened to the ark, he falls dead on the spot (4:18). Gloom and misery now descend on Israel.

For their part, the Philistines do not benefit from the captured ark, for whenever they put it beside their idols, the latter fall down and break in pieces (5:3–4). In exasperation, and after much misery, the priests of Philistia deposit the ark on an ox-drawn cart near the borders of Israel, and in time the oxen wander into the fields of some Hebrew farmers, who receive the holy shrine with great rejoicing and piety (6:15).

Note: The Philistines heap the ark with bejeweled offerings in hopes of appeasing the wrath of Yahweh. These offerings are described as "five golden emerods, and five golden mice" (6:4), representing two plagues that afflicted Philistia while it retained the ark—the disease of hemorrhoids and the infestation of mice.

Samuel as Leader

Chapter 7 begins the reign of Samuel as prophet and judge. His first sermon to the people deals with their repeated transgressions and idolatry (7:3). So effective are Samuel's words that the Hebrews return to the proper worship of God and expiate

The American painter John Singleton Copley shows Samuel reporting to the priest Eli that he has heard the voice of God.

Surviving from a 3rd-century synagogue (see p. 285) is this chunky relief carving of the Ark of the Covenant, shown here on wheels for easy transport.

their former sins by fasting and prayer. Now when the Philistines attack, they are routed; captured territories are restored to Israel, and peace commences. For years Samuel journeys from his home in Ramah, going from place to place preaching God's word and establishing shrines. He is the chief religious and political ruler of Israel—but he is not quite a king, and before long, as Samuel grows old, the people begin clamoring for a king "like all the nations" (8:5).

It was doubtless God's will that such a king be found, for Samuel now suffers the same fate as his predecessor, Eli; his sons are wicked men, ill fit to assume the priesthood when he dies. Knowing this, the prophet accedes to the people's cry (and to God's instruction), warning the elders, however, that the king they want will "take your daughters to be . . . cooks . . . and the tenth of your seed, and of your vineyards . . ." (8:13, 15). The people are not persuaded by Samuel's warnings, and so he reluctantly turns to God for guidance in the proper choice of Israel's first real monarch.

Saul—the Tragic King

The choice falls on a tall, strapping herdsman named Saul, who comes upon Samuel at Ramah one day while searching for some runaway cattle (9:5–6). God has prophesied Saul's arrival, and Samuel is prepared. At dawn the old prophet takes the future king to the roof of his house and anoints him on the forehead with oil as a sign of holy ordination. At the same time he tells Saul that he is to be Israel's king by God's command (9:25–10:1). To convince the baffled herdsman of his destiny, Samuel describes several events that will occur as omens of God's will, including the fact that Saul will find that the missing cattle are safely returned to his ranch (10:2).

The story of Saul as king of Israel is one of the most pathetic in the Bible. Some say it is reminiscent of a Shakespearean tragedy (such as *Macbeth*), for the king is a good warrior and often means well. But he is also an unsophisticated man who apparently loses favor with God through inadvertent blasphemies. Even so, Saul's tragedy is gradual. In the beginning of his monarchy, he seems destined for success as he emerges heroically from battle with the Ammonites and wins the people's hearts. Gladly they proclaim him, shouting "God save the king" (10:24 and 11:15). Unfortunately for Saul, Samuel still resents the ascension of a monarch, as Chapter 12 clearly relates. In fact, at times, Samuel sounds downright petulant (see 12:3) and only gradually becomes resigned to the historical necessity of a kingdom (12:23–25).

As Saul continues to demonstrate military skill, Samuel recedes into the background. But when the king takes it on himself to offer sacrifices as though he were a priest (13:9–10), Samuel returns to the forefront in wrath. A careful reading of this section (especially 13:6–8) indicates that Saul probably meant well in his heart. Before undertaking the ritual sacrifice himself he did wait, after all, seven days for Samuel to begin it. Was the old prophet setting a snare for the king? You must evaluate Saul's argument (13:11–12) against Samuel's condemnation (13:13–14) and draw your own conclusion.

But even if Saul meant well concerning the sacrifice, we must wonder about his temperament when we read how he almost killed his own son, Jonathan, simply because the boy, by eating some honey, inadvertently broke a fast (14:27). Fortunately, the people prevent Saul from harming Jonathan (14:45), but relations between father and son are forever after strained and difficult. Nor does Saul reduce tension with Samuel. In a battle with the Amalekites, which Samuel ordered (15:1–3), Saul captures Agag, the king, but does not slay him as Samuel demanded. This displeases not only Samuel but God himself, who utters a strange admission of error at 15:10: "It repenteth me that I have set up Saul to be king, for he is turned back from following me, and hath not performed my commandments."

Samuel does not hesitate to report God's anger to Saul and further reproaches him for sparing the heathen king, Agag, and for taking booty in the battle. Saul protests that he meant to do well: I only took these things, he says, in order to sacrifice them to the Lord. But Samuel is unbending: "Hath the Lord as great delight in burnt offerings and sacrifices, as in obeying the voice of the Lord?" (15:22). The two men argue heat-

edly, Saul seeking to redeem himself—for he cannot understand the nature of his sin—and Samuel piously renouncing him in the name of God. At the height of their dialogue, Saul grabs hold of Samuel's mantle and unintentionally tears it in two. Using this incident to establish his point, the old prophet exclaims: "The Lord hath rent [or torn] the kingdom of Israel from thee this day, and hath given it to a neighbor of thine, that is better than thou" (15:28).

Samuel anointed Saul with oil from a vial, but used a ram's horn like this one for David.

129

The ceremony of David's anointing is fitted into the circle of a 7th-century Byzantine silver plate.

This is the first time we learn that a new king will eventually replace Saul on the throne, by God's will (and by Samuel's). Who this king will be is soon revealed.

David—the Singing Shepherd

In secret, Samuel begins to search for Saul's replacement, and God leads him to the house of Jesse in Bethlehem. But none of Jesse's elder sons is to be king of Israel. It is the youngest and humblest of them, the beautiful shepherd and harpist David, who is the choice of the Lord, and so Samuel anoints the boy and bids him patiently await the day of his ascension (16:10–13).

At the same time, the Bible tells us that King Saul begins to lose his mind, or, to put it in Biblical form, "an evil spirit from the Lord troubled him" (16:14). In the hope of comforting Saul, his courtiers send for a musician who may be able to soothe the king with song. As the Lord would have it, David is the one who is chosen to play for Saul, and when he does so the troubled king is comforted. In due time the two men become fast friends; indeed, Saul appoints David to be his armor bearer (16:21) and to live in his palace. This episode demonstrates the effective storytelling techniques of the Bible by the way it employs coincidence, secondary plots, characterization and irony for the purpose of providing memorable literature. The following chapter emphasizes this point.

Goliath—the Giant

Throughout his reign Saul had to contend with the Philistines, a fearsome kingdom of idolaters who now gather for a decisive battle at the valley of Elah. At the head of their troops the Philistines place a monstrous warrior named Goliath, who, according to the Bible, stands almost nine feet tall. In addition to his frightening height, Goliath is adorned in brass armor weighing about 150 pounds; his spear, we read, is "like a weaver's beam," its head nearly twenty pounds in weight (17:7). Each day this formidable giant appears in the valley, and each day he taunts the Israelites, saying: "Choose you a man for you, and let him come down to me. If he be able to fight with me, and to kill me, then will we be your servants: but if I prevail against him and kill him, then shall ye be our servants, and serve us" (17:8–9).

Though Saul and his bravest men quail at this challenge, David, the shepherd,

fearlessly offers himself. Saul at first refuses to consider this offer, but he is eventually convinced by David's entreaties, for the lad reminds the king that many times, while tending his flocks, he has slain both bear and lion by dint of his skill, courage and piety (17:34–37).

Rejecting the use of weighty armor and setting aside even a sword, David takes to the field against Goliath armed only with his trusty sling. The big, brash giant is at first insulted when he sees the young shepherd scampering toward him, accept-

The illustrations on this ceremonial axe associated with Pharaoh Ahmose show how it was used: to hew a conquered enemy. Possibly Saul used such a weapon against the Philistines.

David plays his harp to comfort a troubled Saul. The warm colors and deep shadows of Rembrandt's painting symbolize the contrasting natures of the two men.

ing his challenge. "Am I a dog? . . ." he cries in scorn and anger (17:43). Undaunted, David invokes the name of the Lord of Hosts, God of the armies of Israel, then he "put his hand in his bag and took thence a stone, and slang it [put it in his sling] and smote the Philistine in his forehead, that the stone sunk into his forehead; and he [Goliath] fell upon his face to the earth" (17:49). And when "the Philistines saw their champion was dead, they fled" (17:51).

The Rise of David

Such a triumph raises David to the heights of fame, and we read how he is rapidly exalted as a captain of the armies in Israel and how he becomes an intimate friend of Jonathan, Saul's son and heir (18:1–4). But throughout these happy days for David, King Saul's attitude worsens, as he broods and grows jealous. From the streets he hears people singing: "Saul hath slain his thousands, and David his ten thousands" (18:7). One day the troubled king goes so far as to attempt murder by hurling a javelin at David while the shepherd is playing his harp. And yet in the face of this danger David "behaved himself wisely in all his ways; and the Lord was with him" (18:14). Then Saul promises to give his daughter Michal in marriage to David if the young hero can triumph over the Philistines, for Saul hopes that David will be killed in battle. But the anointed one, as a favorite of God, survives and triumphs greatly so that Saul is obliged to fulfill his pledge. David marries Michal, but Saul "was yet the more afraid of David; and Saul became David's enemy continually" (18:29).

A break was inevitable between the king and his son-in-law (who is, unknown to Saul, also his successor). David therefore realizes that he must escape Saul's clutches lest the next javelin flung by the king find its mark. With the help of Michal, David flees the palace (19:12) and seeks the advice of Samuel at Ramah. Saul follows close behind but is unable to recapture him.

Determined to make peace, David asks Jonathan to intercede for him with Saul and find out, once and for all, his fate in the king's palace (20:1). Jonathan promises to do so and tells David to hide in the fields nearby. If Saul is in a peaceful mood,

The even roundness of these stones suggests that they were used, like David's, for slingshots.

Andrea del Castagno, painting on leather, presents a determined young David triumphant over Goliath's head.

Jonathan will fetch David back to the palace. But if the king is vengeful, as ever, Jonathan will shoot his arrow across the field as a signal of danger.

Unfortunately for all concerned, Saul is as irrational as ever, and when Jonathan raises the question of David, Saul flings a javelin at his own son! "Whereby Jonathan knew that it was determined of his father to slay David" (20:33). Seeking David in the fields, Jonathan signals the bad news with his arrow. Then in an emotional farewell he bids David flee and hide himself far from Saul's intemperance (20:41–42).

Civil War in Israel

The split between David and Saul is the cause of the first in a series of civil wars that is to plague the kingdom of Israel for centuries. A war builds up between the outlawed forces of David and those loyal to Saul. As we have seen from Chapter 16, it is God's will that David be monarch over Israel. Not only is Saul emotionally unfit to rule, but his attitude toward the priesthood and toward his subjects becomes ruthless and unpredictable. At one point he

Part of bronze gates sculptured at Balawat. Saul and his sons were impaled after their deaths; their bodies were displayed in the manner seen here.

orders the execution of an entire congregation of priests because they aided David in his flight (22:17). At another, as we shall see, he bows to the impious practice of witchcraft in a vain attempt to save his power.

David meanwhile hides in the hills with his loyal followers (who more and more flock to him), and though he has repeated opportunities to kill Saul, he reverently restrains himself, for Saul is, after all, God's anointed (24:4–6). Years of strife deepen Saul's misery and strengthen David's resolve. When the two men finally face each other at a place called En-gedi, David attempts a reconciliation by reminding Saul how he could have killed him many times were it not for the fact that he respected his position and remembered their bonds of kinship and affection. "The Lord judge between me and thee," cries David to the king, "and the Lord avenge me of thee; but mine hand shall not be upon thee" (24:12). Saul is at first moved by this plea and in a lucid moment repents his wrath. But even so the strife continues.

Throughout this time, David gains strength. At one point he marries Abigail, the widow of a mighty chieftain, thereby gaining the chieftain's estates (25:39). *Note:* Multiple marriages were common among nobility in those times. David also allies himself with Saul's traditional enemies, for the young man knows that, one way or another, the king must fall (Chapter 27 and 28:1–2).

The tragedy of Saul now gathers momentum. Forsaken by God, the king turns to the occult and to conjuring (28:6). Then, believing he might consult with Samuel, who has recently died (25:1), Saul invokes the aid of a witch at a place called Endor. We can measure the troubled man's

Among the chalky hills of Judah were deep caves of refuge for David and his companions.

confusion by the fact that he himself had earlier outlawed witchcraft in Israel (28:9) and yet now, disguised, he seeks this very same impiety. The witch of Endor manages to raise the ghost of Samuel—or some such phenomenon (on this point the Bible is unclear). Saul throws himself at the prophet's mercy, begging for guidance now that "God is departed from me, and answereth me no more . . ." (28:15). But Samuel has no words of comfort or advice, ominously saying: "Tomorrow shalt thou and thy sons be with me . . ." (28:19).

Saul at first collapses with this grievous news. But he soon revives and in a new mood of resolve heads out toward Mount Gilboa, where the Philistines have launched a massive attack. *Note*: David did not join the Philistines against Saul, for they mistrusted him. Probably he was glad of their decision; read Chapter 29.

On Mount Gilboa, Saul and Jonathan are hopelessly surrounded. Unwilling to be taken alive, the tragic king falls on his own sword—a suicide (31:4). Jonathan and his brothers are also slain, and the Philistines, finding the royal corpses, behead them and fasten the severed bodies to the walls of a temple at Beth-shan. (Such a temple, dating from the period in question, has been unearthed at that spot, a temple dedicated to the Philistine gods.) Fortunately, certain tribesmen of Israel remember Saul and his days of greatness. At night they secretly reclaim his body and those of his sons and give them a decent burial not far from the site of Saul's first and most glorious victory (31:11–13).

On this sorrowful note the First Book of Samuel comes to an end. But its epilogue may be found in Chapter 1 of the Second Book of Samuel, for here we read of

David's lament for the fallen Saul and Jonathan (1:17–27). In utter grief the shepherd, who is soon to be king and who was, besides, the greatest poet and psalmist of Israel, lifts up his voice and exclaims: "The beauty of Israel is slain upon thy high places: how are the mighty fallen. . . . Saul and Jonathan were lovely and pleasant in their lives, and in their death they were not divided: they were swifter than eagles, they were stronger than lions. . . . How are the mighty fallen, and the weapons of war perished!"

Second Samuel, First and Second Kings, First and Second Chronicles

The following five books of the Bible are devoted to the kings and queens of Israel and Judah (as we shall see, the country is soon split into two separate kingdoms). Most of these rulers were dissolute and impious. But the reign of David and that of his son Solomon (II Samuel–I Kings) were glorious indeed and established Israel as a significant and powerful civilization in the Middle East.

Saul's death occurred around the year 1000 B.C. As we learn from Chapter 2 of II Samuel (so called out of respect for the old prophet, whose preparations are responsible for the events in this book), Saul's only living son, Ishbosheth, declared himself king in his father's stead. With the aid of a powerful general named Abner, he managed to establish his reign in the northern part of the country. David, for his part, declared himself king of the southern region of the land, the one dominated by the tribe of Judah. Ishbosheth's partial reign, though it lasted only seven years, was clearly an affront to God, for as Samuel had

told Saul and David, no one of the dead king's family was ever to rule in the Holy Land. Knowing this, David resigned himself to the rigors of continued civil war. There could be no peace in Israel until the house of Saul was thoroughly demolished.

For a while the two kings refrained from actual contact in battle. David, remembering his affection for Jonathan, probably felt reluctant to harm Ishbosheth. But Abner, the general of the north, and Joab, who was David's commander, were restless for a fight and went so far as to initiate war games in a place called Gibeon, the same place where Joshua had caused the sun to stand still. During these bloody events Abner killed Joab's brother, and the latter swore eternal revenge (2:12–24).

This Abner is an interesting and disturbing Biblical character. At first devoted to Ishbosheth, he eventually decides to switch sides and join David as the result of a dispute with Saul's son over the rights of inheritance (3:8). David welcomes Abner to his fold, especially because the general brings Michal, daughter of Saul and David's wife, to Judah, which helps David establish his claim to Saul's throne by right of marriage. Unfortunately, Joab resents Abner as the murderer of his brother; he is also jealous of the general's growing power. One day Joab treacherously "took [Abner] aside in the gate to speak with him quietly, and smote him there under the fifth rib, that he died . . ." (3:27).

The murder of Abner challenges David's rule, and we see from this section

This "Tree of Jesse" illuminates a medieval Psalter and shows the ancestors of Jesus, beginning with Jesse, in blue at the bottom; King David above him; then King Solomon with his Sceptre; and finally Mary and her Son.

how effectively the young king manages to keep the peace. He publicly laments for the murdered general but does not punish Joab lest he stir up resentment among his own followers. The Bible constantly shows how David wisely and sincerely manages the delicate affairs of state and how strictly he upholds his sacred oaths. For example, when Ishbosheth is finally slain (by his own followers), David does not rejoice and reward the assassins; rather he has them executed (4:12) in remembrance of the sanctity of Saul and Jonathan. Likewise, he sends for Jonathan's son, Mephibosheth, a crippled lad of five, establishes the boy in his own palace and protects him throughout his life (9:7–8 and 13).

David—King of a Unified Land

Chapter 5 of II Samuel launches the reign of David as sole king of Israel and Judah. He was a mere thirty years old at the time and was to rule for some thirty-three years over the united kingdom. Apparently the leaders of both areas, north and south, regard him as an excellent leader, for they now declare themselves kinsmen with him; "we are thy bone and thy flesh" (5:1). For the most part they are faithful to him and to their oaths throughout his reign.

An air view of Jerusalem that centers on the Temple Mount, the former site of Solomon's temple, where now stands the Muslim Dome of the Rock (with golden dome). Just above is St. Stephen's Gate, where the apostle was martyred; from there (upper left) is the Via Dolorosa. Just below the Dome of the Rock is the Western or Wailing Wall (center). The slope half way up the right edge belongs to the Mount of Olives, and the wooded area it leads to is the Garden of Gethsemane. Across to the left, the Via Dolorosa leads off the edge of the picture, to the Church of the Holy Sepulchre and the traditional site of Jesus' crucifixion.

David knows that as king of a unified nation he would do best to establish a central location for his palace. His choice falls on the sacred city of Jerusalem, which is henceforth to be known as "the City of David." It was a fortress controlled by Canaanites in the area of the tribe of Benjamin, situated squarely between Israel and Judah. After a brief battle, David and his troops secure this "fortress of Zion" (as Jerusalem was also known), making sure to spare the inhabitants as an act of peace. In this sacred place, on its central mount, Abraham had brought Isaac for sacrifice; here God had intervened in the fate of Israel by stopping Abraham's hand at the critical moment (see page 54), and here too would someday rise the sacred temple of Yahweh. Jerusalem was ideally suited to the young king's dynamic plans for the nation. Neither belonging to the north nor the south, sacred in Jewish memory and set high on a natural fortress-hill, the City of David would be a symbol of unification, peace (the word "Jeru-salem" means "city of peace"). Here a palace would be built for David made of cedars from Lebanon (5:11), and in this palace David was to rear his family of princes.

But warfare still plagues the land, for the Philistines and their allies continue to threaten the provinces. The fact that David decisively defeats this foe and breaks through from Jerusalem to the Mediterranean coast signifies to all the people that God is truly with him. As the Bible says, "The Lord preserved David whithersoever he went" (8:6). Indeed from this point on in Jewish history, the Philistines seem to have lost all significant military power and were content to remain a secondary influence in the area. We remember them mainly today because they lent their na-

These surviving Cedars of Lebanon rise as high as 115 feet. Wood from such trees was used to build the royal compound of King David.

tional name, Philistia, to the geographical lexicon of world history. The area of Israel and Judah in modern times has been known as Palestine (from "Philistian") and was so called until the founding of the modern Jewish state of Israel in 1948.

The Sacred Kingdom

More than the glorification of conquest and power, David wished to establish the authority of God in the new dominion. For this purpose he arranged to bring the sacred Ark of the Covenant from the farmlands, where it had resided for more than a generation. Accordingly, when the ark arrived at the gates of Jerusalem, "David danced before the Lord with all his might . . ." (6:14). Michal, his wife, watching

this display of joy, grows contemptuous of the king. Apparently she considered his actions out of place with his exalted station. Her displeasure is significant, for we may assume that the royal couple drifted apart from that moment on. Thus David was susceptible to infidelity (6:20–23).

But joy in the love of God was an honest emotion for the king. So moved, David plans to build a mighty temple in which to house the ark. His religious counselor, Nathan, however, advises him to wait with such plans since the people, he says, are used to a simple tent, or tabernacle, for their holy place (as Moses had erected in the desert). Rather, Nathan prophesies, David's son will be the one to build such a temple. The Lord's desire on this point seems to startle the king, and he goes before the ark and cries out: "Who am I, O Lord God . . ." (7:18), questioning his remarkable fate that he, a shepherd, has risen to be a mighty king, a king who has now learned that his son—and even his grandsons—shall also rule in Israel. Humbled and filled with a sense of destiny and gratitude, David prays to God: "Therefore now let it please thee to bless the house of thy servant, that it may continue for ever before thee: for thou, O Lord God, hast spoken it: and with thy blessing let the house of thy servant be blessed for ever" (7:29).

In that great body of religious poems known as the Psalms, King David repeats this theme of an enduring household born out of Israel (see Psalms 89:3–4 and 132:11). In many Christian minds this prophecy implies the coming of Jesus Christ, who is regarded as a descendant of David and whose throne indeed "endureth forever" (see Luke 1:30–33). In the Hebrew faith the eternity of David's throne is symbolic and reflects the redemption of Israel as a modern homeland for the Jewish people. For David and his followers, in the tenth century B.C., the promise of endurance meant peace, prosperity and God's love.

The Ups and Downs of David's Life

The amalgamation of neighboring kingdoms with Israel followed the rout of the Philistines (Chapter 10). Before long David's empire extended to the borders of Mesopotamia, beyond the Jordan, to the fringes of Egypt (see II Chronicles 9:26), practically the same territory that God had promised to Abraham in Genesis (15:18).

But for all his glory and wisdom, his

David was one of the significant figures in the 13th-century "Bible in Pictures" (see page 44). Here, carrying a harp, the King triumphantly brings the Ark of the Covenant into Jerusalem.

piety and power, David sinned like any other man. In Chapter 11 we read how he desired Bathsheba, the beautiful wife of a soldier named Uriah. David stopped at nothing to win Bathsheba and wickedly disposed of Uriah by sending him alone into the "forefront of the hottest battle . . . that he may be smitten, and die" (11:15). Uriah is indeed killed as David hoped, and, soon after, the king takes Bathsheba for his wife. "But the thing that David had done displeased the Lord" (11:27).

David's sin is to plague him—and even his children—all their lives. When Bathsheba gives birth, the child dies soon after. Then Nathan, the prophet, publicly condemns the king, saying, "Now therefore the sword shall never depart from thine house . . ." (12:10); in other words, strife and bloodshed will afflict the royal family and eventually bring about civil war, assassination and ruin. God's curse upon David is fearful, and yet the Lord spares the king's life, for David becomes sorely repentant of his crime. In several of the Psalms he apparently wrote during this painful period, his bitter sorrow and penance may be felt. Psalm 32: "Blessed is he whose transgression is forgiven, whose sin is covered. . . . I acknowledged my sin unto thee, and mine iniquity have I not hid . . . ."And Psalm 51: "Have mercy upon me, O God . . . wash me throughly from mine iniquity, and cleanse me from my sin . . . Create in me a clean heart, O God; and renew a right spirit within me."

Sadly, for all his sincere penance, the mighty king cannot escape trouble and strife—as Nathan had warned. Beginning

Rembrandt's compassionate insights enhance David's reconciliation with his rebellious son Absalom; we see the long hair that was to be Absalom's undoing.

with Chapter 13, we read of dissent among David's sons and shameful acts that lead to brotherly murder. We see the rise of Prince Absalom, David's most handsome son, who leaves the palace and begins plotting to usurp his father's throne and who, indeed, before long wins many followers to his cause. David is grief-stricken over Absalom's defection, but even so eventually pardons him (14:21–23).

Absalom

Absalom returns to the palace but continues to plot against his aging father. Finally he has himself secretly anointed king (15:10–12). The Bible leads us to believe that Absalom's plot was a long-term affair—forty years, according to Verse 7, Chapter 15 (it may have been shorter, forty being a common denotation of time, possibly representing a decade). During his conspiracy many of David's courtiers defect to the attractive young prince, who has clearly managed to steal "the hearts of the men [or soldiers] of Israel" (15:6).

While all this dissent and strife ensues, while the sword cleaves the house of David, the king himself seems powerless. Perhaps he is still weighed down by grief over his adultery with Bathsheba, or perhaps his preoccupation with religious thoughts, as reflected in the Psalms, causes him to remain aloof from daily political affairs. In any case, David does not at first take up arms against the rebellious Absalom, but simply allows history to take its course. Ultimately this inconclusiveness gets the best of the king, and he is reluctantly forced to flee Jerusalem as Absalom's army approaches (15:30).

Joab and others loyal to David have been making their own plots against Absalom, sending spies and detractors into his camp.

When the usurper finally arrives in Jerusalem as conqueror, he heeds the advice of counselors who are, in fact, loyal to David. As a result, Absalom fails to consolidate his victory and indeed is beaten in battle. While galloping away from his defeat, Absalom is accidently caught by his luxuriant hair in a branch of a tree so that he hangs helplessly "between the heaven and the earth" (18:9). The vengeful Joab, finding him in this posture, "took three darts in his hand, and thrust them through the heart of Absalom . . ." (18:14).

With his rebel son's death, David returns, all-powerful, to Jerusalem. But his victory is meaningless, for David dearly loved his troublesome son and now grieves for him without cease: "O my son Absalom, my son, my son Absalom! would God I had died for thee . . ." (18:33). Angered by this grief, Joab reminds the

This 2,000-year-old monument has become popularly known as Absalom's Tomb.

king of the young man's treachery and wickedness, asking: "Do you love your enemies and hate your friends?" (19:1–7). David finally leaves off his mourning and resumes the throne, but the glory and vigor of his youth are clearly gone.

The effects of Absalom's rebellion are long felt in Israel, and other local leaders also try their hands at usurpation (see Chapter 20 re the uprising of Sheba). Even the Philistines reappear in the story (21:15), giving rise to the question of sequence in this section of the Bible. Some scholars believe Chapter 21 concerns events that occurred earlier in David's career, since the reference to the Gibeonites (21:1, etc.) and their claims against Saul would most likely have surfaced nearer to the beginning of David's reign. Also we read in 8:1 that David decisively smote and subdued the Philistines; yet here they are again in Chapter 21 back to their warlike ways. David's glorious hymn of praise and thanksgiving that follows in Chapter 22 would more logically complement Chapter 20, which reports the triumph of Joab over the rebellious Sheba. This again implies that Chapter 21 is out of place.

David's exultation "The Lord is my rock, and my fortress, and my deliverer . . ." (22:2) bears the same quality of devotion and inspiration as do many of the Psalms (Psalm 18 for example, which begins: "I will love thee, O Lord, my strength. The Lord is my rock, and my fortress, and my deliverer . . ."). It is a fitting end to the great king's career. Yet two more chapters follow in II Samuel. Chapter 23 gives us David's legacy, along with a list of the king's trusted companions, oddly enough including Uriah the Hittite, the husband of Bathsheba, whom David had sent to his death (23:39). Chapter 24 relates the curious story of an ill-fated census ordered by the king. By numbering the people, David seemingly doubted God's promise of prosperity and expansion. As punishment for this arrogance, the Lord sends a pestilence upon Israel, and 70,000 people fall victim. As the angel of death is about to strike Jerusalem, "The Lord repented him of the evil, and said to the angel . . . It is enough: stay now thine hand . . ." (24:16). David erects an altar at the place where the plague abated, and here, in time to come, King Solomon will build his great temple to God (see II Chronicles 3:1).

The Reign of Solomon

David's death is not reported in II Samuel but in the middle of Chapter 2 of I Kings. The great monarch was seventy years old—a fairly young age in Biblical reckoning—when his life began to ebb. Weak as he was (I Kings 1:1), the king retained his power—no one dared usurp it. His eldest living son, Adonijah, begins, however, to prepare for the throne. Bathsheba, knowing of Adonijah's plans and believing that her own son, Solomon, has been ordained by God to rule in his father's place (see II Samuel 12:24), wins a pledge from David that Solomon is his lawful heir. Adonijah, meanwhile, is arranging a sacred sacrifice in the company of the veteran general, Joab. He believes such a display will confirm his ascension. In the midst of his preparations, Adonijah hears the street criers proclaiming that Solomon is king (1:39).

Fearfully, Adonijah rushes to the tabernacle, where he throws himself upon the sacred altar, for there in that holy place he knows no one will dare to harm him (1:50). Solomon is lenient with his elder half bro-

The "horns" of such altars as this, from Megiddo, were a symbol of sacred refuge, such as that sought by Adonijah, Solomon's rival for the throne.

ther and swears to spare him so long as he holds his peace. With Adonijah's apparent submission, the new king seems firmly established on his throne.

The year of Solomon's ascension was 963 B.C., a year during which the peace of Israel tottered and the religious conviction of the people weakened as well. At such a time it was clearly God's will that an inspired, devout and steadfast leader be enthroned in Israel. Solomon's expansion of the empire and his building of the holy temple forever after cemented Yahweh to the Jewish people despite the corruption of later kings and the dispersion of the Hebrew kingdoms several centuries later.

Before the story of Solomon goes on any further, the Bible relates the passing of

David. "I go the way of all the earth," he says to his son, the newly crowned king, "be thou strong therefore, and shew thyself a man; and keep the charge of the Lord thy God, to walk in his ways, to keep his statutes . . . as it is written in the law of Moses, that thou may prosper in all thou doest . . ." (2:1–3).

Then we read: "David slept with his fathers . . ." (2:10); the "sweet psalmist of Israel," as he is called in II Samuel 23:1, who began life as a humble shepherd, dies in glory and is buried on Mount Zion in Jerusalem, the holy city he founded, where his tomb may be seen today.

Solomon's Wisdom and Wealth

Adonijah did not for long hold his peace and soon attempted to wheedle his way to the throne. In a decisive step, Solomon ordered the usurper's execution, along with that of Joab and other court functionaries loyal to Adonijah (I Kings 2:24–34). Indeed, Solomon's reign begins with quite a bit of bloodshed, for it seems that the young king wished to secure his rights to the throne lest usurpation interfere with his nobler ambitions – those of peace and piety. Accordingly, at the end of Chapter 2, with the various executions accomplished, we read: "the kingdom was established in the hands of Solomon" (2:46).

Now begins the great work of statesmanship and the proverbial wisdom associated with Solomon (Chapter 3). At an elaborate sacrificial ceremony, the young king prays to God "for an understanding heart to judge thy people, that I may discern between good and bad . . ." (3:9). God is pleased that Solomon has chosen wisdom over wealth and long life. In a dream, the Lord promises even these to the king, along with great intelligence. There was "none like thee before thee," God reveals to Solomon, "neither after thee shall any arise like unto thee" (3:12).

To demonstrate the new king's wisdom and justice, the Bible now relates a famous story concerning two women who claim motherhood of the same baby. Solomon satisfactorily resolves this dilemma, and how he does so is well worth reading in the original text, Chapter 3, Verses 16–28. (Perhaps you might hold off the "punch line"—26–27—to see if your child can guess the outcome of Solomon's seemingly frightful plan.)

Wisdom, wealth, honor and glory— these were the handmaidens of King Solomon. To Israel he brought peace, prosperity and power, and to the world he left a legacy of literature unrivaled for its scope and meaning—some 3,000 proverbs, over 1,000 songs and psalms, discussions and essays on botany, zoology, geology (see 4:32–33). In addition, he probably wrote the Biblical books called Ecclesiastes and the Song of Solomon. All that he did was larger than life. For instance, to feed his household for one day required thirty measures of flour and seventy measures of meal (a Biblical measure may have equaled ten pounds), along with ten fat oxen, twenty grazing oxen, one hundred sheep, in addition to rabbits, roebucks, deer and fatted fowl (4:22). He owned forty thousand stalls of horses (the ruins of which were uncovered near Megiddo in the Holy Land) and employed twelve thousand horsemen (4:26). As part of his political treaties with foreign kings, he married seven hundred royal princesses and the daughters of local rulers (11:3). These wives were to be his undoing, as we shall see. Concerning his wealth, it is said that Solomon was the richest man of his time (10:23), given to much luxury: "And all King Solomon's drinking vessels were of gold . . . none were of silver: [silver] was nothing accounted of in the days of Solomon" (10:21)—in other words, silver was worthless compared to the huge quantities of gold at Solomon's disposal. One estimate of the great king's wealth implies a fortune worth ten billion dollars, much of it brought to him as gifts from neighboring monarchs like the Queen of Sheba, who came bearing "spices and very much gold, and precious stones . . ." (10:1–2). She spent most of her visit questioning Solomon on matters of his wisdom (what precise questions she asked we are not told). When Sheba left Jerusalem, she declared: "I believed not the words [about your wisdom and wealth], until I came, and mine eyes had seen it; and, behold, the half was not told me: thy wisdom and prosperity exceedeth the fame which I heard" (10:7).

The Temple of Solomon

Solomon's greatest work was the building of the holy temple in Jerusalem. Chapters 5 to 8 recite the details of this fabulous undertaking (repeated in II Chronicles 2 to 7). While reading this section you should recall Exodus 35 to 40, where the building of the desert tabernacle was described by Moses. Now, some 480 years later, in their own homeland, in the sacred city of David and by means of great devotion, labor and cost, a similar but permanent structure will be built to house the sacred ark and to glorify God. Throughout history, this temple and its successors have represented to the Jewish people, and to all Bible read-

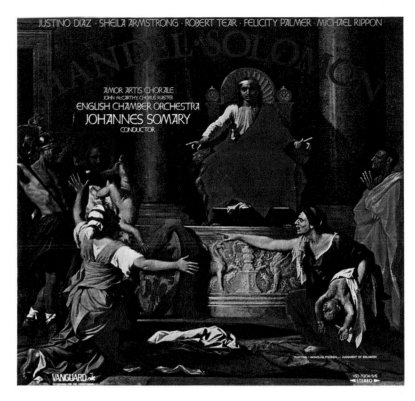

The 18th-century composer Handel told the story of Solomon and the two mothers in a massive oratorio; at about the same time, the French artist Poussin organized the event in dramatic opposing forms and colors. Here it all comes together in a record album.

ers, a concept that mingles national and historical pride with love of God. David had not undertaken this sacred project, tainted as he was by sin. But Solomon, at the zenith of his power and reverence, could finally begin the long-awaited construction, replacing a desert tent with an edifice that would be, in King David's words, "exceeding magnifical, of fame and of glory throughout all countries" (I Chronicles 22:5).

The building of the temple took twenty years (II Chronicles 8:1); its cost has been estimated at some two billion dollars. It was fashioned of huge, close-fitting stones, cedar beams and boards overlaid with gold (I Kings 6:14–22; 7:9–12) and, as noted, was conceived on the general plan of the tabernacle. However, it was twice the size of that desert structure, or about ninety feet long, thirty feet wide and forty-five feet high (I Kings 6:2). It faced east, and its portals of gold were flanked by two impressive free-standing columns of bronze, each given a name: Jachin (the right column, as one faced it) and Boaz (the left) (7:21).

Within the sacred structure, as in the tabernacle, was the altar court and beyond that the holy of holies, where the Ark of the Covenant resided. No idol of any sort stood in this shrine (an occurrence unique in the world of the time); candelabra, braziers, altars, thrones, wall hangings of great beauty and splendor and elaborate carvings of gilded cedar adorned the sacred interiors.

For the common people, prayer and sacrifice were assigned to the spacious courtyards around the temple; there was an inner and outer court, the latter probably dominated by Solomon's splendid palace. Nearly fifty thousand people worked on this holy temple and on its fixtures, assembling each finished component on the site without use of hammer or any metal tool (I Kings 6:7). And when the structure was completed, a solemn dedication was convened by Solomon (8:1–3), and God himself descended into the temple to dwell "in the thick darkness" of it (8:12). At the same time, the holy rituals were established and the laws and ordinances of temple life set forth (8:31–43). Withal, the people were "joyful and glad of heart for all the goodness that the Lord had done . . ." (8:66).

Note: There were three major temples built on the same site throughout Jewish history: the one of Solomon, which stood four hundred years; the temple built by Zerubbabel, which stood five hundred years; and Herod's Temple, restored in 25 B.C., which stood only ninety years. The western wall of this last temple still remains in Jerusalem and is venerated by Jews today. On the mount above this wall, where the temple once stood, there is now a Muslim mosque, known as the Dome of the Rock. In this building one may see the altarlike ridge believed by many Muslims, Christians and Jews to have been the site of Abraham's attempted sacrifice of Isaac.

Solomon's stables at Megiddo: partially restored in a model, and as they are today.

The Breakup of the Kingdom

Solomon's vast building programs—the great buildings and fortresses he constructed, the navy he maintained (9:26)—eventually became a financial burden on

This Dutch 18th-century engraving attempts to convey the busy construction scene described in the Bible. No one knows for sure what Solomon's temple looked like.

the Hebrew people, particularly those in the northern half of the country (specifically called Israel, as opposed to the southern section, called Judah). In I Kings 11 we read of rumblings and dissent. An Edomite prince called Hadad and an Israelite chieftain named Jeroboam began envisioning power for themselves (11:17–19 and 29–31) and started plotting with the Egyptian pharaoh, who was a longtime enemy of Solomon's. God, as well, resented the many idolatrous shrines erected in Jerusalem for the benefit of Solomon's seven hundred foreign wives. As we read in 11:2, the Lord had warned the king that such marriages "will turn away your heart after their gods . . ." and so it happened even to the great and noble Solomon. He who had built the holy temple now erected idols and burned incense and sacrificed to heathen images (11:7). "And the Lord was angry with Solomon . . . wherefore the Lord said unto Solomon, Forasmuch as this is done of thee, and thou hast not kept my covenant and my statutes . . . I will surely rend the kingdom from thee, and will give it to thy servant . . . notwithstanding, in thy days I will not do it. . . . But I will rend it out of the hand of thy son. . . . I will not rend away all the kingdom; but will give one tribe to thy son . . ." (11:11–13).

After Solomon's death (11:43), his son, Rehoboam, ascends the throne. Immediately the northern tribes break away, forming their own kingdom with Jeroboam as monarch. Naturally, idol worship soon takes over the land, not only in Israel (the north), where Egyptian influence is great, but also in Judah, for Rehoboam falters in his faith. As a result, the magnificence of Solomon is soon stripped away by invading enemies, who "took away the treasures . . . took away all . . ." (14:25–27).

As reported in First and Second Kings and First and Second Chronicles, the history of these divided kingdoms is fairly repetitious, consisting of deepening idolatry, corruption, war and sin. (First Chronicles also treats us to a lengthy genealogy, starting with Adam!) It is no wonder that eventually both kingdoms were destroyed by enemies. In 721 B.C., Israel, after two hundred years, was captured and its people so thoroughly dispersed that they disappeared without a trace: the so-called Ten Lost Tribes. Judah (along with the tribe of Benjamin) was defeated in 600 B.C., its people made slaves and wanderers. Even so, because the kings of Judah were, on the whole, somewhat more pious than those of Israel, the fate of these southern people under kings such as Hezekiah and Josiah was generally better and they survived to become modern-day Jews. On several occasions they have returned to reclaim the Holy Land—as recently as 1948, when the Jewish state of Israel was founded.

During the time these monarchs ruled in the divided kingdoms, many devoted and inspired prophets arose in the land forcibly to remind the people of the Lord God and of proper worship. We will pursue the story of two such prophets, Elijah and Elisha, who had to contend with some of the most wicked rulers in history.

Note: The stories of Elijah and Elisha are told only in Kings and Chronicles. Prophets such as Amos, Isaiah and

Inside the ornate Dome of the Rock is the sacred area known as Mount Moriah, where it is believed Abraham offered his son to God.

A relief carving from Nineveh shows the burning of an ancient building by the Assyrians, who were to do the same to the Hebrew temple.

Jeremiah have their own books, which we will study shortly.

First, a list of the better-known kings of Israel and Judah:

Jeroboam—first king of the separate kingdom of Israel, reigned twenty-two years.

Rehoboam—Solomon's son, king of Judah, reigned seventeen years.

Omri—of Israel, reigned twelve years; "and did worse than all that were before him" (I Kings 16:25).

Ahab and Jezebel of Israel (see below).

Jehoshaphat—of Judah, best remembered for his lengthy name, though a good and pious king (I Kings 22:41–43).

Athaliah—queen of Judah; a usurper of extreme wickedness, daughter of Jezebel. She massacred her own grandchildren (II Chronicles 22:10–23:21), except for

Joash—who began his reign in Judah at age seven; restored the temple and was generally a decent ruler (II Chronicles 24).

Uzziah—of Judah, reigned fifty-two

More Assyrian warmaking: shielded archers storm a fortress as a siege engine moves up to batter a tower. Hanging overhead are the bodies of three citizens.

One of the few contemporaneous portrayals of a Hebrew king is the one of Jehu, prostrated before a conquering Assyrian ruler. This relief is found on the so-called Black Obelisk, dating from about 830 B.C..

years as a good king, but in the end became arrogant, contracted leprosy and had to live apart (II Chronicles 26:21).

Zachariah—of Israel, reigned only six months—an evildoer (II Kings 15:8–9).

Hoshea—the last king of Israel, who bowed before the Assyrian hordes (II Kings 17:18).

Hezekiah—of Judah; one of the best of all kings, a great warrior and builder who repelled the mighty Assyrian king, Sennacherib, with aid from the angel of God (II Kings 19:35).

Josiah—of Judah, a noble king, who reinstituted the book of Deuteronomy around 620 B.C. (see II Kings 23:1–3) and who restored the sacred temple.

Jehoiakim—of Judah, who undid Josiah's good works. He tried to kill the great prophet Jeremiah and "did that which was evil in the sight of the Lord" (II Kings 23:36–37).

Zedekiah—last king of Judah, who fell before Nebuchadnezzar, emperor of Babylon, and was blinded by him, but not before he witnessed the burning of Jerusalem: "and the city was broken up, and all the men of war fled by night . . ." (II Kings 25:4–7).

The longest reign in Israel was that of Jeroboam II, forty-one years, all bad; the shortest, Zimri, seven days. In Judah, the idolatrous Manasseh reigned fifty-five years, more than any other king, and two monarchs, Jehoahaz and Jehoiachim, reigned only three months each—but even in these short reigns, evil was the rule.

Note: You have seen concurrent references to Kings and Chronicles. By and large, I and II Chronicles repeat the events reported in I and II Kings, though primarily emphasizing the history of Judah. A reading of I and II Kings often suffices for historical background. The themes of power corrupting and idolatrous backsliding are evident in both sets of books.

The Ordeals of Elijah and Elisha

We first hear of Elijah in I Kings, Chapter 17, when he appears abruptly before King Ahab of Israel to warn of a punishing drought that will afflict the land. Immediately thereafter, at God's instruction, the holy man flees to the wilderness "by the brook Cherith" (I Kings 17:3), where he may be safe from Ahab's cohorts. Ravens sent by God feed Elijah and the brook furnishes his water; he is one of the few to have water, for the drought hangs heavy on the land.

The great prophet soon after journeys to the town of Zarephath, where he is fed by a generous woman whose son later falls ill and "there was no breath left in him" (17:17). In great passion for the mother, Elijah "stretched himself upon the child three times, and cried unto the Lord, and said, O Lord my God, I pray thee, let this child's soul come into him again . . . and the Lord heard the voice of Elijah; and the soul of the child came into him again, and he revived" (17:21–22).

Several such miracles occur at Elijah's behest, and it becomes clear that God has chosen this man to combat the most evil of all Israelite kings, Ahab, and his heathen wife, Jezebel.

I Kings 16 to II Kings 10 concern themselves directly or indirectly with these dissolute monarchs of Israel, who completely turned from God and established the wor-

Giovanni Savoldo, a 16th-century artist from Brescia, shows Elijah in the wilderness about to be fed by a raven. A foretelling of his ascent in the fiery chariot is seen in the sky (left).

Carved ivory brought richness to the decoration of Samarian houses. This "cherub" was found in what may have been Ahab's palace.

larly fond of erecting ivory-paneled houses (I Kings 22:39). Jezebel, as a priestess of Baal, busied herself establishing altars to her god on places formerly sacred to Yahweh. In addition, she set about murdering God's priests and prophets in a wholesale fashion (18:13).

When he hears of Jezebel's slaughterings, Elijah can contain his anger no longer and, at great personal risk, emerges from hiding to confront Ahab (I Kings 18:17). Boldly, he demands that the king stage a public contest between the idol Baal and God Almighty on Mount Carmel in northern Israel. Four hundred and fifty priests of Baal assemble on the mount with their idol of stone, and Elijah stands facing them alone. The Baalists offer prayers and sacrifices to be consumed by their god. But Baal does not reply to their entreaties. They leap about and gash themselves in the hopes of eliciting some reaction from him—but to no avail.

"Cry aloud!" Elijah says in mockery; perhaps Baal is sleeping "and must be awaked" (18:27). By evening the priests of Baal finally give up their efforts in defeat. Now Elijah turns to God, and in the name of Abraham, Isaac and Jacob he prays for a sign of divine power. Though the sacrificial animals and wood arranged by Elijah are repeatedly drenched in water

ship of the idol Baal—a worship that consisted of brutal child sacrifice. The clash between the fiery prophet Elijah, who appears and disappears with dramatic suddenness, and the wicked rulers is one of the most suspenseful in the Bible, for the antagonists are very well matched. Ahab is a skillful warrior and a devious politician, with a passion for luxury that bleeds the people of their livelihoods. He was particu-

In going to Mt. Carmel (seen here from the west) for his trial of strength, Elijah with superb confidence chose the place most sacred to his antagonist, "Baal of the Heavens."

(18:33–35), even so "the fire of the Lord fell, and consumed the burnt sacrifice, and the wood, and the stones, and the dust, and licked up the water . . ." (18:38) The people who witness this miraculous event turn from their idolatrous ways and resume the worship of God. Even Ahab, who is ever a vacillating man, seems repentant and willing to return to Yahweh. He is no doubt moved to do so when Elijah blames him and his wickedness for the unrelieved drought that has wasted the land for all these years. Because of Ahab's apparent but short-lived penance, Elijah now miraculously brings forth rain from a cloud no bigger than a man's hand, a wisp that grows into a drenching storm cloud (18:44–45). Ahab is duly impressed, but the real power behind his throne is the haughty Jezebel, and her response to Elijah's miracles is hatred and scorn. In fact, she sets out to murder him (19:2). Elijah flees again into the wilderness and there falls into a mood of great despair and discouragement, unique in Biblical accounts.

"It is enough; now, O Lord, take away my life . . ." he cries (19:4). The evil Ahab and Jezebel "have slain thy prophets with the sword; and I, even I only, am left . . ." (19:10).

Hearing this, God appears to Elijah and teaches him a powerful lesson about faith that forms the nucleus of this entire recounting. The lesson is this: God is not only in the miraculous feats such as Elijah has been able to perform, nor is he evident alone in the roaring wind, or in earthquakes, or fire. Beyond all such things and all such obvious signs, God remains "a still [that is, peaceful], small voice" that fills the heart and soul; a voice that convinces not by magical or miraculous means, but by an

The ancient Syrian legal case documented here implies a land seizure similar to the one undertaken by Ahab and Jezebel. In this case the king had to pay compensation.

irresistible appeal to goodness, reason and truth. Elijah is renewed by this lesson and goes on to fight idolatry and sin. In the course of his mission, he chooses a young plowman named Elisha as his disciple, passing on his mantle to him as a sign of acceptance (19:19).

Ahab and Jezebel continue their horrendous ways. They murder a wealthy landowner named Naboth in order to seize his estate (Chapter 21). This last scandal enrages Elijah anew, and he curses husband and wife, predicting an end to their reign and an inglorious death for each. And so it comes to pass. Ahab is killed in battle after much suffering (22:34–37), and Jezebel is eventually assassinated and her body thrown to the dogs, as Elijah foretold. Truly, "there was none like unto Ahab, which did sell himself to work wickedness in the sight of the Lord, whom Jezebel his wife stirred up" (21:25).

Elijah's end is exactly opposite that of his enemies. He is taken up to heaven in a

Elijah's fiery chariot ride to heaven contrasts in splendid baroque style with the earthbound figure of Elisha, who kneels enraptured before the event depicted in Giovanni Piazzetta's Venetian painting.

chariot of fire, drawn by horses of fire (II Kings 2:11), as witnessed by Elisha. Only his mantle is left behind, and this Elisha places on his own shoulders so that he may continue the great prophet's work. This he does in like fashion, even raising a dead child as his master had done (4:32–37). Elisha also warns the wicked kings of Israel who follow Ahab of their fate—kings such as Jehoram and Jehu.

The two prophets, Elijah and Elisha, were very different in the way they pursued God's call. Elisha was gentle, diplomatic and patient. Elijah, a man of the wilderness, of fiery speech and dramatic gesture—a forerunner, some say, of John the Baptist—could neither be gentle nor diplomatic in his mission to trample out Baalism and its evils. The fact that Elisha dies peacefully in bed (II Kings 13:14) and that Elijah was lifted alive to heaven in a miraculous fashion further symbolizes the difference between the two and sets the style for the later prophets of Judaism,

never technically died, he is easily available for such visits.

Musically, Elijah is the subject of a great oratorio by the German composer Felix Mendelssohn (1809–1847). Using the Biblical text, the composer contrasts the pagan rituals of Baal with the holy reverence for God exemplified by Elijah. This contrast is especially vivid during the contest on Mount Carmel, where we can hear—in the oratorio—Elijah taunting the Baalists: "Cry aloud!" Jezebel's wrath and Ahab's wickedness are also depicted in Mendelssohn's score. But nothing equals for beauty and drama God's message to the prophet in which he reveals the glory of the "still small voice; and in that still voice, onward came the Lord."

Summary of the Biblical Books in this Chapter

Joshua: the conquest of Canaan.

Judges: the period of national adjustment.

Ruth: the forebears of King David.

I Samuel: the prophet Samuel; King Saul and David.

II Samuel: David as king.

I Kings: Solomon; the temple; the divided kingdoms.

II Kings: the kings and queens of the divided kingdoms.

I Chronicles: the genealogy of Israel and Judah (David as king).

II Chronicles: Solomon as king; the history of Judah.

Note: Some scholars refer to I and II Samuel as I and II Kings, thus making what we call I and II Kings into III and IV Kings.

some of whom were fiery, some gentle, all devoted to God and justice.

The figure of Elijah has inspired many legends and artistic interpretations, and it furnishes an incident in the New Testament that we will explore later (the Transfiguration—Luke 9:30). Among the most venerable of the legends is the one concerning Elijah's Cup, which is offered for the prophet during the Passover feast. At such times Elijah is supposed to visit every Jewish home and partake of the celebration by sipping wine. As one who

CHAPTER FOUR

ADVENTURE AND ROMANCE

Ezra · Nehemiah · Esther · Job · Jonah

The link between the preceding four books of the Bible and the ones we are about to explore is so strong that we find the last two verses of II Chronicles are identical to the first two verses of the book called Ezra. This is no accident or literary oddity. It was extremely important for the scribes who wrote these books to confirm the fact that God has not abandoned the Jewish people despite the collapse of their kingdoms, and it is this message that dominates the repeated verses.

To be sure, a huge jump in history occurs during the last chapter of II Chronicles, specifically at Verse 20. In fact, sev-

enty years pass between the Babylonian captivity of Judah and the events repeated in II Chronicles 36:22–23 and Ezra 1:1–2. During these seventy years two prophets are the inspirations of the captive people, Ezekiel and Daniel. Their stories, however, are delayed until the section of the Bible that deals with the prophets as such.

Suffice it now to say that between 606 B.C. (II Chronicles 36:1–21) and 536 B.C. (when Ezra begins), the following major events occurred in Jewish history:

609 B.C.—Nebuchadnezzar emerges as the leader of the Babylonian (or Chaldean) empire.

606–600—He takes captive thousands of Jews from Judah (the prophet Jeremiah urges submission; see the prophet section).

586—Nebuchadnezzar burns Jerusalem and completes his conquest of the Judean kingdom (see Jeremiah 34:17–22).

In Nebuchadnezzar's time, the enameled brickwork of the huge, ceremonial Ishtar gate at Babylon was originally ornamented with 13 rows of animals, alternating bulls with serpent-headed dragons like this one.

This clay cylinder, with its many columns of text, was inscribed at Nebuchadnezzar's order soon after 586 B.C., during Daniel's time at court.

582–572—Nebuchadnezzar conquers most of the Middle East (during this time Daniel is influential at the emperor's court).

562—Nebuchadnezzar dies.

560–538—The Jews are captives in Babylon (the prophet Ezekiel is prominent at this point, as we shall see in the prophet section).

538–536—The Persian empire asserts itself and conquers Babylon. Darius and Cyrus are emperors of Persia (again Daniel is prominent).

536—Cyrus orders the repatriation of Judah (as prophesied by the prophet Isaiah; see Isaiah 45:1–2 and 13).

The books of Ezra, Nehemiah and Esther tell of Jewish life during this Persian period (roughly 536 to 331 B.C., when Persia was conquered by Alexander the Great of Greece). The stories of Job and Jonah are from an earlier period. Job is unique in the Bible for its theological message. But Jonah fits in with this section as a fascinating story of adventure and the mingling of Jewish thought with alien ideas.

The Hebrews in Captivity

Though dispersed and resettled in Babylon, the exiles of Judah kept alive their hopes of returning to the homeland some thousand miles away. It would be more accurate to say that their prophets and religious leaders kept the hope alive—both those prophets of the past, such as Isaiah (read his Chapters 40 to 66) and Jeremiah, whose works were remembered, and also the new breed of exile leaders, such as Ezekiel. These men had an especially difficult task in reviving Jewish national feeling and the love of Yahweh. Babylon was not a particularly oppressive conqueror, and in fact many Jews lived very well and prospered, in accordance with Jeremiah's advice that they "build ye houses, and dwell in them; and plant gardens . . . and seek the peace of the city whither I [God] have caused you to be carried away captives . . ." (Jeremiah 29:5 and 7). Besides, how could ordinary people retain their faith in a God whose temple lay in ruins and whose grace and favor seemed departed? The gods of Babylon were attractive for many reasons, and the tendency to assimilate was a compelling one indeed. Yet, save for a few exceptions, the spiritual leaders held fast and remembered their heritage, remembered Jerusalem and Yahweh. As the great Psalm of Exile tells us (Psalm 137):

By the rivers of Babylon, there we sat down,

Yea, we wept, when we remembered Zion.

We hanged our harps upon the willows in the midst thereof. For there they that carried us away captive required of us a song; and they that wasted us required of us mirth, saying Sing us one of the songs of Zion.

How shall we sing the Lord's song in a strange land?

If I forget thee, O Jerusalem, let my right hand forget her cunning.

If I do not remember thee, let my tongue cleave to the roof of my mouth;

If I prefer not Jerusalem above my chief joy.

The leaders of the Hebrew faith knew, as Jeremiah had prophesied and as Ezekiel had commanded, that a true love of God potentially lay within each human heart and was not necessarily tied to a specific building or even a specific city. But they also realized how important a return to Judah might be for a people growing comfortable in captivity. So it was that when the Persians conquered Babylon and the new ruler, Cyrus, announced his policy of repatriation, Jewish leaders were quick to accept the opportunity.

It is God who directly inspires Cyrus, though a Persian, to the task of repatriating the Jews and, in addition, to rebuilding Jerusalem and the sacred temple (Ezra 1:2). Cyrus even bestows on the former captives countless treasures of gold and silver to accomplish this task. (In this way, he may remind you of how leaders in the United States treated the people it conquered after World War II.) All the precious objects Nebuchadnezzar had looted from Jerusalem would now be returned, and so would over fifty thousand people (Ezra 1 and 2).

The Rebuilding of Jerusalem

After about a year, the returning Jews crossed into the sacred city of Jerusalem, a place in ruins for the most part and populated by a mere remnant of Hebrews, descendants of those whom Nebuchadnezzar thought too old or too unimportant for captivity some seventy years before. The leader of the repatriates was Zerubbabel, a relative of King Jehoiakim, appointed by Cyrus as Governor of Judah (3:8). Under his authority a new temple is begun, one smaller than the building of Solomon—or so the older men who had seen the original complain (3:12). It is to be fifteen years, however, before even this temple is completed, not because of its ornate structure but owing to the interference of non-Hebrew tribes now settled throughout the Holy Land. As the Bible reports: "Then the people of the land weakened the hands of the people of Judah, and troubled them in building . . ." (4:4).

The good king Cyrus dies in Persia and is succeeded by Ahasuerus I, who does not lift a finger to help the Jews. Only when Darius the Great becomes king is work on the temple resumed (around 519 B.C.; see 4:24). This is the same King Darius whose record of conquests was carved into the living rock of a mountainside called Behistun (or Bisutun) near present-day Baghdad and who also began the building of the magnificent royal city of Persepolis in Persia.

The completion of the temple in Jerusalem, though encouraged by Darius, is not an easy matter, as we learn from reading the books of Haggai and Zechariah, two prophets of the period who are referred to at the beginning of Chapter 5. These leaders taught something new in the Hebrew faith, a messianic spirit, a direct redemption by God that could be expected if the Jews repented their ways and trusted in Yahweh. Urging them to finish their temple, as a sign of faith the prophets tell of a descendant of King David who shall "grow up out of his place, and he shall build the temple of the Lord . . . and he shall bear the glory, and shall sit and rule upon his throne . . ." (Zechariah 6:12–13). To the Jews of captivity, this message implied a possible restoration of the Davidic kingdom. To many Christians today it forecasts the coming of Christ.

The Work of Ezra

The man whose name is given to this book, Ezra, does not appear until Chapter 7, where the text suddenly veers into a first-person narrative style. Some eighty years have passed since Zerubbabel led the repatriates into Jerusalem. The temple is more or less completed and a semblance of normal life has returned to the beleaguered city and to the battered people, who, for all their hardships, celebrate the Passover as a recognition of their sacred obligations (6:19–20). But something vital was still missing in the land of the Jews (which the Bible refers to as Israel even though only Judah remained). The true religious love of God had badly faltered. This the priest Ezra learned about while still living in Babylon. He determined to go to Jerusalem, "for Ezra had prepared his heart to seek the law of the Lord, and to do it,

These stately steps, columns and carved figures are all that remain of the audience-hall at Persepolis, begun by Darius and completed by Ahasuerus (Xerxes).

and to teach in Israel statutes and judgments" (7:10).

In order to carry out what might be called the second repatriation, Ezra appealed directly to the new Persian monarch of the day, Artaxerxes I, to provide funds and a military escort to ensure the success of the venture. Artaxerxes was generous and quick to reply (read 7:11–26). The year was about 457. Some two thousand Jews accompanied Ezra on the four-month trek to Jerusalem.

We may assume that smaller groups of repatriates had been trickling back to the Holy Land in the decades since Zerubbabel's mission. But none was to be as significant as this one, for Ezra had the spirit of the old prophets, and the children of Israel badly needed spiritual guidance. As we read in Chapters 9 and 10, intermarriage with foreigners threatened to reinstitute idolatry again in the Holy Land (as had happened with Solomon's wives), and this once more threatened national safety. Had not God punished the Jews with captivity as a result of their pagan practices? It could happen again.

Ezra, aware of this possibility and so grief-stricken by the spiritual void that he found in Israel, says that "[I] rent my garment and my mantle, and plucked off the hair of my head and of my beard, and sat down astonied" (although it looks like a misspelling of "astonished," "astonied" is a seventeenth-century word meaning bewildered, translated as "appalled" in the Revised Standard Version, 9:3).

Drastic acts were apparently required to purge the people of their sins, and these Ezra enforced in the name of Artaxerxes. He called a mass meeting of leaders in Jerusalem and warned that those who failed to appear would be "separated from the congregation . . ." (10:8). Furthermore, leaders who had married foreign wives were obliged to give them up (10:17). A whole new form of religious observation was gradually to emerge under Ezra's guidance. This system was based on several concepts founded by Ezra, among them the establishment of the synagogue, or a meeting place for prayer, and the study of Torah (the Law of Moses). Ezra's ideal of Torah study, observance in the synagogue, and ethical conduct based on the Law, all centered around devotion to the one God, Yahweh, is the essence of Judaism as we know it today.

Nehemiah

Ezra's work was spiritual and legalistic (he established judges and courts again in Israel). But practical matters such as reinforcing the crumbling city walls were to be left to another Jew of the Exile, a court official of Persia named Nehemiah. His book follows Ezra's.

The Bible tells us that the younger man arrived about thirteen years after Ezra's mission began. He came from Sushan, the royal capital of Persia, with explicit orders from his friend and protector King Artaxerxes (whose cupbearer he was). As governor of Judah, Nehemiah's chief responsibility was to reinforce the city by rebuilding its defensive walls. Until that was done, the repatriates were at the constant mercy of their enemies and the Second Temple (humble as it was) in danger of annihilation. A devout man, Nehemiah spent four months in prayer before undertaking his journey (see Nehemiah 1:1 and 2:1). Finally in the year 444, with Artaxerxes' edict in hand, he set forth.

Note: Esther, the Hebrew maiden and

later queen of Persia, was Artaxerxes' stepmother and was probably still alive at this time. Is she the queen who is mentioned in Nehemiah 2:6 sitting beside Artaxerxes? We may believe she was and that her great influence on behalf of her people lay behind the friendly attitude Persia maintained toward the repatriates of Judah (see following book).

The City Walls

As we learn from Nehemiah's own words, Jerusalem was militarily in a sorry state (2:17). Accordingly, the governor first repairs the city gates (Chapter 3), some parts of which are still extant, according to archaeologists (e.g., "the tower that lieth out," or David's Tower, 3:26). Rebuilding the actual walls is a far more difficult task for Nehemiah, owing to attacks and distractions by neighboring tribes. A new spirit of resolve, however, seems alive in the land—no doubt due to Ezra's influence and reforms—and the people, under Nehemiah's insistence, complete the walls in only fifty-two days (6:15), a triumph "wrought of our God" and one that causes Israel's enemies to be "much cast down in their own eyes . . ." (6:16).

Now, once again, after 142 years—since the time Nebuchadnezzar's hordes sacked the city—Jerusalem stands fortified.

The next two chapters of Nehemiah (7 and 8) tell of the listing of the people (the genealogies) and the great public reading of the Torah that was given under Ezra's direction. For seven days, from early morning until noon (8:3), this event took place. It was, in short, a wide-scale reeducation of the people, instituted so that the letter of the Law could be clearly understood by everyone capable of hearing. As a result of this unique religious experience, many wept for their sins. But the priests forgave the sinners and bade them "neither be ye sorry; for the joy of the Lord is your strength" (8:10). Then the grateful congregation celebrated the holiday of Succoth, or Booths, commemorating the time of the Exodus when their forebears dwelled in booths in the desert (8:17).

Ezra was not finished in his campaign to rededicate the people to God. Now he called for a new covenant, a public ceremony reaffirming the bond between the Hebrew people and Yahweh as Abraham had conceived it centuries before. Repeating the history of the Jewish nation from Abraham's time to the Second Temple (9:7–32), Ezra invited the princes and leaders of Israel to step forth and sign a scroll of dedication "to observe and do all the commandments of the Lord our God . . ." (10:29).

Susa—or Sushan—was the winter capital of Persia and the scene of Esther's triumphant story. This air view shows something of the vast excavation process.

The Western or Wailing Wall in Jerusalem's Old City, with stones as old as 2,000 years, is said to be a remnant of the third temple and is a shrine of remembrance and worship.

The remainder of the Book of Nehemiah is devoted to ordinances and rules of daily life, taxation, worship and to the genealogies so vital to Biblical records. The walls are dedicated (12:27) amid exultant joy, "with cymbals, psalteries, and with harps," and Nehemiah is praised for his leadership and perseverance. All is well in Judah. Indeed, a new era of peace and dignity begins for the repatriates, who are now, in fact, natives of their native land. There were still to be problems of idolatry, of foreign intrusions and the like. But the age of the Second Temple generally seems a noble one. To be sure, Judah was no longer a great world power. Nevertheless, as a protectorate of Persia, she could live in peace, develop her prosperity and, above all, be dedicated to the God of Israel, whom Nehemiah called "the great, the

mighty . . . who keepest covenant and mercy . . ." (9:32).

From this point on in our story—and, more important, in the chronology of the Bible as we know it—events are not sequential. In fact, with the close of Nehemiah, the Old Testament chronology actually comes to an end; in other words, no book to follow relates information about a later period (except for the Apocrypha, but this is not technically the Old Testament—as we shall see).

The incidents and events that occupied the period between the fall of Judah and the Book of Ezra are related in sections still to be read. One of these is the Book (or, more specifically, the Scroll) of Esther—a delightful and dramatic story of the Persian captivity and of a beautiful woman who saved her people from extermination and

The Story of Esther

Historically, as we have noted, this story comes *before* that of Nehemiah—about thirty years before. The scene is again Persia—in fact, Sushan, the city from which Nehemiah journeyed to Jerusalem. The king is not the friendly Artaxerxes but rather his father, called Ahasuerus (Xerxes I), an illustrious ruler who reigned from "India even unto Ethiopia . . ." (Esther 1:1), one given to luxury and gala festivities. Indeed, it is one of Ahasuerus's lavish parties that sets the wheels in motion for the ironic story that is to follow. On the eve of some great event—possibly a battle with the Greeks—Ahasuerus inaugurates a seven-day feast amid gorgeous decorations

A gold goblet from Persia of the 6th or 5th century B.C. is like the one used by Nehemiah, the cupbearer.

Persian guardsmen still parade in glazed brick along walls from the royal city of Susa; these walls survived the city's conquest by Alexander the Great and are now to be seen in the Louvre.

169

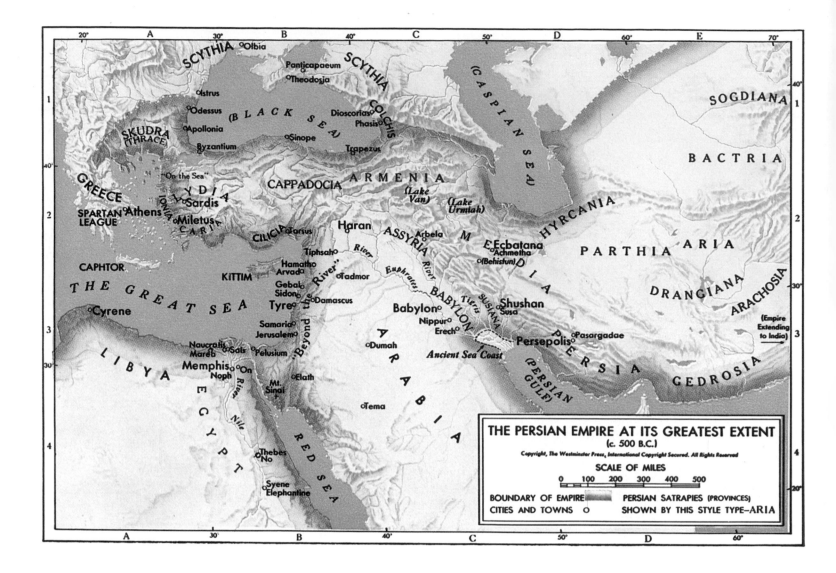

THE PERSIAN EMPIRE AT ITS GREATEST EXTENT
(c. 500 B.C.)

Copyright, The Westminster Press, International Copyright Secured. All Rights Reserved

SCALE OF MILES

0   100   200   300   400   500

BOUNDARY OF EMPIRE   PERSIAN SATRAPIES (PROVINCES)
CITIES AND TOWNS O   SHOWN BY THIS STYLE TYPE—ARIA

rarely described anywhere else in the Bible (1:6–7). At the same time the king is feasting, his wife, Queen Vashti, is holding her own banquet for the honored ladies of Sushan. In the midst of the revelry, an unfortunate domestic squabble arises between the king and the queen. Ahasuerus wishes Vashti to appear, with her royal crown, at the men's banquet so that they may see her beauty. The lady flatly refuses (1:12), causing the king's anger to "burn" in him. His ministers warn that Vashti's disobedience might be the signal for an outbreak of female rebellion in the empire, whereupon every wife "shall despise their husbands in their eyes..." (1:17). Ahasuerus agrees. Rather impetuously, as is his wont, the king sends word throughout the country that Vashti is no longer

queen—and she disappears from the story.

Ahasuerus now orders a search among the maidens of his kingdom for one both beautiful and obedient to replace Vashti as his queen. The elements of a Cinderella-type story creep through as we read of royal messengers searching the provinces for such a girl. Their choice is not a Persian native but one of the Jewish captives. She is Hadassah, a maiden reared by an older cousin called Mordecai (2:7). This Mordecai had been taken captive by the Babylonians and had then adopted Hadassah, whose parents were dead; he had renamed her Esther, in keeping with Persian styles.

Ahasuerus is smitten by the beautiful girl, and after much ceremonious delay—and what seems to be a sort of beauty contest (2:12)—the king finally crowns Esther queen in place of Vashti (2:17). He does not know her to be a Jewess.

Mordecai meanwhile sets himself up in the royal gate lodge of the palace, where he becomes a doorkeeper, or sentry. There one day he overhears a plot to murder Ahasuerus. This he reports to Esther, who in turn warns the king. The matter is quickly settled; the would-be assassins are hanged and Mordecai's good deed recorded in the chronicles of the kingdom (2:21–23).

All this clever plotting in the story so far is still but a prelude to the main action, which follows with the introduction of the character Haman, one of the most artful villains in Biblical literature. As prime minister to the king, Haman spares no effort to glorify himself. One day he issues an order that obliges everyone at the palace to bow down and revere him. Only Mordecai, being a Jew and therefore not bowing to any man, refuses (3:2). Angered by the doorkeeper's pride and learning of Mordecai's religion, Haman institutes a frightening plan in which he "sought to destroy all the Jews that were throughout the whole kingdom of Ahasuerus . . ." (3:6).

To determine the precise day and month on which his scourge of genocide is to take place, Haman casts a lot (called *pur* in Hebrew), probably by means of dice, hitting on "the thirteenth day of the twelfth month, which is the month of Adar . . ."

The story of Esther tells of Haman's plan to annihilate the Jewish people. In modern times, such a crime was almost carried out by the Nazis. A memorial to the heroic Jews who resisted their enemies stands today in Israel at Yad Vashem, the documentation center dealing with Nazi crimes.

for the slaughter (3:13). Next in his plan, Haman convinces the king, who is clearly disinterested in the whole affair, of the value of this genocide. Ahasuerus gives Haman his ring as a sign of agreement, saying "do with them [the Jews] as it seemeth good to thee" (3:11).

And so the evil plan is put into motion, and according to the ancient laws of the Persians and the Medes, once sanctioned, a rule can never be revoked, even by the king. All over the kingdom people read the following edict: "to destroy, to kill, and to cause to perish, all Jews, both young and old, little children and women, in one day, even upon the thirteenth day of the twelfth month, which is the month of Adar . . ." (3:13).

Mordecai's Grief

Mordecai is quick to read this notice and in great anguish goes into mourning. He hopes by this means to attract Esther's attention, for she is apparently cut off from all such worldly matters (4:1–3). Word does reach the queen of widespread lamentations among the Jews and particularly Mordecai's "loud and bitter cry" (4:1). But it is clear from the text that the queen is ignorant of the cause behind her people's misery and fear. Will this delay be fatal?

Through a trusted intermediary, Mordecai finally passes a copy of Haman's decree to Esther in the palace, with a message that she must save her people at all costs. Indeed, he says, this crisis is probably the reason why God destined Esther for such a high position; or as Mordecai asks her rhetorically in his message: "Who knoweth whether thou art come to the kingdom for such a time as this?" (4:14).

No doubt Esther is willing to do what she can, but the rigid laws of the palace prevent her from simply walking in on the king without a summons. Death is the penalty for such an affront, unless "the king shall hold out the golden sceptre . . ." (4:11). Boldly, Mordecai informs the queen—again by messenger—that she will die anyway as a Jewess if Haman's plan is carried out, for none shall be spared. The suspenseful back-and-forth nature of these messages by means of intermediaries reaches a fervent climax as Esther, bravely, lets it be known that she will pray and fast and then take her chances before the king. With audacious pluck she announces: "And if I perish, I perish" (4:16).

Chapter 5 is an extraordinarily clever piece of melodramatic writing. Adorning herself, the brave young queen approaches the king's throne room. What will be his reaction to her sudden appearance, unsummoned to boot? We read: "When the king saw Esther the queen standing in the court, she obtained favor in his sight: and the king held out to Esther the golden sceptre that was in his hand" (5:2). So far so good. But now Esther has to convey publicly her dramatic message and consequently admit that she is Jewish. Unwilling, it seems, to be so forward at this point, she cleverly pretends that she has come simply to invite the king and his prime minister, Haman, to a private banquet.

The king and Haman readily comply, and while enjoying the first day of the feast (for these affairs, as noted, ran several days), Ahasuerus exclaims to Esther: "What is thy petition?" He clearly recognizes that she has something to ask of him. "It shall be granted thee . . ." he continues, "even to the half of the kingdom it shall be performed" (5:6).

Suspense is unrelenting as we read that Esther does not at once reveal her purpose

A ceremonial relief sculpture from Persepolis shows the kind of procession by means of which Ahasuerus honored Mordecai.

but further requests that the king and Haman come again on the following day to a similar feast.

The Downfall of Haman

Throughout this build-up Haman has been in very high spirits. Not only will he soon wreak vengeance on his hated enemies, the Jews (particularly Mordecai), but he has now become a favorite of the queen, invited twice to her private banquets. Of course, every time he catches sight of Mordecai unbowing at the gate he becomes more enraged. "All this [glory] availeth me nothing . . ." he tells his wife (5:13). On her advice, he then decides to put Mordecai to death on the gallows even before the thirteenth day of Adar.

The plot thickens in Chapter 6 as Ahasuerus, unable to sleep one night, turns to his chronicles of good deeds and there discovers the unrewarded action of Mordecai in saving his life from assassins. At this very moment Haman approaches, planning to request permission to execute Mordecai on the gallows. Ahasuerus, now anxious to reward his gatekeeper, calls Haman forward to ask his advice on how he might honor "the man whom the king delighteth to honour . . ." (6:6). Naturally, thinking himself the man in question, Haman suggests a royal parade with the honored man adorned in princely garments led on horseback by the king's most noble ministers. Ahasuerus is pleased with the suggestion and tells Haman: "Make haste . . . do so even to Mordecai the Jew, that sitteth at the king's gate . . ." (6:10). We can imagine Haman's astonishment and horror at this turn of events. Though the Bible does not reveal his immediate reaction, it tells how after leading Mordecai in glory through the streets of the city, Haman rushed back to his house and covered his head in mourning. So bereft is the arrogant man that he nearly forgets Queen Esther's banquet and has to be summoned there by messenger (6:14).

The climax of Esther's plan approaches.

While dining with the king and his prime minister on the second day of her feast, she finally petitions her husband. "If I have found favour in thy sight, O king," she says, " . . . let my life be given me at my petition, and my people at my request: for we are sold, I and my people, to be destroyed, to be slain, and to perish . . ." (7:3–4).

Ahasuerus is amazed. Who in the world dares seek the queen's death? he demands.

"The enemy is this wicked Haman," Esther declares, causing Haman to shrink in fear where he sits.

Ahasuerus, given as usual to explosive outbursts, rushes from the room to get some air in the garden. Thus he leaves Haman alone with the queen. In panic for his life, the vicious man throws himself at Esther's mercy, going so far as to fall on the couch where she sits. Ahasuerus, returning and seeing this outrage of decorum, orders Haman executed on the very gallows the villain had prepared for Mordecai (7:9–10).

The Thirteenth Day of Adar

The blood-and-thunder story is not yet over, for as you will remember, the law of Persia cannot be revoked even by the king, and despite the fact that Haman is dead, his monstrous plan of genocide must be carried out on the thirteenth day of Adar as decreed.

Esther goes before Ahasuerus and proposes a counterplan to be enforced by Mordecai, who is now promoted to prime minister. On the thirteenth day of Adar, she suggests, let every Jew throughout the empire be armed to defend himself and his family so effectively that none will dare rise against him, knowing that "the Jews should be ready against that day to avenge themselves on their enemies" (8:13). This decree is widely publicized and proves eminently effective; in fact, not only do most of the Persians refrain from initiating the slaughter, but we also learn that many of them "became Jews; for the fear of the Jews fell upon them" (8:17).

Instead of a horror, the Jews celebrate "gladness and joy and honour" on that fateful day and do so to this day in the feast called Purim, named for the lots (or dice) Haman cast to determine the date of genocide.

Chapter 9 reports in some detail just how the slaughter was avoided. (The Jews, it seems, were obliged to fight at Sushan, killing five hundred of Haman's diehard followers.) When the bloodshed was over, however, Mordecai emerged undisputed second in command of the kingdom (or really third, after Ahasuerus *and* Esther). The Jews settled down to a peaceful life. So it was that Ezra and Nehemiah could rise to such heights under Artaxerxes, the son of Ahasuerus and the stepson of Esther.

What Does This Story Tell Us?

The Scroll of Esther was one of the last books accepted into the Old Testament by the Hebrew scribes (around A.D. 100). Even so, some did not think it appropriate as a Biblical book. For one thing, nowhere in the text is there a single mention of God in any way, a situation unique in the Bible (although we are aware of God's *will* working through Mordecai). For another, the story seems rather overly dramatic and posited on rather illogical premises, such as the rigid laws of the Persians and the Medes, which even threaten Queen Esther's life when she first approaches

Jan Steen, in 17th-century Holland, paints Ahasuerus' tempestuous anger on learning that Haman (cowering at the left) has been plotting to kill all the Jews, including Queen Esther (right).

Ahasuerus to invite him to her banquet. The bloody ending of the tale, where the Jews turn into a punishing horde, also seems out of keeping with the tone of Purim, a joyous, carnival-like holiday.

On the other hand, few stories in the Bible are so compelling and so rich in characters: the quick-to-anger Ahasuerus; the haughty Vashti; Mordecai, proud, emotional and courageous; Haman, sinister, crafty and arrogant; and the supreme heroine, Esther, a paragon of beauty and bravery. In addition, the twists and turns of the plot are the stuff of great fiction, and

thus the story is appealing. Consider the exciting literary devices used in this story, from the ironic turnabout that takes place at Mordecai's procession of honor to Esther's dramatic denunciation of Haman to the even more startling turnabout that enables the Jews to save themselves.

The scribes of Biblical times, who decided to include the story in Scripture, appreciated these literary values, and though Esther does not relate any specific ethical teaching or theology, it does give heart to all who read it in times of peril. Such times were sadly repetitious in Jewish history.

Ahasuerus on his throne, with Esther on the right, hands a decree to an attendant in a 3rd-century synagogue fresco.

Under the Syrian tyrant Antiochus IV (165 B.C.), genocide once again almost destroyed the Jews (as we shall see in the Apocrypha), and, in our own time, within living memory, the evil of Haman arose in the person of Adolf Hitler, who, like the wicked villain of this book, desired to kill and slay and cause to perish every Jew in the world—a plan that nearly succeeded.

The Book of Job

There follows now, in strong contrast to Esther, what many believe to be the most profound and amazing of all Biblical books. Victor Hugo, the eminent French novelist, called it "perhaps the greatest masterpiece of the human mind," and Thomas Carlyle, the Scottish historian, said "this book, apart from all theories about it, [is] one of the grandest things ever written. Our first, oldest statement of the never-ending problem: Man's destiny and God's ways with him in the earth."

Because of its power and greatness and its pertinence to Jewish and Christian beliefs, the Book of Job requires a slightly different approach where the average child is concerned. Though it can be told as a cautionary story of a man who loses everything but remains faithful, it must nevertheless also somewhere touch on the question of God's purpose regarding man, as Carlyle noted. It must also ask the question: Why do the good suffer? We will approach the basic themes of Job within the story, but for now we begin with a schematic breakdown of the book—namely, who wrote it, when, its form, plot and so forth. Unfortunately, this scheme may only add to the imponderables concerning the text, since very little is entirely conclusive about Job—except its greatness and the forty-two chapters it comprises.

Author of the Book

No one can say for sure who wrote the Book of Job. Generally it is thought to have been the work of Moses, written sometime during the Exodus. Job may have been an Edomite chieftain. It is therefore believed that Moses heard his story when the Israelites were camped near Edom and went on to use it as the jumping-off point for an ethical lesson about man's fate and God's will. This means that the Book of Job would belong to the pre-kingdom period of Israelite history, or about 1150 B.C.

Most modern Biblical scholars, however, think the date of authorship to be much later, since the story reflects ideas about God that evolved during prophetic times (ninth to second centuries B.C.). This opinion fits in well with the possibility that the prophet Jeremiah may have been the author of Job. Two reasons are given. For one thing, Jeremiah was the prophet of the Exile, that time in history when Judah fell before the Babylonians and all seemed lost

for the Hebrews. The theme of Job is faith in adversity, or how to remain God-fearing though bereft of all joy and sustenance. Isaiah also concerns himself with this theme. Indeed, some say that the prophet known as Second Isaiah may have written Job. But the case for Jeremiah is stronger insofar as we know this prophet to have been a prolific author (as we shall see he even had a secretary named Baruch to do his transcribing), and there are several passages in Job that seem very close to Jeremiah's thoughts and style. For example, Job's heartbreaking lament "Let the

Somehow embodying the "patience of Job" in its ageless style is this 3,000-year-old likeness of an ancient official, carved in tough diorite.

day perish wherein I was born . . ." (Job 3:3–6) is very much like Jeremiah's lament "Cursed be the day wherein I was born . . ." (Jeremiah 20:14–16). Job's recognition of God's unknowable powers (as reflected in God's answer to Job, 38:4–5) "Where wast thou when I laid the foundations of the earth . . . ?" sounds like Jeremiah's realization that God will never abandon Israel, until ". . . the heaven above can be measured, and the foundations of the earth searched out beneath . . ." (Jeremiah 31:37).

The debate goes on as to the authorship of this book. Suffice it to say that it was a devout Hebrew scholar who wrote it with a great gift for both poetry and philosophy.

The Form of the Book

Job is divided into several sections that together resemble an epic poem. It begins with a prologue (1:1 to 2:13) and closes with an epilogue (42:7–17). The body of the poem, which lies between the prologue and the epilogue, consists of three parts: 1) the argument of Job's three visitors, each of whom speaks three times (except for Zophar, who speaks twice) and Job's replies to each of them; 2) the speeches of Elihu (32 to 37), which may have been later additions; and 3) God's message and Job's humble reply (38:1 to 42:6), which are, in fact, the climax of the story—the epilogue notwithstanding.

The Style of the Book

These sections are written in an advanced form of Hebrew literary style (or poetry), which depends for its powerful effects on several striking devices: first, the use of mirror images, or subtle repetitions of the same idea, such as "Let the *day* perish wherein *I was born*," followed by "and the *night* in which it was said, there is a man *child conceived*." Second, the impact of unusual and memorable imagery: "Yet man is born unto trouble, as the sparks fly upward" (5:7), conveying the idea that trouble is as inevitable as natural phenomena. Third, the dialogue concept, resembling a drama, in which characters speak back and forth, creating a feeling of immediacy and reality. And fourth, the ringing quality of religious sentiment couched in stunning first-person prose: "I know that my redeemer liveth, and that he shall stand at the latter day upon the earth . . ." (19:25).

These stylistic devices, plus the greatness of the theme, are the essence of Biblical literature and nowhere more evident than in Job.

The Plot

Simply told, the story of Job is as follows: A wealthy man named Job, in the land of Uz (possibly Edom), is considered the most righteous, noble and devout of men. But Satan, the adversary of God, believes Job's goodness is the result of his material well-being. "Put forth thine hand now, and touch all that he hath," says Satan to God, "and he will curse thee to thy face" (1:11). God allows Satan to deprive Job of all his worldly possessions and even to destroy his family—sons, daughters and grandchildren—in order to test his religious faith. Though grief-stricken, Job remains faithful to God, saying: "The Lord gave, and the Lord hath taken away; blessed be the name of the Lord" (1:21).

Satan again approaches God and implies that Job remains faithful only because he himself has not been afflicted with personal physical pain. "Touch his bone and his flesh," the adversary says, "and he will curse thee to thy face" (2:5). God allows Satan to inflict the suffering man with a multitude of diseases. Even so, Job is faithful, despite the entreaties of his wife that he "curse God, and die" (2:9). "Shall we receive good at the hand of God," the sickened man says, "and shall we not receive evil?" (2:10).

Now three visitors appear. They have come, they say, to comfort Job. Their names are Eliphaz, Bildad and Zophar (later a younger man named Elihu joins them). Unfortunately, their presence greatly upsets Job, who by this time is covered in boils and forced, as a mourner, to sit naked on a pile of ashes in great agony, pain and bereavement. His condition is so appalling that the comforters cannot begin to comfort him and remain at his side one full week without a word.

It is Job who begins the dialogue, bewailing his fate (3:3), saying: "Why died I not from the womb? Why did I not give up the ghost when I came out of the belly?" (3:11). Though miserable, bitter and despairing, Job does not curse God.

The friends begin to question him as to why he may be suffering as he does. What did he do to deserve such punishment? All suffering, they say, is the result of sin. Therefore, those who suffer must have sinned either openly or in secret, knowingly or even unwillingly. This is the theme they repeat in various, often complicated, phrases.

ELIPHAZ: ". . . they that plow iniquity, and sow wickedness, reap the same." (4:8).

BILDAD: "If thou wert pure and upright; surely now [God] would awake for thee . . ." (8:6).

ZOPHAR: "If iniquity be in thine hand,

An amulet worn by Babylonians to chase away the demon of disease such as plagued Job.

put it far away, and let not wickedness dwell in thy tabernacles" (11:14).

To all these statements Job replies in the same vein; he is disappointed that his friends believe him to be sinful, for he is not at all a wicked man. "To him that is afflicted pity should be shewed from his friend," he says (6:14). "Thou knowest that I am not wicked" (10:7); besides, God sometimes afflicts the righteous as well as the guilty (9:22). Perhaps it is the fate of all men to suffer, he says. "Man that is born of woman is of few days, and full of trouble" (14:1). Perhaps the wicked prosper and the righteous suffer: "Wherefore do the wicked live, become old, yea, are mighty in power?" (21:7). Whatever the situation, the so-called comforters have only increased Job's sorrow and pain by doubting his integrity and accusing him of wickedness. "How hast thou helped him that is without power?" (26:2), he cries and launches a lengthy parable, or comparison story, justifying his innocence. In this impassioned speech, which covers six chapters (26 to 31), Job alludes to many images in nature and everyday life in order to make his point: "But where shall wisdom be found? and where is the place of understanding? Man knoweth not the price thereof; neither is it found in the land of the living. The depth saith, It is not in me: and the sea saith, It is not with me. It cannot be gotten for gold, neither shall silver be weighed for the price thereof" (28:12–15).

Then at 31:40, "The words of Job are ended." He has complained bitterly of his fate and gravely questioned God, but throughout he has never denied his creator. In fact, as he earlier declared in a great hymn of faith: "I know that my redeemer liveth, and that he shall stand at the latter day upon the earth: and though after my skin worms destroy this body, yet in my flesh shall I see God" (19:25–26).

Now Elihu, the youngest of the group, speaks up for the first time (Chapters 32 to 37). He contributes two new ideas to the discussion. First, he says, God often punishes men in order to teach them the error of their ways. By this means they can correct their faults even though the faults be unwillingly committed. Thus would Job be wise to say: "That which I see not, teach thou me: If I have done iniquity, I will do no more" (34:32), because "God exalteth by his power: who teacheth like him?" (36:22).

But Job's suffering implies an even greater conclusion, and this is Elihu's second idea; it concerns the nature of God more so than the nature of man. "God is great, and we know him not . . ." (36:26), the young man declares. "God thundereth marvellously with his voice; great things doeth he, which we cannot comprehend" (37:5); "touching the Almighty we cannot find him out . . ." (37:23).

As though to compound Elihu's realization of God's mysterious powers, the Almighty himself now speaks to Job out of a storm cloud (38 to 41). In thrilling poetry, the Lord tries to show the suffering man how little he really understands of the world and how, in fact, "God thundereth marvellously . . . great things doeth he, which we cannot comprehend." Here are some of the awesome questions the Lord asks of Job, knowing full well he cannot answer them:

"Hast thou entered into the treasures of the snow? or has thou seen the treasures of the hail?" (38:22). "Who can number the clouds in wisdom? or who can stay the bottles of heaven . . .?" (38:37). "Knowest thou the time when the wild goats of the rock bring forth, or canst thou mark when the hinds do calve?" (39:1). "Hast thou given the horse strength? hast thou clothed his neck with thunder?" (39:19—read this section for a glorious description of the horse as a creature of God). "Canst thou draw out leviathan with an hook?" (*Note:* Leviathan is believed to be a sort of sea monster, or possibly a crocodile.) "None is so fierce that dare stir him up: who then is able to stand before me?" (41:10).

In short, "Shall he that contendeth with the Almighty instruct him?" (meaning God himself) (40:2). "Hast thou an arm like God?" When man comprehends the mystery of God, only then can he say that he is righteous or wicked, deserving of punishment or not deserving of it, or that he knows anything at all, for "whatsoever

William Blake found a variety of meanings in Job's sufferings. In this brush drawing the three friends seem weighed down, listening in silent sympathy to Job (center) and his wife.

is under the whole heaven is mine," God declares (41:11).

Job fully accepts this powerful message. Why he suffers has suddenly become of less importance than the fact that God exists in a wondrous and mysterious fashion. He accepts his lot, realizing that he tried to speak of things "that I understood not; things too wonderful for me, which I knew not" (42:3). Now, instead, Job comes to understand that man's relationship to God must be a personal one. Man must "see" God with his eye—that is, his inner eye or his soul. He must not simply speak of God or take for granted what others tell him (42:5).

The final chapter of the book may seem an anticlimax. In it the Lord reprimands the unfeeling "comforters" who misrepre-

sented God and his ways. Only Job, by his devotion, has come near the understanding that surpasses understanding. For this wisdom, the ailing, suffering man is rewarded with a complete turnabout of his troubles. "So the Lord blessed the latter end of Job more than his beginning" (42:12). New sons and daughters are born to him, his wealth restored, and at the age of 140 Job dies "full of days" (42:17).

The Theme of Job

We have referred to the essential themes of this book in the plot outline above. They may be summed up in the following "collage" of quotes from the text itself:

"What is man, that thou [God] shouldest magnify him? and that thou shouldest set

thine heart upon him? and that thou shouldest visit him every morning, and try him every moment?" (7:17–18).

"Man that is born of a woman is of few days and full of trouble. He cometh forth like a flower, and is cut down . . ." (14:1–2).

"What then shall I do when God riseth up? and when he visiteth, what shall I answer him?" (31:14).

"Behold, God is great, and we know him not, neither can the number of his years be searched out . . ." (36:26); ". . . great things doeth he, which we cannot comprehend" (37:5). "Touching the Almighty, we cannot find him out . . ." (37:23).

"Shall he that contendeth with the Almighty instruct him?" (40:2). "Wilt thou also disannul my judgment? Wilt thou condemn me, that thou mayest be righteous?" (40:8); ". . . whatsoever is under the whole heaven is mine" (41:11).

"The Lord gave, and the Lord hath taken away; blessed be the name of the Lord" (1:21).

Jonah

And now we jump a bit ahead, breaking the order of the standard Bible this one time to include here a great adventure story: the Book of Jonah. By rights this book should be included with the so-called Minor Prophets (see following chapter), where Jonah stands between Obadiah and Micah. But the four short chapters of Jonah are so unlike these other prophets

Christopher Plummer played Satan (left), Raymond Massey God, and James Daly (kneeling) the tormented Job-like character in the 1959 production of Archibald MacLeish's play *J. B.*, a modern retelling of the Biblical story.

that they seem to require a place of their own in this section of Adventure and Romance. The fact is that Jonah is not so much a prophet as he is the leading character of a story that in itself teaches us a prophetic message concerning God's universality and love.

The story begins when the Lord commands Jonah to go to the great city of Nineveh and preach to the people, whose wickedness has become an affront to heaven. Nineveh was, at that time, among the most prosperous, powerful and beautiful cities of the world, the capital of Assyria. In recent times, much archaeological work has uncovered the site of this ancient city and revealed that in its heyday it covered some thirty miles, including suburbs, and was protected by five sets of walls and three moats. Among its most impressive buildings was the library of King Ashur-bani-pal, believed to have contained 100,000 volumes in the form of clay tablets (many of which are now in the British Museum).

From the Book of Jonah we can calculate the population of Nineveh during the time of the story (about 780 B.C.). Chapter 4, Verse 11 refers to "sixscore thousand persons that cannot discern between their right hand and their left hand," meaning 120,000 little children. If there were about ten times that many adults (the usual ratio), then the population consisted of over a million people.

God wishes to communicate with these people, now fallen to great wickedness. Their aggressive ambition, the "violence" in their hands, referred to at 3:8, would eventually cause the fall of Israel, around 720 B.C. Possibly God wished to postpone that terrible event by softening the hearts of the Assyrians. We learn from II Kings

A model of an Egyptian boat, probably like the one in which Jonah tried to escape his mission.

14:25 that Jonah was responsible for the restoration of certain lands taken by Assyria from Israel, implying that God's intention was realized for a short period of good neighborly relations between the two countries. It is also the clear purpose of this book to convey the message of God's compassion for all peoples—not only the Hebrews—wherever they might be.

Unfortunately, Jonah cannot appreciate this idea. Rather than preach to the hated Ninevehites, he boards a ship at Joppa (present-day Jaffa) and heads toward the coast of Spain, as far away in the opposite direction as he can get from Nineveh.

Naturally God is aware of this evasion and sends a "mighty tempest" to rock and wreck Jonah's ship (1:4). The sailors and other passengers of that ship are exceedingly afraid and toss off all cargo in order to lighten the weight of the foundering vessel. Everyone prays to his God for safety, everyone except Jonah, who lies "fast asleep" in the hold (1:5).

The captain of the storm-tossed ship, realizing this is to be a most unnatural storm, decides to cast lots "that we may know for whose cause this evil is upon us" (1:7). By this means they discover that Jonah is the sinner, that God has sent this terrible tempest as a means of forcing Jonah to undertake his sacred mission. The sailors are desperate and even more fearful when Jonah tells them that he is a Hebrew escaping Yahweh. "What shall we do unto thee," they ask, "that the sea may be calm

In this painting by Rubens, Jonah's robust fellow-sailors are linked together rhythmically as they reluctantly lower him into the sea, where the great fish waits (right).

unto us?" (1:11). Jonah bravely tells them to toss him into the sea; "so shall the sea be calm unto you: for I know that for my sake this great tempest is upon you" (1:12). At first the men attempt to outrun the storm, since they do not want to kill Jonah. But when they see that the sea grows even more tempestuous, they relent and, praying for forgiveness, toss Jonah into the thick of the billowing waves.

As soon as they have done so, the storm abates. But what of Jonah? Chapter 1:17 puts it quite simply: "Now the Lord had prepared a great fish to swallow up Jonah. And Jonah was in the belly of the fish three days and three nights."

The "Whale" and the Worm

Exactly what kind of fish swallowed Jonah we cannot say. Many believe it was a whale (which is technically not a fish but a sea mammal). A whale's throat, however, is too small to accommodate a whole man alive, and so it must be assumed that some other, more unusual, creature arose to fulfill this need. Since Verse 17 above clearly states that God "*prepared* a great fish," one can infer that this was a special fish created especially for this occasion.

Deep in the belly of the fish, Jonah repents his cowardly ways and resolves to do his duty as God commanded. The prophet's near drowning has scared him dreadfully, for he remembers how "the waters compassed me about, even to the soul: the depth closed me round about, the weeds were wrapped about my head" (2:5). With great passion, he begs forgiveness of the Lord.

Now God causes the fish to spew up Jonah "upon the dry land" (2:10), probably near the coast of Israel. The prophet proceeds to Nineveh, a three-day journey.

It is Jonah's belief that the Lord wishes him to alarm the Ninevehites by publicly proclaiming the imminent fall of their city. This he does with great enthusiasm, for clearly Jonah despises the Assyrian enemy. But his zealous message frightens the Ninevehites so greatly that they earnestly repent. Even the mighty king puts on sackcloth and sits on ashes as a sign of contrition.

"And God saw their works, that they turned from their evil way; and God repented of the evil that he had said that he would do unto them; and he did it not" (3:10). Jonah perceives that Nineveh will not be destroyed as he had prophesied in the streets. He at once turns angry and begs God to let him die rather than be thus humiliated.

Sulking and embittered, the prophet leaves the city and takes up a post nearby to await a possible change in God's plan. He actually wants to see Nineveh destroyed. To protect himself from the hot sun of the desert, Jonah erects a booth, or lean-to, in the shade of a leafy gourd, or vine, which God purposely allowed to grow where it was. Jonah, we are told, was "exceeding glad of the gourd" (4:7). Now, further in his lesson, "God prepared a worm" to nibble at this gourd so that it eventually withers and dies. "And it came to pass, when the sun did rise, that God prepared a vehement east wind; and the sun beat upon the head of Jonah, that he fainted . . ." (4:8). Without the shade of his gourd, Jonah is in great agony and cries out pitifully for the gourd, lamenting that it has withered and died.

God proceeds to announce the message and moral of this entire story. "Thou hast had pity on the gourd," he says to Jonah,

Jonah is greeted by an angel as he comes up out of the great fish, seen in vivid patterns by a 14th-century Persian artist.

but not on Nineveh, where scores of thousands of people live, not to forget "much cattle" (4:10–11).

With these words, the Book of Jonah abruptly ends, and we are left with the task of "completing" it, or resolving its message. It does not specifically say that Jonah repented his anger at God's decision to save Nineveh. Nor does it spell out the concept of universal mercy in so many words. But in this reading we must examine details as though they were clues in a mystery. Only then is the message evident.

First we see the elements "prepared" by God (the storm, the fish, the gourd, the worm, the hot east wind), all to convince Jonah of his rightful mission. Secondly, we learn of God's compassion to non-Hebrew peoples (the Ninevehites, the sailors on the storm-tossed ship and even for the cattle of the Assyrians). Finally, there is God's willingness to forgive Nineveh its sins (3:10), even as he forgave the Children of Israel time after time.

No doubt Jonah came to understand this lesson of forgiveness and of God's universal power. In any case, his story has represented this theme thoughout the ages. In the New Testament, Jesus himself speaks of it (Matthew 12:39–41), even comparing himself to Jonas (Jonah). For many this is validation enough of an unusual tale.

הָאִישׁ אֲשֶׁר לֹא הָלַךְ בַּעֲצַת רְשָׁעִים וּבְדֶרֶךְ חַטָּאִים לֹא עָ
עָמָד וּבְמוֹשַׁב לֵצִים לֹא יָשָׁב: כִּי אִם בְּתוֹרַת יהוה חֶפְצוֹ וּבְ
וּבְתוֹרָתוֹ יֶהְגֶּה יוֹמָם וָלָיְלָה: וְהָיָה כְּעֵץ שָׁתוּל עַל פַּלְגֵי מָיִם
אֲשֶׁר פִּרְיוֹ יִתֵּן בְּעִתּוֹ וְעָלֵהוּ לֹא יִבּוֹל וְכֹל אֲשֶׁר יַעֲשֶׂה יַצְלִ
יַצְלִיחַ: לֹא כֵן הָרְשָׁעִים כִּי אִם כַּמֹּץ אֲשֶׁר תִּדְּפֶנּוּ רוּחַ: עַל
עַל כֵּן לֹא יָקֻמוּ רְשָׁעִים בַּמִּשְׁפָּט וְחַטָּאִים בַּעֲדַת צַדִּיקִים:
כִּי יוֹדֵעַ יהוה דֶּרֶךְ צַדִּיקִים וְדֶרֶךְ רְשָׁעִים תֹּאבֵד:
לָמָּה רָגְשׁוּ גוֹיִם וּלְאֻמִּים יֶהְגּוּ רִיק: יִתְיַצְּבוּ
מַלְכֵי אֶרֶץ וְרוֹזְנִים נוֹסְדוּ יָחַד עַל יהוה וְעַל מְשִׁיחוֹ: נְנַתְּ
נְנַתְּקָה אֶת מוֹסְרוֹתֵימוֹ וְנַשְׁלִיכָה מִמֶּנּוּ עֲבֹתֵימוֹ: יוֹשֵׁב
בַּשָּׁמַיִם יִשְׂחָק יהוה יִלְעַג לָמוֹ: אָז יְדַבֵּר אֵלֵימוֹ בְאַפּוֹ וּבַחֲ
וּבַחֲרוֹנוֹ יְבַהֲלֵמוֹ: וַאֲנִי נָסַכְתִּי מַלְכִּי עַל צִיּוֹן הַר קָדְשִׁי: אֲ
אֲסַפְּרָה אֶל חֹק יהוה אָמַר אֵלַי בְּנִי אַתָּה אֲנִי הַיּוֹם יְלִדְתִּיךָ:
שְׁאַל מִמֶּנִּי וְאֶתְּנָה גוֹיִם נַחֲלָתֶךָ וַאֲחֻזָּתְךָ אַפְסֵי אָרֶץ:
תְּרֹעֵם בְּשֵׁבֶט בַּרְזֶל כִּכְלִי יוֹצֵר תְּנַפְּצֵם: וְעַתָּה מְלָכִים הַשְׂ

CHAPTER FIVE

GREAT THOUGHTS AND WISDOM

Psalms · Proverbs · Ecclesiastes · Song of Solomon ·

The Major and Minor Prophets · Lamentations

The remaining sections of the Old Testament are generally considered the spiritual core of the Bible. There are few real stories in these books, except for the events surrounding the messages of the prophets. But even these stories are secondary to the wisdom of the text. Poetry, philosophy, theology and general knowledge are the essences to be sought when reading Psalms, Proverbs, Ecclesiastes, the Song of Solomon and the Prophets. Taken together, these books represent the basic philosophies of the Judeo-Christian tradition and round out the historical information presented so far (this is particularly true of the Books of Daniel and Ezekiel).

The first page of Psalms with the word "happy" or "blessed," written in Hebrew and "illuminated" with a bright-colored miniature of King David, from a late 15th-century Italian manuscript.

But unlike the sections we have already explored, these writings, especially Psalms, Proverbs, Ecclesiastes and the Song of Solomon, require direct confrontation with the text. One can hardly retell the essence of the Psalms in language more explicit or revealing than the King James or Standard Revised English translations. Therefore, this part of our investigation will necessarily concern historical and literary questions, leaving to the reader the direct pleasures of the poetry itself. We will, however, try to show in Psalms—with a few famous examples—just how the poetic images themselves evolved. Themes, authorship, style and the like will similarly be explored.

The Psalms

Martin Luther called the Psalms "the immortal songbook of the human heart,"

These Elamite musicians, strumming, blowing, drumming, and singing in victory, suggest the musical fervor that fills so many of the Psalms.

and there is much reason to believe that these exquisite religious poems were indeed meant to be sung to music. "I will sing unto the Lord . . ." the psalmist writes in Psalm 104:33, and in many places specific musical instruments and notation are indicated. Psalm 8, for example, is prefaced: "To the Chief Musician upon Gittith," the gittith thought to be a musical instrument from the city of Gath (also see Psalms 81 and 84). It is further believed that the *neginoth* in the preface to Psalm 4 was a stringed instrument and the *nehiloth* of Psalm 5 a flute. Fifty-five psalms are headed "To or For the Chief Musician." Whether individually sung or performed by chorales, these lyrics no doubt echoed

in the chambers of the temples of Jerusalem and even today may be heard in musical settings.

There are a total of 150 psalms in the Bible, together known as the Psalter (or Book of Psalms). Seventy-three of them are ascribed to King David, either as author or patron (the one who may have commissioned them). Two are under the name of Solomon (72 and 127), one authored by Moses: "Lord thou hast been our dwelling place in all generations . . ." (Psalm 90). Fifty are anonymous, and the

Winnowing grain, as in this tomb painting from Thebes, produces the windblown chaff spoken of in the first Psalm.

remaining twenty-four are by various other authors. Tradition, of course, considers David the author of most of the psalms, the anonymous ones included.

Tradition also groups the psalms into five sections (1 to 41; 42 to 72; 73 to 89; 90 to 106; 107 to 150) in imitation of the first five books of Moses. Whatever their grouping or authorship, every one of the psalms concerns itself with man's relation to God. Sometimes this is a joyous, heartfelt relation; sometimes one of sorrow, penitence and personal contrition. In some cases the psalms seem full of thunder, in others full of sweet murmurings. They are reverent, inspired, passionate and, above all, bespeak an outpouring of man's faith and trust as he approaches the Lord. The words "praise," "rejoice," "shout for joy" and the famous expression "Hallelujah" or "Praise to Yahweh" fill dozens of these poems. Many also resound with Messianic

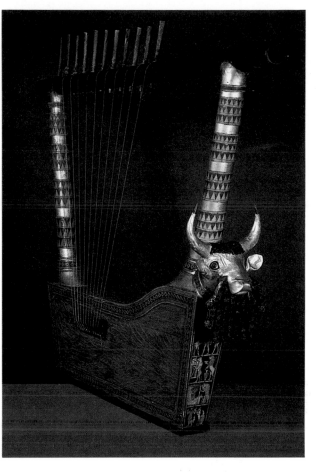

A reconstructed lyre from Ur of the 25th century B.C., possibly like one used to accompany the Psalms. Strings were supported by mosaic-studded uprights.

Sheep, and even young shepherds, seem almost as timeless as the Bible lands themselves and recall the famous Shepherd's Psalm, Number 23.

fervor, the promise of God's redemption by means of his personal messenger and a coming age of righteousness and peace.

There follows now a brief survey of some of the more famous psalms with excerpts from each. Again, you are urged to read aloud—or have your child read—these masterworks in their entirety from the Bible.

Psalm 1: "Blessed is the man that walketh not in the counsel of the ungodly . . ." (1)—a hymn to the righteous person warning against idolatry and irreverence. "The ungodly . . . are like the chaff which the wind driveth away" (4), sings the psalmist, setting the tone for the poems that follow.

Psalm 2: Takes up the same theme; the "heathen" is deplored and the reverent man called by God ". . . my Son; this day have I begotten thee" (7). This last phrase is believed by many to be a foreshadowing of Jesus Christ.

Psalm 8: Philosophically, this psalm resembles the Book of Job and contains a line almost identical to one in Job (7:17), "What is man, that thou art mindful of him?" (4). "For thou hast made him a little lower than the angels . . ." (5). God's creations are extolled in this psalm, and it is said that his words shall come forth even "out of the mouths of babes and sucklings . . ." (2).

Psalm 16: A hymn of trust. The Lord is called "the portion of mine inheritance and of my cup . . ." (5) who will gladden the heart of the faithful even in death.

Psalm 19: A poem exalting God. "The heavens declare the glory of God; and the firmament showeth his handiwork . . ." (1). It ends with a universally effective prayer: "Let the words of my mouth, and the meditation of my heart, be acceptable in thy sight, O Lord, my strength, and my redeemer" (14).

Psalm 22: A tragic, melancholy psalm, quoted by Jesus as he suffered on the cross: "My God, my God, why hast thou forsaken me?" (see also Mark 15:34). The singer here (David) seems bereft of hope and feels abandoned. "I am poured out like water" (14). In the end, his faith is renewed because "all the ends of the world shall remember and turn unto the Lord" (27).

Psalm 23: The Shepherd's Song—perhaps the most famous and well loved of all psalms, often recited at funerals or in times of peril. Closely drawn to actual practices among the herders of Biblical times, this psalm compares God to a shepherd who "maketh me to lie down in green pastures: he leadeth me beside the still waters" (2). Shepherds, we know, do indeed lead their flocks to quiet brooks, since sheep will not drink from bubbling waters. In Biblical times there was a treacherous path near the Dead Sea called "the Valley of the Shadow of Death," which is referred to at line 4. Here the shepherd, by proper use of his rod and staff, safely guides the sheep over the path to pasture. Thus the reference is both literal and poetic, for it also implies the difficult journey through life (valley of the shadow of death), through which God guides the righteous. *Note*: This psalm should be read in full and even memorized by the child so that he or she may fully learn the power of Biblical meter and style.

Psalm 24: Almost as well known as the preceding psalm, this one affirms God's mastery of the universe. "The earth is the Lord's, and the fulness thereof . . ." (1). The singer here is so ecstatic that he calls upon the very gates of the temple and its doors to "lift up your heads . . ." (7). Many believe this is one of David's earliest psalms, composed by him when the Ark of the Covenant was returned to Jerusalem.

Psalm 37: A psalm of comfort for those beset by the evils of life. "Fret not thyself because of evildoers . . ." (1). "Trust in the Lord, and do good . . ." (3). "Rest in the Lord, and wait patiently for him" (7). A phrase in this psalm appears in the Beatitudes of Jesus (see Matthew 5:5); it is "But the meek shall inherit the earth" (11), meaning those who wait with trust will live to reap the bounty of the earth. Psalm 40 takes up this very theme.

Psalm 42: "God is my Rock"—a psalm of confidence in the Lord's unending strength and security. Psalm 46 is similar: "God is our refuge and strength, a very present help in trouble" (46:1).

Psalm 51: This prayer of David was composed during the crisis over his adultery with Bathsheba (see preface to the psalm itself) and is filled with contrition and remorse. "Have mercy upon me, O God . . ." (1), "for I acknowledge my transgressions: and my sin is ever before me" (3). Psalm 55 is similar.

Psalm 63: Probably composed by David when he was fleeing from the vengeful Saul; a reaffirmation of faith in God, wherein the young rebel cries out: "My soul thirsteth for thee" (1).

Psalm 85: This psalm was likely written after the Jews returned from captivity, and it is full of thanksgiving to God who "hast brought back the captivity of Jacob . . ." (1). A popular psalm recited on Christmas Day in many Protestant churches.

Psalm 88: Despair again motivates faith as the psalmist cries out his prayer "day and night before thee" (1), ". . . for my soul is full of troubles" (3). Some say this is the most agonized of all the psalms, ending appropriately with the word "darkness."

Psalm 90: The Psalm of Moses, source of the popular hymn "O God Our Help in Ages Past" (by Isaac Watts). It reflects hope in a time of peril (possibly the Exodus), recognizing that God's ways are not the ways of men, "for a thousand years in thy sight are but as yesterday when it is past . . ." (4).

Psalm 91: God as a great winged protector who "shall cover thee with his feathers, and under his wings shalt thou trust" (4); ". . . thou shalt not be afraid for the terror by night; nor for the arrow that flieth by day" (5). Here, as in the Shepherd's Song (Psalm 23), the literary metaphor, or comparison, is taken from everyday life, from the bird hunter and the warrior.

Psalm 95: A great paean of joy and thanksgiving. "Let us make a joyful noise to the rock of our salvation" (1). It is similar to Psalm 98: "Make a joyful noise unto the Lord . . ." (4) and Psalm 100.

Psalm 103: The Lord is exalted as "merciful and gracious, slow to anger . . ." (8) and his personal communion with man greatly advocated. "Like as a father pitieth his children, so the Lord pitieth them that fear him" (13). Psalm 139 is akin.

Psalm 104: The avowal of One God "clothed with honour and majesty . . ." (1); the Supreme Creator, who appeared to Job in the whirlwind. "He appointed the moon for seasons: the sun knoweth his going down . . ." (19). "O Lord, how manifold are thy works" (24). One of the very greatest of all psalms.

Psalm 107: The famous nautical psalm which tells of "they that go down to the sea in ships, that do business in great waters . . ." (1); a favorite of seafaring men.

Psalm 109: Represents a style found occasionally in the Psalter but an unusual one nevertheless. Here the psalmist seems to be asking God to curse his enemies in a vengeful manner: "Let his children be continually vagabonds, and beg . . ." (10). "Let his posterity be cut off . . ." (13)—all this because the victim of the curse has "rewarded me evil for good, and hatred for my love" (5).

Psalms 113 to 118: The Praise, or *Hallel*, Psalms, recited during the Passover celebration since ancient times. They retrace the Exodus story (114) and other related events. All are included in the Passover *Haggadah*, or storybook. Were these the hymns referred to in Mark 14:26, which Jesus and his disciples sang at the Last Supper?
Note: The shortest of all the psalms, and

The decorations for Psalm 51 in Humphrey de Bohun's 14th-century Psalter include Biblical scenes such as Jacob wrestling with the angel (lower left), plus many others.

Jerusalem, in several of the Psalms, signifies a longed-for home both terrestrial and spiritual—a tangible heaven on earth, a place to praise and from which to send forth praises.

the shortest chapter in the entire Bible, is Psalm 117.

Psalm 119: This is the longest of the psalms and the longest single chapter in the Bible (176 verses). Each section is headed by a letter of the Hebrew alphabet. In theme, Psalm 119 concerns the keeping of God's laws and statutes. "O, how love I thy law! it is my meditation all the day" (97).

Psalm 121: A song of degrees, or pilgrimage, sung as the faithful journeyed to Jerusalem, or other holy shrines, for prayer and sacrifice. "I will lift up mine eyes unto the hills, from whence cometh my help" (1). Many good examples of the literary device known as "mirroring" (explained in the Book of Job) occur here, such as "The *sun* shall not smite thee *by day*, nor the *moon by night* . . ." (6).

Psalm 122: A prayer for the "peace of Jerusalem: they shall prosper who love thee" (6), clearly representing a pilgrimage, or ascent, to the temple.

Psalm 127: A strong affirmation of God's omnipotent influence in the world. "Except the Lord build the house, they labor in vain that build it . . ." (1). The joy of children is also extolled in this psalm (3 to 5).

Psalm 137: The Song of the Exiles quoted on page 163 in relation to the Babylonian Captivity.

Psalm 139: As mentioned, along with Psalm 103, this expression of faith relates God to man in intimate terms. "Thou knowest my downsitting and mine uprising . . ." (2). "Search me, O God, and know my heart: try me, and know my thoughts . . ." (23). Psalms 145 and 146 are parallel in mood and theme.

Psalm 146: Beginning "Praise ye the Lord" (Hallelujah), this psalm ushers in the final, or Hallelujah, group, alive with reverent praise for God and familiar in the musical setting of the Hallelujah Chorus from Handel's oratorio *Messiah*: "The Lord shall reign for ever . . ." (10). Psalm 148 contains the passage "Praise ye him, sun and moon: praise him, all ye stars of light . . ." (3). "Praise the Lord from the earth, ye dragons . . ." (7). All creatures, large and small, are called upon to praise God.

Psalm 150: The final psalm takes up the song of praise, calling upon the faithful to exalt the Lord "with the timbrel and dance . . . upon the loud cymbals . . . Hallelujah!" (4 to 6).

Proverbs

According to the dictionary, a proverb is a "short popular saying . . . embodying some familiar truth or useful thought in expressive language; a wise saying." No better description could be found for the Proverbs of the Bible, except to add that the truths they espouse are not only familiar but sacred.

Composed for the edification of young people and for easy learning, the Proverbs have universal appeal, since they are very often quite shrewd, even humorous, and cause us to reflect not only on God but on human nature as well. "Pride goeth before destruction, and a haughty spirit before a fall" (16:18) is one example out of many of the humanistic, as opposed to purely religious, sayings in this book.

Divided into five parts, like the Psalms,

Proverbs covers the entire scope of earthly foibles and concerns, stressing that love of God is the source of all good conduct. King Solomon is generally regarded to be the author of Proverbs 1 to 24, co-author of 25 to 29 and the patron of the remaining two chapters (those of Augur and Lemuel). Stylistically, Proverbs offers a perfect example of the mirroring device explained earlier and further exemplifies the skillful use of metaphor and imagery. Almost every sentence demonstrates the double-edged thought so common in Hebrew verse: "Faithful are the wounds of a friend; but the kisses of an enemy are deceitful" (27:6). Or "Better is a dinner of herbs where love is, than a stalled ox and hatred therewith" (15:17). Note that in both examples the idea swings on a conjunction, like "but" or "than." The other most prevalent poetic form in Proverbs is the cumulative list: "There are six things doth the Lord hate: yea, seven are an abomination unto him . . ." (6:16). etc.

For a more enjoyable reading of Proverbs, it is suggested that selective groupings be studied along the lines offered in the Dartmouth Bible, edited by R. B. Chamberlain and Herman Feldman of Dartmouth College. These scholars compiled the Proverbs into thematic chapters, drawing together similar thoughts scattered throughout the thirty-one chapters of this book. We will follow their outline in our brief description of these wise and pleasurable sayings.

Proverbs begins with a glorification of wisdom and piety. "The fear of the Lord is the beginning of knowledge" (1:7), it says. The words that follow are offered for instruction, understanding and justice. "Fools despise wisdom and instruction," King Solomon warns, but "whoso hark-eneth unto [wisdom] shall dwell safely, and shall be quiet for fear of evil" (3:3).

Speaking through the mouth of Solomon, Wisdom herself addresses the reader: "I love them that love me" (8:17), she says. "My fruit is better than gold, yea, than fine gold; and my revenue than choice silver" (8:19). Before all life began, there was Wisdom—God's own close companion—"therefore get wisdom: and with all thy getting get understanding" (4:7). "Blessed is the man that heareth me," Wisdom announces (8:34).

Having vigorously set forth her principle, Wisdom now launches into the specific proverbs that make up the bulk of this book. As noted, they fall into several thematic groupings, such as:

THE NATURE OF FOOLS

"As a jewel of gold in a swine's snout, so is a fair woman which is without discretion" (11:22). "He that walketh with wise men shall be wise: but a companion of fools shall be destroyed" (13:20). "Let a bear robbed of her whelps meet a man, rather than a fool in his folly" (17:12). "Answer not a fool according to his folly, lest thou also be like unto him" (26:4).

TRUST IN THE LORD

"Trust in the Lord with all thine heart; and lean not unto thine own understanding" (3:5). "Every word of God is pure: he is a shield unto them that put their trust in him" (30:5).

HUMAN NATURE

"There be three things which are too wonderful for me, yea, four which I know not: the way of an eagle in the air; the way of a serpent upon a rock; the way of a ship in the midst of the sea; and the way of a

The sage and kingly figure of Solomon—author of many Proverbs—is framed by parts of his temple in this brilliantly illuminated 15th-century Italian manuscript from Ferrara.

man with a maid" (30:18–19). "The spirit of man is the candle of the Lord, searching all the inward parts of the belly" (20:27).

RIGHTEOUSNESS

"To do justice and judgment is more acceptable to the Lord than sacrifice" (21:3). "The wicked flee when no man pursueth: but the righteous are bold as a lion" (28:1).

CHILDREN AND PARENTS

"A wise son maketh a glad father: but a foolish son is the heaviness of his mother" (10:1). "He that spareth his rod hateth his son: but he that loveth him chasteneth him betimes" (13:24). "Hearken unto thy father that begat thee, and despise not thy mother when she is old" (23:22).

LOVE AND CHARITY

"The rich and the poor meet together: the Lord is the maker of them all" (22:2). "Hatred stirreth up strifes: but love covereth all sins" (10:12). "If thine enemy be hungry, give him bread to eat . . ." (25:21).

PRAISE AND EMOTION

"Hope deferred maketh the heart sick: but when desire cometh, it is a tree of life" (13:12). "Pleasant words are as a honeycomb, sweet to the soul, and health to the bones" (16:24). "As cold waters to a thirsty soul, so is good news from a far country" (25:25). "Let another man praise thee, and not thine own mouth" (27:2).

ANGER

"He that hath no rule over his own spirit is like a city that is broken down, and without walls" (25:28). "A soft answer turneth away wrath: but grievous words stir up anger" (15:1). "Whoso keepeth his mouth and his tongue keepeth his soul from troubles" (21:23).

INDUSTRY AND SLOTH

"Slothfulness casteth into a deep sleep; and an idle soul shall suffer hunger" (19:15). "Go to the ant, thou sluggard; consider her ways, and be wise: which having no guide, overseer, or ruler, provideth her meat in the summer, and gathereth her food in the harvest" (6:6–8).

WEALTH AND SOBRIETY

"Wealth maketh many friends; but the poor is separated from his neighbor" (19:4). "Be not among winebibbers; among riotous eaters of flesh: for the drunkard and the glutton shall come to poverty: and drowsiness shall clothe a man with rags" (23:20–21). "Hell and destruction are never full; so the eyes of man are never satisfied" (27:20).

MARRIAGE AND WOMEN

"It is better to dwell in the wilderness, than with a contentious and an angry woman" (21:19). "Who can find a virtuous woman? for her price is far above rubies. . . . She will do [her husband] good and not evil all the days of her life" (31:10 and 12). "She is not afraid of the snow for her household: for all her household are clothed with scarlet" (31:21).

GOVERNMENT

"The king's wrath is as the roaring of a lion; but his favor is as dew upon grass" (19:12). "When the righteous are in author-

A richly illuminated manuscript—from a 15th-century Italian Bible, introducing Ecclesiastes. Directly below the initial is the key word "Vanitas"–vanity.

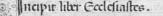

Incipit liber Ecclesiastes.

Verba ecclesiastæ filii dauid regis

ierusalem. Vanitas uanitatum dixit ecclesiastes uanitas uanitatum et omnia uanitas. Quid habet amplius homo de uniuerso labore suo quod laborat sub sole. Generatio preterit et generatio aduenit, terra uero in eternum stat. Oritur sol et occidit, et ad locum suum reuertitur: ibiq: renascens gyrat per meridiem et flectitur ad aquilonem. Lustrans uniuersa in circuitu pergit spiritus, et in circulos suos reuertitur. Omnia flumina intrant in mare et mare non redundat. Ad locum unde exeunt flumina reuertuntur ut iterum fluant. Cuncte res difficiles non potest eas homo explicare sermone. Non saturatur oculus uisu nec auris impletur auditu. Quid est quod fuit? ipsum quod futurum est. Quid est quod factum est? ipsum quod faciendum est. Nichil sub

sole nouum, nec ualet quisquam dicere ecce hoc recens est. Iam enim precessit in seculis que fuerunt ante nos. Non est priorum memoria, sed nec eorum quidem que postea futura sunt erit recordatio apud eos qui futuri sunt in nouissimo. Ego ecclesiastes fui rex israel in ierusalem, et proposui in animo meo querere et inuestigare sapienter de omnibus que fiunt sub sole. Hanc occupationem pessimam dedit deus filiis hominum ut occuparentur in ea. Vidi cuncta que fiunt sub sole, et ecce uniuersa uanitas et afflictio spiritus. Peruersi difficile corriguntur et stultorum infinitus est numerus. Locutus sum in corde meo dicens: Ecce magnus effectus sum, et precessi sapientia omnes qui fuerunt ante me in ierusalem, et mens mea contemplata est multa sapienter et didici. Dedique cor meum ut scirem prudentiam atque doctrinam erroresque et stultitiam. Et agnoui quod in his quoque esset labor et afflictio spiritus, eo quod in multa sapientia multa sit indignatio, et qui addit scientiam addit et laborem.

Dixi ego in corde meo: Vadam et affluam deliciis, et fruar bonis. Et uidi quod hoc quoque esset uanitas. Risum reputaui errorem, et gaudio dixi: Quid frustra deciperis? Cogitaui in corde meo abstrahere a uino carnem meam, ut animum meum transferrem ad sapientiam, deuitaremque stultitiam, donec uiderem quid esset utile filiis hominum, quo facto opus est sub sole numero dierum uite sue. Magnificaui opera mea. Edificaui michi domos, et plantaui uineas. Feci ortos et pomeria et consui ea cuncti generis arboribus. Et extruxi michi piscinas aquarum, ut irrigarem siluam lignorum germinantium. Possedi seruos et ancillas, multamque familiam habui, armenta quoque et magnos ouium greges ultra omnes qui fuerunt ante me in ierusalem. Coaceruaui michi argentum et aurum, et substantias regum ac prouinciarum. Feci michi cantores et cantatri

The Song of Songs and many of the Psalms were meant to be sung. Here two Israeli children are playing some Biblical-looking instruments, made from natural objects.

ity, the people rejoice: but when the wicked beareth rule, the people mourn" (29:2).

Ecclesiastes

In Latin this word, Ecclesiastes, means "the preacher," from the Hebrew *Koheleth*. It is thought to be a pseudonym of King Solomon himself. Certain scholars disagree with the idea that this book was actually written by Solomon and date its composition nearer to 200 B.C., since, they say, it contains a great deal of Greek philosophy. It wasn't until after the second century B.C. that the Jews fully came under Hellenistic influence, with its genial but consistent pessimism and skeptical criti-

cism of the material world (which is, by and large, the theme of Ecclesiastes).

If Solomon were, in fact, the "preacher" in question, his appraisal of luxury, wealth and status as nothing more than "vanity" would be all the more impressive. Solomon, after all, was the wealthiest, most luxury-bent and greatest man in the world of his day. When he wrote "Vanity of vanities . . . all is vanity," he must have spoken from his heart—and a slightly bitter heart it is. "What profit hath a man of all his labour which he taketh under the sun?" the great king asks (1:2–3). "I have seen all the works that are done under the sun; and behold, all is vanity and vexation of spirit" (1:14).

Modern readers especially find this book

compelling and rewarding, comparing it to the *Rubáiyát* of Omar Khayyam or the *Meditations* of Marcus Aurelius, two other examples of world-weary observation. But despite this tone, the religious or spiritual side of Ecclesiastes is subtle and not to be minimized. Solomon, as the preacher, concludes that though vanity rules the secular world, God unquestionably rules the spirit. "Fear God, and keep his commandments: for this is the whole duty of man" (12:13–14).

The Book of Ecclesiastes, while primarily an essay on the vanity of material life—and the glory of spiritual fulfillment—is at the same time one of the most startling anthologies of great poetry to be found in one place. In fact, it is composed of at least half a dozen prose-poems world-famous for their style as well as their message. Preeminent is the one beginning: "To everything there is a season, and a time to every purpose under the heaven . . ." (3:1). This outpouring of emotion should be read in its entirety, for it is incomparable. In addition, it may strike a familiar chord with many young people, since it has been set to music by the popular folksinger Pete Seeger.

A group of proverbs (not unlike those of the preceding book) is offered at 7:1, beginning: "A good name is better than precious ointment; and the day of death than the day of one's birth . . ." (meaning that a man's reputation at the end of his life is naturally bound to be greater than that of his infancy). These proverbs should also be read through (7:17 and also 10:1 to 11:6) for fullest appreciation.

Solomon covers a wide field of human interests in this remarkable text—habits of eating (9:7, etc.); attitudes toward money and status (5:10, etc.); and the nature of youth and old age. This latter theme is dominated by the powerful passage beginning: "Rejoice, O young man, in thy youth . . ." (11:9), adding, "remember now thy Creator in the days of thy youth . . ." (12:1), "for all these things God will bring thee into judgment" (11:9).

Though possibly a bit too subtle for most children (especially pre-teens), this section of the Bible is worth careful exploration for the beauty of its language alone. If indeed some flavor of the theme emerges in the young mind, what harm can there be? In the end, though everything is "vanity and vexation of the spirit," Solomon reaffirms God's inimitable power: "For God shall bring every work into judgment, with every secret thing, whether it be good, or whether it be evil" (12:14). This, says Solomon, is "the conclusion of the whole matter" (12:13).

Note: A moving piece of modern music by the Swiss-American composer Ernest Bloch captures the emotional power of Ecclesiastes in rich orchestral tones. The work is entitled *Schelomo* (Hebrew for "Solomon"). In it, the great king's voice is heard as a mournful, passionate cello solo.

The Song of Solomon (or The Song of Songs)

If the previous book, Ecclesiastes, may be called subtle and possibly out of the reach of the average child, even more so may be Solomon's masterpiece, known as *The Song of Songs*. For one thing, this lavish poem may appear out of place in the Holy Scriptures, confusing to the reader who has so far been exposed only to pious and reverent sentiments. For another thing, the sensuous nature of the lyrics may provoke questions in areas far removed from religion or theology. Nevertheless, it would be a deprivation indeed to exclude such a famous section from our exploration on the grounds of its subtlety or sensuality. The exceptional child will be able to handle both; the less sophisticated will enjoy the rich poetry and colorful images.

To bridge the unusual nature of this work and even to justify its place in Scripture, many scholars and churchmen have explained that rather than being a purely sensuous love poem (as it seems), the Song of Solomon is actually an allegory (or symbolic comparison) related to what is called the I-Thou relationship, or the communion between man and God. Thus such phrases as "I sat down under his shadow with great delight, and his fruit was sweet to my taste" (2:3) may refer to the protective shadow of God and the sweetness of his commandments. This allegoric interpretation of the poem is especially strong in terms of the many allusions to marriage and wedded bliss in the verses. These are said to imply the wedding of the Christian Church (the Bride) to Christ (the Bridegroom). Since marriage is a holy sacrament, ordained by God, it follows that a love poem about a wedding may indeed be a subtle description of God himself in various roles. Other scholars look upon this work as typical of the poetry popular in the Middle East of Solomon's day, poetry extolling nature, luxury, love and pleasure. At the same time, they say, the Song (or Canticle) gives us information about many charming customs of courtship, weddings and life among courtly women in the ancient world.

When all is said and done concerning the theme and purpose of the Song, we are still left with its somewhat bewildering style and form. Few readers jumping right to the verses can make sense of their ever-shifting moods. In the first few verses of Chapter 1, for example, a woman is clearly speaking. "Let him kiss me with the kisses of his mouth," she says. She then addresses herself to other women gathered before her: "Ye daughters of Jerusalem" (1:5). Next her attention shifts to a young shepherd whom she loves. "Tell me, O thou whom my soul loveth" (1:7). Abruptly, at 1:8, the shepherd seems to take up the reply: "If thou know not, O thou fairest among women . . ."

In the next verse (9), the king, possibly Solomon himself, appears and speaks; he is no doubt wooing the maiden despite her love for the shepherd (a sort of lover's triangle ensues). It is the maiden, or the bride-to-be, who carries the main part of the Song, telling of her great love (2:3), of the dream she had of her lover (3:1–4) and of nature in all its glory. "Awake, O north wind; and come, thou south; blow upon my garden . . ." (4:16).

The king reappears at 4:1 pressing his love, but to no avail. The shepherd, however, seems more successful (4:9) as he compares the bride to all manner of beautiful things—"a garden inclosed" (12), "an orchard of pomegranates . . . spikenard and saffron" (13–14), (two valuable spices).

A long duet between the maiden and her lady friends follows as the shepherd withdraws (5:1), the girl complaining of being lovesick (5:8) and restless. Once more the king returns to admire the bride, "fair as the moon, clear as the sun" (6:10) —and we learn here that she is a "prince's daughter" (7:1). But all of the king's elaborate words do not move the maiden.

"I am my beloved's, and his desire is

toward me," she protests (7:10). Deeply moved, the king now gives his blessing to the young lovers and orders a wedding to be held in the vineyards (as was Oriental custom). The shepherd and the maiden—bridegroom and bride—now rejoice in union. "Set me as a seal upon thine heart," he sings (8:6), and she replies: "Make haste, my beloved, and be thou like to a roe or to a young hart upon the mountains of spices" (8:14).

In one sense, the Song of Songs may be compared to a play, made up of the following characters: a maiden who is also a princess (she first appears at 1:1); a group of court women, or the "daughters of Jerusalem" (1:5); a shepherd, soon to be a bridegroom (1:8); and the king, possibly Solomon himself (1:9). The setting of this play is the palace garden of the king. The action concerns the attempts of the monarch to woo the maiden away from her lover. As a climax to the drama, however, we learn that the king defers to young love and, in fact, orders the wedding of his rival and the girl he loves.

Several references in the lyrics require specific translation or explanation, no matter in what spirit the poem is read. For example, the maiden's "I am black. . . . Look not upon me, because I am black, because the sun hath looked upon me" (1:5 and 6) refers to sunburn and not to race. The maiden has apparently been waiting for her lover too long in the sun, and this has spoiled her complexion. The expression "I am sick of love" (2:5 and 5:8) is better understood as "I am lovesick." The roe and young hart the maiden speaks of are poetic allusions to young vigorous animals (a deer and a rabbit); this is how she thinks of her lover. The many references to jewels, plants, animals and exotic

The Song of Songs is a hymn of springtime joy in this Florentine Jewish prayerbook dating from 1492. The large gilded word is the Hebrew word for "song"; it begins Chapter 1 of this Book.

places are all part and parcel of the lyrics, easily explained in any dictionary. The Song of Songs is a challenging and unusual Biblical book, certainly worthy of exploration, despite the obstacles.

The Prophets

To many people, the books of the prophets represent the most significant ideas of the Old Testament, for they integrate the Laws of Moses with great outpourings of ethical and religious philosophy. These powerful and meaningful ideas developed from men who were very often outcasts in Israel, despised by the ruling classes (as was Elijah) and frequently

Zechariah was one of the so-called minor prophets of Israel. His message was the reunion of all the faithful. Michelangelo painted him in vivid colors, reading his book, high on the walls of the Sistine Chapel.

persecuted. Today we honor and respect them; in their own time many were known as "crazy men" or rabble rousers. In fact, the Hebrew word for the prophets is *neviim*, or "wild ones"!

Our word "prophet" is really just as awkward, if we accept the common meaning often given today in occult circles. These men did not prophesy like twentieth-century fortunetellers, pretending to tell about future events unrelated to religious ideas. Their prophecy concerned the values and ethics of the people in har-

mony with God. When Isaiah, Jeremiah, Ezekiel and Daniel foretold dire or wondrous events to come, they were not conjuring or dealing in magic; they were inferring the logical result of piety or iniquity.

The prophets are divided into two categories: major and minor (referring mainly to the length of their books). The major prophets, whom we will explore in some detail, are Isaiah, Jeremiah, Ezekiel and Daniel. The minor prophets are listed below with a brief commentary concerning their themes. But first, a basic outline.

There are seventeen books collected under the label "Prophets": the four major prophets (above), the twelve minor ones, and Lamentations, a special text written by Jeremiah. Thirteen of these books are connected with the fall of the Hebrew nation and three with its restoration (Haggai, Zechariah, Malachi). Some of the prophets preached to foreigners as well as Jews; remember Jonah in Nineveh (Nahum also preached there). Obadiah's message was intended mainly for the Edomites.

Originally the work of the prophets began when the kingdom was split up after Solomon and the subsequent rise of idolatry. Priests, appointed by the kings, were a hereditary class and often corrupt. They did not do much to rescue the people from their sins; they became part of the problem. Prophets were from the people; they were not appointed and, as Amos said in great modesty: "I was no prophet, neither was I a prophet's son; but I was an herdsman . . . and the Lord said unto me, Go, prophesy unto my people Israel" (Amos 7:14–15). In other words, these men drew their authority not from class, royal appointment or factional instruction but solely from God.

Their purpose was manifold: first, to try to rescue the nation from idolatry and corruption; failing this, to warn of national ruin; to prepare the people for captivity and exile in face of this ruin by instilling a respect for religion in the remnants of the nation; and finally, to give promise of greater days, often by predicting the coming of a Redeemer or Messiah.

Their messages were heard over a period of four hundred years (approximately 800 B.C. to 400 B.C.) and centered around the fall of Jerusalem and the temple. Their task at this point was to warn of this calamity and then to explain it in religious terms once it happened. The collapse of the nation, they cried, did not mean the end of God's love or plan for Israel, or the rupture of the Covenant. From such tragedy the people could—and must—rebuild their lives, and the prophets offered them the process for doing so. First, they said, cast off idolatry and return to Yahweh; two, live by ethical and righteous codes of the law; three, reform the corruptions of politics; and four, reform all aspects of life infested with moral rot and selfishness. In addition to these corrective themes many of the prophets preached elevated theological ideas such as the universality of God; the inwardness of faith (man must feel God's truth within his heart); that law and justice in the name of God are superior to hollow ritual. The temple, they said, is a lofty symbol needed in a complex world, but God must essentially dwell within each man for a true religious revival. No political or social leader is allowed special privilege; the poor and humble are equal to all others in God's eyes; the future is a time of hope as God's plan for the world unfolds—these were the dominant messages of the prophets.

The Minor Prophets

Each of the so-called minor prophets had a message of his own. We give them here, in the prophet's own words, each man listed chronologically:

Joel (about 840–830 B.C.): "And it shall come to pass, that whosoever shall call on the name of the Lord shall be delivered . . ." (2:32). "I will also gather all nations . . . (3:2);" "the Lord also shall roar out of Zion [Israel], and utter his voice from Jerusalem" (3:16).

Jonah (790–770): "And the word of the Lord came unto Jonah the second time, saying, Arise, go unto Nineveh, that great city, and preach unto it the preaching that I bid thee" (3:1–2). A daring ecumenical theme in its time.

Amos (780–740): "Seek good, and not evil, that ye may live . . ." (5:14). "I hate, I despise your feast days . . . though ye offer me burnt offerings and your meat offerings, I will not accept them" (5:21–22). "Behold, the days come, saith the Lord God, that I will send a famine in the land" (8:11); "And I will bring again the captivity of my people of Israel, and they shall build the waste cities, and inhabit them" (9:14).

Hosea (760–720): "I will not execute the fierceness of mine anger . . . for I am God, and not man . . ." (11:9). "Yet I am the Lord thy God from the land of Egypt, and thou shalt know no God but me: for there is no saviour beside me" (13:4). "O Israel, thou hast destroyed thyself; but in me is thine help. . . . I will ransom them from the power of the grave" (13:9 and 14).

Isaiah (745–695): See below.

Micah (740–700): "And he shall judge among many people, and rebuke strong nations afar off; and they shall beat their swords into plowshares, and their spears into pruning hooks: nation shall not lift up

An angel points the way for the prophet Isaiah, who appears to have been reading, in this painting by Michelangelo on the Sistine Chapel ceiling.

a sword against nation, neither shall they learn war any more. But they shall sit every man under his vine and under his fig tree; and none shall make them afraid . . ." (4:3–4). "And we will walk in the name of the Lord our God for ever and ever" (4:5).

Note: This stirring call to universal peace is almost identical to Isaiah 2:2–3 (see below).

Nahum (630–610): "The Lord will take vengeance on his adversaries" (1:2). " . . . Who can stand before his indignation?"

(1:6). "The Lord is good, a stronghold in the day of trouble; and he knoweth them that trust in him" (1:7).

Zephaniah (639–608): "Hold thy peace in the presence of the Lord God: for the day of the Lord is at hand" (1:7). ". . . That day is a day of wrath, a day of trouble and distress . . ." (1:15). "Seek ye the Lord, all ye meek of the earth, which have wrought his judgment . . ." (2:3).

Jeremiah (626–586): See below.

Ezekiel (592–570): See below.

Obadiah (586): "Shall I not in that day, saith the Lord, even destroy the wise men out of Edom . . ." (1:8). "For thy violence against thy brother Jacob shame shall cover thee, and thou shalt be cut off for ever" (1:10). *Note*: Obadiah is the shortest book of the Prophets.

Habakkuk (606–586): "For the vision is yet for an appointed time; but at the end it shall speak, and not lie: though it tarry, wait for it; because it will surely come, it will not tarry" (2:3).

Daniel (606–534): See below.

Haggai (520–516): "Now therefore thus saith the Lord of hosts; Consider your ways. Ye have sown much, and bring in little" (1:5). "Go up to the mountain, and bring wood, and build the house [the temple]; and I will take pleasure in it, and I will be glorified, saith the Lord" (1:8), ". . . and I will shake all nations, and the desire of all nations shall come" (2:7).

Zechariah (520–516): "Thus saith the Lord of hosts; My cities through prosperity shall yet be spread abroad; and the Lord shall yet comfort Zion . . ." (1:17). "Sing and rejoice . . . for, lo, I come, and I will dwell in the midst of thee, saith the Lord. And many nations shall be joined to the Lord in that day, and shall be my people . . ." (2:10–11). "Rejoice . . . behold, thy King cometh unto thee: he is just, and having salvation . . ." (9:9).

Malachi (450–400): "Return unto me, and I will return unto you, saith the Lord of hosts . . ." (3:7). "Behold I will send you Elijah, the prophet before the coming of the great and dreadful day of the Lord: And he shall turn the heart of the fathers to the children, and the heart of the children to their fathers, lest I come and smite the earth with a curse" (4:5–6).

Below are a few other quotations from the minor prophets well worth committing to memory for their beauty and pertinence.

"They have sown the wind, and they shall reap the whirlwind" (Hosea 8:7).

"Your old men shall dream dreams, your young men shall see visions" (Joel 2:28).

"What doth the Lord require of thee, but to do justly, and to love mercy, and to walk humbly with thy God?" (Micah 6:8).

"The Lord is in his holy temple: let all the earth keep silence before him" (Habakkuk 2:20).

"Not by might, nor by power, but by my spirit, saith the Lord of hosts" (Zechariah 4:6).

"Have we not all one father? hath not one God created us?" (Malachi 2:10).

The Wise Isaiah

The "messianic" prophet, as he is called, conducted his mission in Judah during the time Israel (to the north) fell to the Assyrians. Kings Uzziah, Jotham, Ahaz and Hezekiah ruled in Judah at the time. Isaiah's active ministry was thus somewhere between 745 and 695 B.C. In some traditions it is said that Isaiah was of noble blood, descended from King Amaziah.

Whatever his background, the young prophet was deeply affected by the collapse of Israel and decided to devote his life to saving Judah, that "sinful nation, [its] people laden with iniquity . . . they have forsaken the Lord" (1:4). He lived to see the Assyrian hordes attempt to sack Jerusalem (around 700 B.C.), but largely owing to his divinely inspired prophecy, the fall of the sacred city was postponed.

By and large, the body of the Book of Isaiah (which in many opinions is the work of two separate prophets by the same name) deals with Isaiah's warnings and religious preaching. But there are narrative, or story, sections as well that should be known for a fuller picture of this great man's life. Briefly told, his biography reads thus:

Touched by an angel as a young man, Isaiah became pure of word and fit to preach the Lord's message (6:6–7). God told him: "Go, and tell this people, Hear ye indeed, but [ye] understood not; and see ye indeed, but perceive not" (6:9). King Uzziah was ruler of Judah at the time of Isaiah's calling. He was a moderately pious king. But soon after Isaiah began preaching, the wicked Ahaz ascended the throne of Judah (not to be confused with Ahab of Israel). God warns this king, through Isaiah, of dire consequences should idolatry and corruption persist (Chapter 7).

Two sons are born to Isaiah. Prophetically he names them Shear-jashub (7:3), meaning "a remnant shall return," and Maher-shalal-hash-baz (8:3), meaning "the spoil speeds, the prey hastens"—or the enemies of Judah shall quickly be defeated. As the Assyrians advance, fresh from their conquest of Israel, Isaiah prays for deliverance. Apparently he knows that eventually Jerusalem will fall, hence "the remnant shall return" (10:21). But he tries to forestall the awful day. Accordingly, he preaches of one who will come to the Hebrews as a redeemer (Messiah) "and the spirit of the Lord shall rest upon him" (11:2). Very often this redeemer is taken to mean Jesus Christ. But in those days the good king Hezekiah seemed a redeemer indeed. His story is taken up at Chapter 36 and tells of the defeat of the Assyrian king, Sennacherib, at the very gates of Jerusalem by divine intervention and as a result of Isaiah's spiritual guidance. Worried by Sennacherib's obvious threat, Hezekiah had put on sackcloth as a sign of mourning and had gone to the house of the Lord (37:1). There he conversed with Isaiah, and the two prayed mightily until God sent his angel of death against the Assyrians, smiting in one blow over 185,000 of the enemy (37:36).

Even as he lay dying, Hezekiah turned to

The universality of Isaiah's famous message is dramatized by its inclusion in the architecture of the United Nations complex in New York City. This area faces the Secretariat and is known as the "Isaiah Wall."

THEY SHALL BEAT THEIR SWORDS INTO PLOWSHARES. AND THEIR SPEARS INTO PRUNING HOOKS. NATION SHALL NOT LIFT UP SWORD AGAINST NATION. NEITHER SHALL THEY LEARN WAR ANY MORE

Several texts in Handel's oratorio *Messiah*, including the chorus "For Unto Us a Child Is Born," seen here in an early score, were drawn from the book of Isaiah.

Isaiah for comfort and guidance (38:1–2). As a result, he was revived to live another fifteen years (38:5) so that he might witness the further deliverance of Jerusalem. At that time Isaiah ministered healing to the king (38:21) and prophesied signs of his recovery and of Judah's salvation. And it came to be, as Hezekiah prayed: "There shall be peace and truth in my days" (39:8).

Beginning with Chapter 40, the narrative portions of Isaiah recede. We know nothing of the prophet's life after Hezekiah's death. What we do learn from the bulk of this lengthy and extremely literary book (it has sixty-six chapters—more than all of Genesis) are the thoughts, fears and aspirations of one of the world's most inspired missionaries.

Isaiah's Ideas

A general survey of the chapters of this book will convey a small part of Isaiah's thoughts and offer a key to Biblical readings in an extremely difficult area.

Chapter 1: Isaiah describes the wickedness of Judah, implying God's vengeance in the form of the Assyrians. Chapters 2 to 4 speak of better days and a peaceful era to come when men "shall beat their swords into plowshares . . . [and] nation shall not lift up sword against nation" (2:4). Yet before that time there will be grief and sorrow. In Chapter 5 Isaiah describes the Lord's vineyard (Israel), soon to be laid waste and overrun with "briers and thorns" (5:6).

The following four chapters (6 to 9) relate some of the biographical material we have already discussed, along with Isaiah's prophecy concerning a mysterious child, born of a virgin, who shall be called Immanuel (7:14). Chapter 9 speaks further of this child "and his name shall be called Wonderful, Counselor, The mighty God, The everlasting Father, The Prince of Peace" (9:6). Jewish tradition regards this child as the Messiah to come, and Christians read a forecasting of Jesus Christ in this message. Chapters 10, 13 and 14 deal with the advancing Assyrian horde and the fall of Babylon to the Persians. Chapters 11 and 12 again prophesy the messianic king, referred to as the Branch (11:1), who shall be the "Holy One of Israel" (12:6).

A catalogue of the fates awaiting the

neighboring kingdoms of Israel and Judah is offered in Chapters 15 to 21. These places are Moab, Damascus (Syria), Ethiopia, Babylon, Edom and Arabia. Chapter 22 deals with the problems of Jerusalem and Chapter 23 with Tyre, the nautical kingdom north of Israel. Several apocalyptic (or futurist) prophecies follow in the next four chapters. Twenty-four deals with world convulsions wherein "the land shall be utterly emptied" (24:3). Death will be abolished, however, at the end of time (25:8). The Lord, Jehovah, is praised in Chapter 26 and his vineyard (Jerusalem) revived at the day of judgment (27).

The cities of Samaria (in the north) and Jerusalem are denounced in Chapters 28 and 29 and the threat of siege repeated (here Jerusalem is called Ariel, or "Lion of God," 29:1–2). Judah's political dependence on Egypt is criticized (30). Chapters 31 and 32 again deal with the Messiah. The tension before battle is described in Judah (Chapter 33). God's wrath upon the nations at the end of time emerges in 34 and 35. The narrative concerning Hezekiah's defiance of Sennacherib's army, with Isaiah's help, picks up at Chapters 36 and 37, while the miraculous cure of Hezekiah is related at 38 and 39.

Second Isaiah

The famous words "Comfort ye, comfort ye my people, saith your God," launches Chapter 40 and that part of the book often called Deutero-Isaiah (Second

The medieval artist of these scenes from the life of Isaiah depicts Isaiah's vision of God (top), his lips being touched with fire (center), his assurance that Hezekiah will recover from sickness (bottom left) and a scene drawn from non-Biblical sources illustrating Isaiah's martyrdom, when he was "sawn asunder."

Isaiah), a masterpiece of theology and religious wisdom, mingled with specific prophecies, such as the rise of Persia and King Cyrus (Chapters 41, 44 and 45). Another vision of the Messiah is offered at 42 and 43, along with a powerful definition of monotheism, which appears at 45:5–7: "I am the Lord, and there is none else. . . . I form the light, and create darkness: I make peace, and create evil: I the Lord do all these things."

In Chapters 46 through 48 the fate of Babylon as a nest of idolaters and sorcerers is outlined. The servant of Jehovah (again the Messiah) is discussed in 49 and 50, and the restoration of Zion after captivity is foretold in the next two chapters.

The Messiah is referred to as one who will bear the woes of Israel, as a "man of sorrows" (53:3). He will help to heal the people, for they are like "sheep . . . gone astray" (53:6). Once restored, Isaiah prophesies in 54 and 55, Zion will greatly influence the world. Another compelling definition of God's nature is offered here (55:8–9). "For my thoughts are not your thoughts, neither are your ways my ways, saith the Lord. . . ."

Isaiah bewails the sins of his day in Chapter 56 to 59 and condemns hypocrisy and meaningless ritual, withal "we grope for the wall like the blind . . ." (59:10). A hymn to the coming Messiah begins at 60 with the thrilling words: "Arise, shine; for thy light is come. . . ." *Note*: The opening sentences of 61 are quoted verbatim by Jesus when he preaches in the synagogue at Nazareth (see Luke 4:18–21).

Because of the redeemer, those who will suffer exile must have faith (63, 64); the Lord will forgive all penitents. The last two chapters of Isaiah reveal the glories of the world to come, "for, behold, I create new heavens and a new earth . . . and I will rejoice in Jerusalem" (65:17 and 19). And it shall come to pass, that . . . from one sabbath to another, shall all flesh come to worship before me, saith the Lord" (66:23).

Archaeological note: One of the oldest handwritten portions of the Bible existing today is a section of Isaiah, written about 200 B.C. (a copy, we think, of the original) and discovered in the late 1940s near the Dead Sea in Israel, hence known as the Dead Sea Scrolls—"the greatest manuscript discovery of modern times," according to archaeologist W. F. Albright.

Jeremiah the Pessimist

Few men in history have had such a thankless task as the prophet Jeremiah, who was called upon to preach defeat and submission in Judah. One hundred years or so after Isaiah had forestalled the Assyrian onslaught, Jeremiah would have to oversee the exile of his people. Though at first he sought to save the kingdom—and protect Jerusalem—it soon became clear to him that God had a meaningful purpose behind the dire events to come, that the Babylonians were to be punishing instruments of the Lord (21:10) and that a greater plan for salvation would arise from the fall of Judah. Hearing such words, the rulers and even the people of the kingdom could think only one thing of Jeremiah—that he was a madman or, worse, a traitor!

His dramatic life story and dynamic philosophy are integrally related, for Jeremiah's life was his prophecy and his prophecy his life. A survey of the fifty-one chapters that make up this book, with a reference to Lamentations (which Jeremiah dictated to his scribe, Baruch), will help explore his lofty thoughts and unusual life. First a few words of introduction:

Jeremiah ministered to Judah from 626 B.C. to the terrible years of the fall of Jerusalem, which he witnessed in 586. He survived this catastrophe and lived out his days a sad, lonely man amid the ruins. Some twenty years before the end, Jeremiah prophesies the destruction of the temple and the exile of the Jews. However, he always interspersed his warnings with the hope that penance might bring redemption. When he realized that the people would not turn from their idolatry and ignorance, he advocated surrender in the face of overpowering odds. His seemingly hopeless message has led many to identify Jeremiah as the prophet of gloom and doom, the pessimist and naysayer. Indeed, his name has become a

A fish-eye lens takes in the whole interior of the Israel Museum's Shrine of the Book in Jerusalem, in which reside the Dead Sea Scrolls (including a copy of Isaiah), made about 100 years before Christ.

Rembrandt's father was the model for this 1630 oil, most likely of Jeremiah lamenting the fall of Jerusalem.

synonym for a pessimist, and the word "jeremiad" now means a lamenting, mournful speech or opinion. As we will see, however, there was always the hope of redemption even in Jeremiah's darkest warnings.

He was contemporaneous with seven kings of Judah, most prominently Josiah, the reformer; Jehoiakim, who defied Jeremiah; and Zedekiah, the weak-willed man who was Judah's final king. Other prophets who lived at the same time as Jeremiah were Ezekiel (in Babylon), Daniel (also in Babylon), Habakkuk and Zephaniah (fellow preachers in Judah) and Nahum and Obadiah, who concerned themselves with the fall of Israel's enemies.

In reading selected excerpts from the Book of Jeremiah you should, of course, remember the two essentials we have so far mentioned: the prophet's philosophy and

A Nubian and a leopard are two images used by Jeremiah in describing the stubborn sins of Jerusalem (13:23). These are from a 15th-century B.C. Egyptian tomb.

his dramatic life. But there is a third element especially pertinent in the case of Jeremiah, and that is his remarkable and exalted literary style, or poetry, if you will, for Jeremiah is the author of such immortal phrases as "the harvest is past, the summer is ended, and we are not saved" (8:20); "Is there no balm in Gilead; is there no physician there?" (8:22); "O, that my head were waters, and mine eyes a fountain of tears, that I might weep day and night for the slain of the daughter of my people!" (9:1); "Can the Ethiopian change his skin, or the leopard his spots? then may ye also do good, that are accustomed to do evil" (13:23–24); and in Lamentations: "How doth the city sit solitary, that was full of people! how is she become as a widow! . . ." (Lamentations 1:1).

The Prophet's Story

Jeremiah's biography begins when the word of God is revealed to him as a child. At first he is reluctant to accept such a lofty calling, but he soon agrees, since God tells him: "I have put my words in thy mouth" (1:9) so that Jeremiah may "pull down" and "destroy," "build" and "plant" (1:10). Early in his ministry the prophet is aware that "out of the north an evil shall break forth upon all the inhabitants of the land" (1:14), meaning the Babylonians. When the Lord compares Israel to a faithless wife and warns that Judah will follow in her neighbor's disastrous path (3:18), Jeremiah grows anxious to spare his country. "How shall I . . . give thee a pleasant land?" he asks God (3:19). "If thou wilt return, O Israel, saith the Lord, return unto me, and if thou wilt put away thine abominations out of my sight, then shalt thou not remove" (4:1). But unfortunately, Judah does not repent or put away its abominations and many "belied the Lord," saying that he no longer existed (5:12).

Now Jeremiah begins specifically preaching about the Babylonian hordes soon to descend. "For evil appeareth out of the north, and great destruction" (6:1), he repeats. Repentance is the only hope to escape the disaster. "Cut off thine hair, O Jerusalem," he cries. "Cast it away, and take up a lamentation. . ." (7:29). Jeremiah's eloquent pleas go unheeded and he is desolate. "Oh that I had in the wilderness a lodging place of wayfaring men; that I might leave my people, and go from them!" (9:2). Idolatry, lustfulness, arrogance and denial of God continue in Judah. Indeed, Jeremiah's warnings of invasion seem to spur the manufacture of idols.

Chapter 11 reveals, for the first time in this story, that Jeremiah's life is endangered. The good king Josiah is now dead and corruption fills the land in high places. "But I was like a lamb or an ox that is brought to the slaughter," he says, "and I knew not that they had devised devices against me . . ." (11:19). But the prophet, though endangered, continues his mission, attempting to persuade the people to return to God by means of colorful and vivid images that mark Jeremiah as a brilliant publicist centuries ahead of his time. Once he compares Judah to a bejeweled girdle (or sash), now threadbare and torn; later he smashes pottery in the streets to demonstrate God's eventual wrath, which will fall on all those "whosoever heareth [the noise], his ears shall tingle" (19:3).

As a sign of things to come, a drought afflicts the land. Even so, the people do not repent and again they plot to murder Jeremiah, who continually confronts them with their sins (18:18). Finally, as he preached one day at the temple, the king's officials come and arrest Jeremiah, putting him in the stocks, wooden yokes that painfully imprison the body. Jeremiah's faith is shaken. "O Lord, thou hast deceived me. . . . I am in derision daily, every one mocketh me . . ." (20:7). He goes so far as to invoke the words of Job (or words very much like them): "Cursed be the day wherein I was born . . ." (20:14).

Chapter 21 (which relates events that occurred toward the end of Jeremiah's story) begins the Babylonian invasion in the reign of King Zedekiah. *Note:* The chronology of this book is hectic; events do not always follow in sequence, as we shall see. Suddenly, Chapter 21 returns to the reign of King Jehoiakim, enemy of Jeremiah. We read of the prophet's agony at the hands of the priests and false prophets in the king's service. Jeremiah stands fast, predicts seventy years of captivity for the Jews (25:9–11) and is taken to trial before his enemies. Fortunately, he is saved from execution by an official named Ahikam (26:24).

Released and free to preach within certain limits, Jeremiah again attempts to bring home his message by dramatic means. This time he places a heavy yoke, such as oxen wear, on his shoulders, saying that only those who allow the yoke of Nebuchadnezzar (also spelled Nebuchadrezzar) upon their necks will survive, for it is God's will that the Babylonians triumph as their punishers.

A gifted poet and writer, Jeremiah also sends frequent messages to those Jews taken captive in the first wave of Babylonian invasion. As ever, he urges submission as part of God's plan, implying the novel idea, for that time, that the Lord can minister to his people even in exile (29:12–

Messages, or "ostraca," were sent in to Lachish on pieces of pottery during the tense, desperate days before the Assyrian attack.

of recent years gives vivid reality to this dire time. A series of tablets (clay letters) found at an outpost called Lachish reports that those manning this post during this period could no longer see the signal fires from the outlying areas of Jerusalem, implying that the Hebrew resistance had crumbled. Lachish is mentioned at 34:7, along with Azekah, another outpost referred to in the tablets.

The Zedekiah episode is again followed by a "flashback" to the reign of Jehoiakim, and we read in 36 how the prophet's books are recklessly burned by this king. Jeremiah and his scribe, Baruch, bravely recompose the documents at God's command (36:27–28).

The Fall of Judah

In Chapters 37 and 38, we learn of Jeremiah's imprisonment (during Zedekiah's reign). Charged with treason and sedition, the prophet is flung into a muddy dungeon, "so Jeremiah sunk in the mire" (38:6). Though Zedekiah is reluctant to harm the prophet, he is equally confused and frightened by impending doom. When Jeremiah is rescued from the pit by an Ethiopian court official (38:7), Zedekiah is actually gladdened, since, in reality, he is desperate for the prophet's advice. Cleaned and refreshed, Jeremiah appears before the king and tells him that it is God's will that Zedekiah surrender to the Babylonians. In this way, Judah *may* be saved. "Obey, I beseech thee, the voice of the Lord . . ." (38:20), he cries. But Zedekiah cannot

14). It is ever Jeremiah's method to mingle hope with the reality of despair. In Chapter 31 he utters perhaps the most significant part of his prophecy. Though beaten and in ruins, he says, Judah and Jerusalem will be restored by the Lord, who will make a "new covenant" for the people, a covenant based on deep, personal faith and integrity. "I will put my law in their inward parts, and write it in their hearts," says the Lord; "and [I] will be their God, and they shall be my people" (31:33). So strong is Jeremiah's faith in redemption and restoration that he buys a field near Jerusalem a year or so before its fall (32:14–15).

Chapter 34 returns to the reign of Zedekiah and the impending invasion of the Babylonians. Archaeological evidence

This low-relief sculpture shows Assyrians pushing a siege engine against the Lachish tower, and meeting a hail of stones and firebrands. Citizens are escaping through the gate below.

bring himself to such decisive action, and, as the Bible relates in its usual brevity (Chapter 39): "in the eleventh year of Zedekiah, in the fourth month, the ninth day of the month, the city was broken up" (39:2). Nebuchadnezzar, "the evil from the north," finally besieges Jerusalem and the fall of Judah begins. Zedekiah is blinded and led off to captivity (his fate is detailed in Chapter 52). But Jeremiah, whose prophecies were known in Babylon, is spared (39:11–12). A governor named Gedaliah is appointed over the fallen kingdom (he is the son of the man who saved Jeremiah in Chapter 26). Nebuchadnezzar invites the prophet to Babylon, where he promises him good treatment; but Jeremiah wishes to remain behind with the remnant for he fears that they too will turn to evil.

Jeremiah's fears are soon realized. Within three months of the siege, the governor, Gedaliah, is assassinated by local dissidents. The new leaders of the remnant, fearful for their lives in face of Nebuchadnezzar's overlords, flee to Egypt, forcing Jeremiah to accompany them. God is wrathful at this flight, for he wishes the remnant to remain in Jerusalem (42:19) and warns them, through Jeremiah, of destruction. But they do not return.

Apparently Jeremiah remained with the fugitives in Egypt, vainly hoping to reform them and bring them back to Judah. He may have died in the land of the pharaohs, possibly murdered by the outcasts. Or he may have returned, alone, or with Baruch, to the ruined city of Jerusalem that he loved so well. In any event, he composed the mournful Lamentations, which describe how the prophet sat among the ruins, bewailing the tragedy, ever hopeful of redemption. "I am the man that hath seen affliction by the rod of [God's] wrath" (Lamentations 3:1).

The final seven chapters of Jeremiah are again "flashbacks" referring to the doom awaiting Egypt, Philistia, Moab and other neighboring kingdoms. Even great Babylon will fall, says Jeremiah, "and Babylon shall become heaps, a dwellingplace for dragons [lizards], an astonishment, and an hissing, without an inhabitant" (51:37). And so it came to be. Today, through the efforts of archaeologists, we can once more see Babylon, and it is but a mass of heaps, or mounds, "without inhabitants."

The Visions of Ezekiel

Of all the major prophets, Ezekiel is the one who most nearly fits the usual definition of a prophet, as one who foretells the future in strange and daring terms. Almost from the outset of this book Ezekiel speaks to us in mysterious phrases, stunning visions and ideas that have an apocalyptic, or Doomsday, quality. For the Jewish people of Biblical times—and also of modern times—these ideas have taken on what might be called a Zionist theme, for Ezekiel preached to the exiles in Babylon of a return to the Holy Land and of a reunification of the Hebrew kingdoms.

To Christians, Ezekiel looms as another of those inspired visionaries who foresaw the coming of Christ and the establishment of God's kingdom on earth. Lovers of language and poetry regard Ezekiel as a master of vivid expression, and many persons of a mystic bent see in his words a treasury of as yet unfulfilled prophecies and signs.

Michelangelo paints his Sistine Chapel Jeremiah as a man weighed down by his own prophecies, and surrounded by lamenting figures.

But Ezekiel, for all this literary power and nationalistic fervor, was essentially a prophet in the style of his great contemporary, Jeremiah. He, too, warned of Judah's sins, and when Jerusalem fell he attempted, like Jeremiah and Nahum, to console the exiles with promises of redemption. Throughout his ministry, however, no matter how threatening or consoling it was, Ezekiel preached faith and worship concerning the one true God of Israel. In hammering home this message he effectively crushed the pagan attitudes of many Hebrews so that they were later able to rebuild their temple and their homeland as devout and purified believers.

Ezekiel's is a difficult book that exists on several levels, and many of its visions and images remain obscure. It is, however, well worth exploring, because we learn a great deal about what concerned Ezekiel, and even some of the details of his life.

What Ezekiel Saw

If you refer back to II Kings 24:14, you will read how Nebuchadnezzar in the year 597 B.C. deported ten thousand captives from Judah to Babylon, in advance of his final siege against Jerusalem. Judah's king Jehoiachin was among the prisoners (II Kings 24:15) and so was a young priest named Ezekiel. Gripped by a passionate faith in God, this captive at once set about preaching to the people regarding the sins of Judah. Several years after his captivity, when Jerusalem finally fell, he changed his message to one of consolation and hope, uttering God's message: "Ye shall know that I am the Lord" (meaning, Yahweh is the one true God of the world). This phrase, which first appears in Ezekiel 6:7, is repeated by the prophet sixty different times (for example: 6:10, 6:13, 6:14, 7:4, 7:27, etc.). Know that God works in mys-terious ways, Ezekiel is saying, and that all the doom and gloom of Judah's destruction and captivity is meant to confirm this fact and purify the chosen nation.

Ezekiel's ministry begins, appropriately enough, with a heavenly vision that comes to the prophet as he stands on the banks of the Chebar River in Babylon (1:1). "A whirlwind came out of the north, a great cloud, and a fire infolding itself, and a brightness was about it, and out of the midst thereof as the colour of amber, out of the midst of the fire" (1:4). This sort of detail and imagery is typical of Ezekiel.

We can already guess that this northern whirlwind is the same evil that came out of the north in Jeremiah's prophecy—namely, the Babylonians. But Ezekiel's vision is not so cut-and-dried. He also sees four "living creatures" who reappear from time to time in his visions (such as at 10:20–21). These cherubim, or angels, are very complicated beings with many faces and feathery wings and odd-shaped feet. Four faces, in fact, emerge from the mass, faces that are to be famous in history: the man-face, the lion-face, the ox-face and the eagle-face (see 1:5–10). Christian scholars have identified these symbols of the Four Evangelists who wrote the Gospels (see Revelations 4:6–7 and 5:6 for further reference to these creatures).

Immediately after seeing these unusual cherubim, Ezekiel discovers another phenomenal sight: celestial wheels within wheels (1:16), whirling, gemlike wheels upon which, or in which, the cherubim were conveyed. "When those went, these

A weird beast from the palace wall at Susa suggests the lion that appeared in Ezekiel's prophetic vision.

Ezekiel is borne by cherubs, an eagle, an angel, a lion and an ox in his visionary flight to Jerusalem, as interpreted by Raphael.

pendence on God, Ezekiel tells how he then ate in his mouth the words God had written on a scroll (3:3). The words were sweet like honey despite the tragic message they foretold. Ezekiel's mission is to be a difficult one but an inspired one as well. So greatly is the spirit of God upon him at this point that the prophet falls dumb and remains that way for seven days (3:15). This condition often befalls him (see 3:26 and 33:22). Again and again Ezekiel is to suffer unbearable agonies for his cause. In 4:4 we

Two Egyptian idols of the kind that appealed to some Israelites and stirred Ezekiel's great indignation (see 20:17). Idols like the goddess Tawert, with her hippopotamus head, and the dwarflike, leering Bez were forbidden by the Ten Commandments.

went" Ezekiel remarks, "and when those stood, these stood" (1:21).

What is all this about, you may ask, these faces, wings, wheels and whirlings? Ezekiel finally tells us: "This was the appearance of the likeness of the glory of the Lord. And when I saw it, I fell upon my face, and I heard a voice of one that spake" (1:28).

God's voice comes to the prophet and he learns of his mission. To dramatize his de-learn how he lay for more than a year on his left side as a symbol of the siege to come, wherein Israel and Judah would be "laid" low. He is moved to eat loathsome things, including manure (4:12); he must cut off his hair (5:1) and burn it to forecast the burning of Jerusalem; his eyes are constantly filled with astonishing visions; his homelife is never serene, and his wife, whom he greatly loves, is taken from him suddenly one evening. Throughout his hardship he is told to "make no mourning for the dead . . ." (24:16–18).

The agony of his own life and the impact of his warnings do little to convince the captives of God's will *prior* to the fall of Jerusalem. Even so, Ezekiel does not re lent, nor does God spare him unbearable visions of things to come. Indeed, one night, in a fantastic dream, the prophet is transported by God to Jerusalem itself (Chapters 8 to 11), where he witnesses idolatrous rituals in the very Temple of the Lord (8:10) and learns in detail of Jerusalem's fall. The multifaced cherubim reappear to him in his dream and bear him in a winged chariot over the city. Along with the disasters Ezekiel witnesses and foresees there also appears God's plan of restoration for Judah (11:17). "And they [the people] shall come thither, and they shall take away all the detestable things [the idols] thereof . . . and I will put a new spirit within you; and I will take the stony heart out of their flesh . . . that they may walk in my statutes . . . and they shall be my people, and I will be their God" (11:18–20). *Note:* This message is reminiscent of Jeremiah 31:33.

Whether Ezekiel dreamed his flight to Jerusalem or secretly made the trip in person (disguising it as a dream to prevent punishment by Babylonian officials) is not known. Despite the vague possibilities, when the actual fall of Jerusalem is at hand, the people finally realize that Ezekiel is truly a prophet of God (33:32–33). For a year since the siege of the holy city began, Ezekiel had lain mute and numb. Now he speaks again, foretelling the downfall of kingdoms such as Edom, Tyre, Egypt and the indictments of Israel's cruel and greedy kings (described as wicked shepherds in Chapter 34). The climax of Ezekiel's prophecy is his thrilling portrayal of Israel's redemption (beginning Chapter 36). God will forgive, "and ye shall dwell in the land that I gave to your fathers . . ." he says, and this land shall "become like the garden of Eden" (36:35). In one of the most vivid and famous parables of the Bible, Ezekiel describes a valley "which was full of bones," the broken, dried-up bones of defeat. God tells Ezekiel to prophesy to the bones and tell them, "O ye dry bones, hear the word of the Lord" (37:4). *Note:* You will recognize this quote as part of the famous spiritual.

As Ezekiel preaches, the dry bones take life; flesh and muscle grow upon them until "they lived and stood upon their feet, an exceeding great army" (37:10). Then God says to Ezekiel, "Son of man" (this is how God consistently addresses his prophet), "these bones are the whole house of Israel . . ." (37:11). The Lord further demonstrates his mercy by causing Ezekiel to write the names *Judah* and *Israel* on two separate sticks. Then Ezekiel is told to hold these sticks together in his hand. "And they shall become one in thine hand" (37:17) "and I will make them one nation . . . and they shall be no more two nations . . . neither shall they defile themselves any more with their idols . . . moreover I will make a covenant of peace

Ezekiel's vision of the dry bones, symbolizing a scattered Israel, is painted along the 3rd-century Dura-Europus synagogue wall. In this version, the bones are clothed with flesh as the prophet's repeated form follows the joining together of the bodies.

with them . . . and will set my sanctuary in the midst of them forevermore" (37:22–26). In this vision Ezekiel also speaks of King David returning to rule the unified nation. Many take this image to represent a foreshadowing of the Messiah. Later Ezekiel speaks of a "Prince" who will come to govern the redeemed in Jerusalem (see 44:3), again implying a Saviour or Deliverer (who many believe is Jesus Christ).

Chapters 40 to 48 of Ezekiel go into great detail concerning the rebuilding of Jerusalem and its temple. Again the prophet conveys his message as part of a visionary trip to the ruined city. A series of complicated and difficult passages seem to point to a Utopian (or heavenly) time when God's temple will stand like a magnificent symbol of all the Hebrew tribes, who will reassemble and sacrifice in the courtyards and at the altars of the Lord. At the height of his inspired and detailed descriptions, Ezekiel breaks off as though overwhelmed by the promises God has put into his mouth (48:35).

The new Jerusalem he has seen has been described by some as the city that arose in the time of Ezra and Nehemiah (see page 163), or as the Christian Church itself, or, in a truly Zionist way, as the modern state of Israel, where the "exiles" of contemporary times have been ingathered and the "dry bones" of the Jews, persecuted by the totalitarian forces of the twentieth century, have indeed been revived, "an exceeding great army."

To all Bible readers, the Book of Ezekiel will always be one of challenge and interpretation. It is also memorable as the source of many colorful ideas and visions: the four cherubim, the wheels within wheels, the boiling cauldron (a frequent reference to Jerusalem destroyed; see Chapter 24), the dry bones and Gog of Magog, a fantastic ruler who probably symbolizes all of Israel's enemies rolled into one. Above all, the Book of Ezekiel is remembered as the repository of the promise that the Lord utters at so many points: "and I will put a new spirit within you . . . and they shall be my people, and I will be their God" (11:18–20).

The Book of Daniel

The fervor of Jeremiah, the foresight of Isaiah and the visions of Ezekiel seem to join forces in the work of Daniel, the last of the four great prophets. Though this book contains some of the most popular stories in the Bible—such as the one about the Lion's Den—it is also the source of extraordinary prophetic passages that even the most devoted scholars have been unable to interpret fully. Indeed, nine of the twelve chapters of Daniel deal with various dreams and visions—and these are puzzles at best when taken in a purely literal sense.

We shall touch on Daniel's philosophies and spiritual message but will stress as well the dramatic portions of his biography, the fascinating and imaginative stories of his life that involve not only his prophecies but his very capable political abilities and worldly views.

Like Ezekiel, Daniel was carried into

The new Jerusalem today appeals to religious people, tourists, scholars and Bible experts, many of whom come to visit the Shrine of the Book.

The looting and burning of Jerusalem, after it fell to Babylonian forces in 586 B.C., seems to foreshadow a super-colossal movie in this 18th-century Dutch engraving.

Babylon during an early invasion of Judah by Nebuchadnezzar. Daniel, being a child at the time, for all intents and purposes could say that he was a Babylonian. Even so, though surrounded by the lavish temples of his adopted land, and no doubt influenced by the glories of Nebuchadnezzar's kingdom—including its fabulous palaces, hanging gardens, armies and the like—Daniel held fast to a deep abiding faith in Yahweh and a strong identification with the Hebrew people. As a result of his faith, Daniel was to be a witness to the redemption of the Jews, for in his lifetime he saw not only the fall of Jerusalem but also the fall of Babylon to the Persians and thus the return of the captives to Judah by edict of the Persian kings. During all

periods Daniel's leadership was of great comfort to his people, who deeply admired him. He was also highly regarded by Nebuchadnezzar himself and later by Darius, the Persian who conquered Babylon. Never has there been a more influential prophet in purely political terms. In fact we may say that Daniel held a post not unlike that of Prime Minister in both kingdoms. Consequently, he managed to introduce the faith in Yahweh even to foreign kings. Nebuchadnezzar, for example, went so far as to admit to Daniel that "your God is a God of gods, and a Lord of kings . . ." (2:47).

Daniel's Adventures

Besides being a wise and inspired youth, Daniel was apparently quite handsome since Nebuchadnezzar, soon after his first invasion of Judah, ordered that all the best-looking, wisest and most promising Jewish boys be brought to live in his palace as though they were princes. Four such youths were selected: Daniel (called Belteshazzar in Babylonian) and Shadrach, Meshach and Abed-nego (1:7). In the palace Daniel and his friends held fast to the Jewish faith and refused to eat nonkosher foods or perform any pagan rituals. Before long this piety and wisdom became famous in the court. Eventually Nebuchadnezzar realized the value of his captives and exalted their rank, for he "found them ten times better than all the magicians and astrologers that were in all his realm" (1:20).

Nebuchadnezzar was soon to put Daniel's wisdom to a test. One morning he awoke disturbed by a frightening dream, some parts of which he couldn't even remember. None of his usual soothsayers and counselors (called Chaldeans in the Bible) could help. Indeed they protested that it was impossible for any man to interpret a dream that the dreamer could not remember. In a rage Nebuchadnezzar decreed that all his wise men be executed, including Daniel.

Now God comes to the lad in a vision and lets him know the king's unusual dream. Calling upon Nebuchadnezzar to postpone the executions, Daniel reveals that the true God of the world, Yahweh, has disclosed the dream *and* the interpretation of the dream. Nebuchadnezzar listens attentively as Daniel describes a huge and terrible figure, or statue, whose "head was of fine gold, his breast and his arms of silver, his belly and his thighs of brass, his legs of iron, his feet part of iron and part of clay" (2:32–33). A great boulder falls from nowhere, says Daniel, describing the dream, and crashes into the statue, knocking it over and smashing it to pieces.

What does all this mean? Four kingdoms will arise, says Daniel, like the various parts of the statue's body—gold for Babylon; silver and brass for the kingdoms that will follow the rule of Babylon; and iron for the fourth kingdom which follows that. All of these kingdoms will fall because the statue stands on feet of iron weakened by clay. Ironically, the rock that smashed the statue shall grow into a mighty mountain surpassing all the kingdoms and filling "the whole earth" (2:35). Here we come upon the first of the puzzling visions of this book. The kingdom of gold we know represents Babylon, for Daniel says to Nebuchadnezzar, "thou art this head of gold" (1:38). Many scholars assume the silver and brass kingdoms refer to the Persians and the Medes, who conquered Babylon. But some say only the silver is the Persians, while the brass is Greece (the kingdom that conquered Per-

sia). This leaves the iron kingdom, which is said to be Rome under the Caesars (Rome conquered Greece). If this interpretation is correct, then Daniel prophesied the rise of an empire, Rome, unknown in his own time. Consequently, the rock that fills the place of the statue—meaning the Roman Empire—is assumed by many to represent a prediction of the Christian Church, which in fact supplanted the Roman religions.

Jewish scholars believe otherwise. The four kingdoms, they say, were Babylon, Persia, Media and Greece, and the stone that overwhelmed them was God's power through Israel. Whatever the true interpretation, whatever the opinions of later minds, Nebuchadnezzar's admiration for Daniel is the key factor in our story. As soon as Daniel has completed his description of the dream, the Babylonian king remembered it at once and was so impressed with the young man's words that he "fell upon his face, and worshipped Daniel . . ." (2:46). Accordingly, the young Hebrew was elevated as "chief of the governors over all the wise men of Babylon" (2:48).

Note: You may be struck by the similarity of this event with the rise of Joseph in Egypt. He too won favor of a mighty foreign king by dint of God's revelation about a problematic dream (see page 69).

The success of Daniel and his companions at court is short-lived. Soon after Nebuchadnezzar falls on his face to worship Daniel, he decides that others should now fall on their faces to worship *him*. He orders the construction of a huge golden idol, in his own likeness, to be erected on the plain of Dura. Here, everyone in the kingdom, from the highest to the lowest, must come and lie down before the image,

A remarkable 12th-century French enamel plaque pictures the three Hebrew youths in the fiery furnace, guarded and preserved by an angel. It was probably part of a four-leafed arrangement of related scenes.

"and whoso falleth not down and worshippeth shall the same hour be cast into the midst of a burning fiery furnace" (3:6).

Possibly this whole spectacle was maneuvered by the enemies of Daniel, who knew that the Hebrews would not obey such an idolatrous order and would thus be subject to a fiery death. We gather this because soon after the decree is issued certain Chaldeans—that is, the soothsayers and counselors of the court—approach the king and report that the Jews, led by Meshach, Shadrach and Abed-nego, re-

fused to bow before the golden image. *Note:* Daniel was apparently out of the country when these events occurred because he does not directly figure in this chapter.

Nebuchadnezzar orders the three Hebrew leaders brought before him and learns from their own mouths that they did indeed refuse to bow before the idol, since it violates their religion. They are not at all afraid to be cast into the fiery furnace, for they know that God will deliver them.

Nebuchadnezzar commands that the

furnace be heated seven times its usual force. So hot does it become that the guards who push the three into the furnace are themselves burned to death. But Meshach, Shadrach and Abed-nego walk directly into the flames and are not burned. To his astonishment, Nebuchadnezzar sees them unharmed and unbound "walking in the midst of the fire" and with them is a fourth figure, an angel, who appears "like the Son of God" (3:25).

The three young Hebrews have conclusively proved the power of God, and again Nebuchadnezzar is contrite. He orders the release of the captives "upon whose bodies the fire had no power, nor was an hair of their head singed . . ." (3:27). They are exalted above all others, and, in addition, "every people . . . which speak anything amiss against the God of Shadrach, Meshach, and Abed-nego, shall be cut in pieces . . ." (3:29).

Note: There is a section of the Apocrypha (which we will explore) called "The Song of the Three Holy Children," which is supposed to have originally been part of Daniel, Chapter 3 (following Verse 23). It is not included in the text, probably because it holds up the action. What it consists of is sixty-eight verses extolling God and calling upon all manner of things to bless him, including the "whales, and all that move in the waters" (Apocrypha: Song, 1:57).

Nebuchadnezzar and Belshazzar

Chapter 4 of the Book of Daniel focuses on the great king Nebuchadnezzar and tells an extraordinary story of his personal anguish and conversion to God. So poignant is this narrative that Nebuchadnezzar himself relates it to us. "I Nebuchadnezzar was at rest in mine house," he says, "and flourishing in my palace [when] I saw a dream which made me afraid . . . and the visions of my head troubled me" (4:4–5). So troubled is the king that he once again calls his sages to his room so that they may interpret his dream. But, as usual, the soothsayers fail to help the king and he turns to Daniel (Belteshazzar). This time Nebuchadnezzar remembers the dream vividly. A great tree (like himself) stood strong and visible over all the earth, crowned with beautiful leaves and much fruit. Suddenly, a heavenly figure descended upon the tree, stripped its branches of leaves, scattered its fruit and chopped down the trunk. Only a stump was left of this once mighty tree. Nebuchadnezzar further relates how, in his dream, his heart was changed from a man's heart to the heart of a beast.

Daniel sadly relates the meaning of this dream. Great Nebuchadnezzar will soon be stricken with insanity and, like a beast, he shall roam in the fields, eating grass. "Seven times shall pass over thee, till thou know that the most High ruleth in the kingdom of men . . ." (4:25). Not only will the king be afflicted with madness but his empire will be chopped down, like the tree, and others will rule over the stump.

The awful prediction soon after comes true. One day, while walking in his palace, Nebuchadnezzar suddenly goes mad and takes to the field like a wild beast on all fours "and did eat grass as an oxen, and his body was wet with the dew of heaven, till his hairs were grown like eagles' feathers, and his nails like birds' claws" (4:33). For about four years the king roams wildly in this fashion, until he realizes the power of God and blesses his name, "and praised and honoured him that liveth for ever, whose dominion is an everlasting domin-

Rembrandt captures the tense drama at Belshazzar's feast, where the king first sees the ominous message: *Mene, mene, tekel. . . .*

ion . . ." (4:34). In the same hour of his conversion, Nebuchadnezzar is healed of his madness and his reason is restored. "Now I Nebuchadnezzar," he writes, "praise and extol and honour the king of heaven, all whose works are truth, and his ways judgment: and those that walk in pride he is able to abase" (4:37).

An interesting archaeological note sheds light on this period of Nebuchadnezzar's madness. Sir Henry Rawlinson, the nineteenth-century historian of Babylon, discovered a scroll of Nebuchadnezzar,

which read in part: "For four years the residence of my kingdom did not delight my heart. In not one of my possessions did I erect any important buildings by my might . . . nor did I worship Marduk, my god. . . ." Was this the period of Nebuchadnezzar's madness in which he would logically take no "delight" in anything?

Nebuchadnezzar's successor was Belshazzar, who, along with his father, Nabonidas, was the last ruler of Babylon. At this time Daniel had risen to "third ruler in the kingdom" (5:29), after the royal father and son. But it seems he had little influence over Belshazzar, who was a decadent king given to lavish banquets and revelry. One night, while enjoying a feast before a thousand people and drinking from sacred goblets looted from God's Temple in Jerusalem, Belshazzar beholds a bone-chilling sight. "Fingers of a man's hand [came forth] and wrote over against the candlestick upon the plaister of the wall . . ." (5:5). Horrified by this mysterious handwriting, the king calls his soothsayers to his presence so that they may interpret the spectral words hovering before his eyes. The man who can do so, says Belshazzar, will be handsomely rewarded. Of course, the king's wise men fail in this problem as they have failed before, and it is left to Daniel to render the correct and ominous meaning. Bravely, the prophet relates how Nebuchadnezzar was also arrogant before the Lord until he was stricken with madness and thus came to worship the one true God. Now such a fate will befall Belshazzar, who has not only ignored God but profaned his sacred temple plates and vessels as well.

The handwriting on the wall is a riddle that reads: *Mene, mene, tekel, Upharsin* (5:25). These words, says Daniel, refer to measurements common at that time. *Mene, mene* refers to a very small coin, *tekel* to a weight and *U Pharsin*, spelled thus, means "given to the Persians." (*Note:* The Bible uses two words for Persians here: *Pharsin* and *Peres*.) In a more poetic translation, the ominous handwriting reads: "God hath numbered thy kingdom, and finished it. . . . Thou art weighed in the balances, and art found wanting. . . . Thy kingdom is divided, and given to the Medes and Persians" (5:26–28).

In that very night the prophecy comes true. Belshazzar is slain and Darius, the Median (from Persia), becomes ruler of Babylon.

Note: We have seen frequent references to "the kingdom of the Medes and the Persians," and the term requires a bit of explanation. Media, the kingdom of the Medes, or Medians, was the ancient name of a region in the northwest of modern-day Iran (or Persia). With its neighbor, Persia, it formed a single political entity in the time of Daniel (and earlier, during Esther's reign). For our purposes here, the generic term *Persia* covers both kingdoms, just as the modern name Czechoslovakia covers both the Czech peoples and the Slovaks.

Daniel Under the Persians

King Darius, and later Cyrus, elevate Daniel to even higher status once they have conquered Babylon. He is so great, in fact, that other princes grow jealous and vindictive. They concoct a plot to cause his downfall, much like the plot that brought Meshach, Shadrach and Abed-nego to the fiery furnace in Chapter 3. In this case, the plotters cause Darius to sign a decree outlawing religious prayer to any god for thirty days (6:7). This law, like all the others of the Persians and the Medes, cannot be revoked even by the king. (You will remember this fact from the story of Esther.) Darius signs the decree with no further thought, not remembering that Daniel must pray three times a day to God in respect of his religion as a Jew. When the jealous princes find the prophet in prayer (as they knew they would) they report him to the king. The punishment, they add, for ignoring this decree is to be cast alive into a den of hungry lions. The Persian ruler is horrified that his trusted counselor Daniel must thus be executed. But as the princes

This 2½-inch-high Babylonian mina (*mene* in Aramaic) was worth about 60 Persian shekels (Aramaic *tekel*). The mina is above and the shekel, with a Persian king as its design, to the left.

remind him, "no decree nor statute which the king establisheth may be changed" (6:15).

Daniel, with utter faith in God, advises Darius to fulfill the punishment, for the Lord will save him in the midst of the lions. The king sadly agrees, and the great prophet—who by now is well past eighty—is cast into the lions' den.

Throughout a sleepless night Darius fasts and prays for Daniel's deliverance. Then, in the morning, he rushes to the den of lions. There he finds the prophet unharmed, because, as he is told, an angel of God had appeared that night and "hath shut the lions' mouths . . ." (6:22). "So Daniel was taken up out of the den, and no manner of hurt was found upon him, because he believed in his God" (6:23). The wicked princes, however, are not so fortunate. Darius has them cast into the den, and there "the lions had the mastery of them, and brake all their bones in pieces . . ." (6:24).

In the twilight of his life, Daniel is visited by a series of astonishing visions and dreams, which he describes in some detail beginning with Chapter 7. Several major themes emerge from these prophecies and relate to earlier elements in Daniel's story. The four beasts he sees in a dream, for example, are, once again, references to the four kingdoms that conquered the Jews: Babylon, Persia, Media and Greece (or, some say, Babylon, Persia, Greece and Rome). All would collapse before "one like the Son of man [who] came to the Ancient of days . . ." (7:13). Many people interpret this phrase to refer to the coming of Christ ("Son of man" is an expression Jesus often uses to describe himself; see Luke 5:24). The Ancient of days is believed to be God, father of Jesus. Other opinions relate this Son of man to the hero Judas Maccabee, who restored the Jewish kingdom during the days of the Syrian persecution (around 165 B.C.). Indeed, many say, the Book of Daniel was really written around this time as a means of giving hope to the people without offending the oppressive Syrian king, Antiochus IV. By casting the story of persecution back in the times of Nebuchadnezzar and Darius, the scribes could avoid arrest. Thus, according to this theory, it is possible to interpret all of Daniel's prophecies in light of the Syrian conquest (initiated by the Greeks after the death of Alexander the Great; see our exploration of the Apocrypha). Whatever the historical background of these visions, they do certainly imply a universal coming to terms with God and the eventual fall of Israel's enemies.

There follows in Chapter 8 a dream in which Daniel sees a ram and a he-goat on the banks of the Persian river Ulai. These creatures have horns of varying lengths, and these horns are taken to represent the conquerors of the world: Alexander, the great horn, and Antiochus, the Syrian

The ram was a familiar symbol for Persia. This richly patterned one, made of gold, recalls the ram of Daniel's vision on the banks of the Ulai.

This subtly shaped mask of bronze is most likely a portrait of the Syrian tyrant Antiochus IV. Daniel called him "the little horn."

The last few chapters of Daniel further relate complicated visions and dreams dealing with the appearance of angels on the earth and other miracles that will occur after the final contingent of Jews returns to Judah with Zerubbabel (see page 163). Further predictions are given about the rise and fall of empires, with hidden references to Alexander the Great (11:3); Seleucus, ruler of Syria after Alexander (11:5); and Antiochus IV, one of the most fearsome enemies of the Jews (11:36–45). These references again imply that the Book of Daniel was written during the Syrian occupation of Judea.

The final chapter of Daniel itself speaks of the "time of the end" (12:9): Judgment Day, when "many shall be purified . . . but the wicked shall do wickedly" (12:10). First great trouble, upheavals and chaos will occur upon the earth. Then "many of them that sleep in the dust of the earth shall awake, some to everlasting life, and some to shame and everlasting contempt" (12:2), a promise of resurrection and judgment. "Blessed is he that waiteth," says Daniel, speaking of those who faithfully believe in God and his Messiah.

A Summary of Daniel's Prophecies

Four kingdoms, beginning with Nebuchadnezzar's Babylon, shall rule in the world, supplanted by God's own kingdom in Israel (Chapter 2).

Nebuchadnezzar will be stricken with madness and recover upon recognition of God's power (Chapter 4).

Babylon will fall to the Persians; the handwriting on the wall (Chapter 5).

The rise of the Greek empire and of the "little horn," or Syria (Chapters 7 and 8).

The coming of the Messiah (Chapter 9).

tyrant mentioned above, as the little horn (8:9).

The angel Gabriel also appears at the river (8:16), and Daniel learns from him of the apocalypse, or end of time (8:19). Before this momentous event, however, a Messiah shall appear who will rebuild Jerusalem. *Note:* This is the only place in the Old Testament where the actual word *Messiah* is written as such.

A sarcophagus, or tomb, from the early Christian period shows Daniel between two lions, whose mouths have been sealed.

The Last Judgment and the end of time (Chapters 11 and 12).

With these ominous, yet hopeful, prophecies, the Old Testament comes to an end. But the story of the Hebrew people from the time of the Second Temple to the birth of Jesus is taken up, more or less, in the Apocrypha, which follows. The Hebrews, throughout the tempestuous times we have just surveyed, have listened to Daniel's advice, for he told them: "Go thou thy way till the end be . . ." (12:13), and this they do and have done—as we all do who "waiteth."

CHAPTER SIX

THE APOCRYPHA

Tobit · Susanna · Judith · The Maccabees

The history of the Jewish people and the wondrous acts of Yahweh did not stop with the close of the Old Testament. This fact is attested to by fourteen books that are included in many Bibles between the Old and New testaments. The section in question is called the Apocrypha, from a Greek word meaning "hidden." In a true sense, these works are not so much hidden as they are unofficial. Jewish tradition regards them as historical but not canonical (or sacred) in value. Many Protestant sects concur. Catholic clergymen, however, see them as continuations of Biblical tradition and entirely God's word in the same sense as the Old and New testaments.

The fourteen Apocryphal books were

Peter Paul Rubens paints the hero Judas Maccabeus as he victoriously re-enters Jerusalem, having defeated the Syrian enemy whose head is impaled on a spear, above.

composed between the first and third centuries B.C. and reflect the ongoing travail of the Hebrews as they fell captive to the Greeks, the Syrians and the Romans. Most significantly, the stories of the Maccabees serve to bridge both the historical and religious gap from Daniel to the birth of Christ. The brief but glorious period of national independence enjoyed by the Jews makes inspired reading. The other books reflect certain religious and cultural trends that are important because of their impact on the New Testament. Two religious parties arose in Israel during the Greek and Roman conquests. These were the Pharisees and the Saduccees. The Pharisees were orthodox, devout and expansive in their interpretation of the Torah. They chose to live apart from the secular and corruptive influences of their day. Indeed, the word "Pharisee" derives from the idea of "separation."

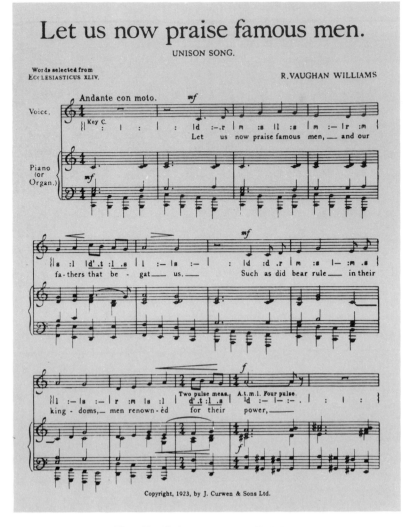

Let us now praise famous men.

UNISON SONG.

Words selected from
ECCLESIASTICUS XLIV.

R. VAUGHAN WILLIAMS

Copyright, 1923, by J. Curwen & Sons Ltd.

The English composer Ralph Vaughan Williams (1872–1958) wrote this striding choral song to words from Ecclesiasticus, Chapter 44.

The Saduccees, though pious and observant, mingled freely with Greek and Roman officials and engaged in temple rituals as a matter of etiquette and custom. Their secular view is reflected in several of the Apocrypha stories (such as I Maccabee and Ecclesiasticus), while the more zealous attitude of the Pharisees emerges in the book of Tobit, the Wisdom of Solomon, I Esdras and II Maccabees.

We will explore the most famous of the Apocrypha books following this capsule of the entire body.

I Esdras—A grouping of ideas and passages from the books of Ezra (Esdras is the Greek form of the name), II Chronicles and Nehemiah, with additional stories about the governor, Zerubbabel. In theme, this book was intended to exhort the Greek rulers to be as generous and forbearing as the Persian kings in the time of Ezra.

II Esdras—Here we read of Ezra's visions and the new era when Israel would be redeemed.

Tobit—See below.

Judith—See below.

Esther Part II—A later version of a portion of the Esther story from the Old Testament. Stressed are the scenes where the Hebrew queen nervously approaches the throne of her husband, Ahasuerus. This book is also interesting for the fact that it mentions the name of the Egyptian queen Cleopatra (Chapter 11), the ruler of the period in which the book was composed.

Wisdom of Solomon—A late compilation of thoughts and proverbs attributed to the famous king. The style of both Proverbs and Ecclesiastes is prevalent: "Better it is to have no children [and] to have virtue; [than for the ungodly to bear children]; for the memorial thereof is immortal . . ." (4:1).

Ecclesiasticus—Sometimes called "The Wisdom of Jesus (or Joshua) Son of Sirach." Not to be confused with the Old Testament book Ecclesiastes, this collection of proverbs and laws was written long after Solomon and stresses the virtues of wisdom. Beginning with Chapter 44, we are treated to a long exultation of famous Biblical heroes, starting with Abraham, Moses, David and ending with the high priest of the day. The section begins with the stirring words: "Let us now praise famous men, and our fathers that begat us" (44:1).

Baruch—He was the scribe or secretary to Jeremiah, the prophet, and this book purports to be his own testimony concerning the great man's final days in Babylon.

Song of the Three Holy Children—We referred to this book in the story of Daniel; see page 227.

Susanna and *Bel and the Dragon*—See below.

Prayer of Manasses—This recites the plea of Manasseh, king of Judah, who was held captive by the Babylonians. It is a short but heartfelt soliloquy.

I and II Maccabees—The core of the Apocrypha, explained below.

A word here is in order concerning many other devotional documents of this period which did not become part of the Apocrypha but which, nevertheless, were of great religious and historical significance. Some of these are known as Apocalyptic books, dealing with the Messianic future. The most famous are the Books of Enoch, telling of revelations given to Noah and to Enoch, his father, who "walked with God" (see Genesis 5:24)—Jesus Christ knew and quoted from these books; the Psalms of Solomon, written probably in the Maccabean period, telling of the Messiah; and the Testament of the Twelve Patriarchs, the legacy of Jacob's twelve sons to their children.

Various versions of the Hebrew Bible appeared in the time between the Old and New testaments, the most prominent being the Septuagint (see Introduction).

The Targum was another translation, this time into Aramaic, a dialect of Hebrew common in Palestine (the Holy Land) around the first and second centuries B.C. Jesus Christ knew this version.

The Talmud is a huge body of commentaries, essays, interpretations and oral explanations about the Old Testament. It was set down in the second century A.D. by Jewish scholars living in Babylon and Palestine. It serves to augment, but never replace, the sacred Scriptures. *The Wisdom of the Fathers* is perhaps the most famous section of this compendium.

Stories from the Apocrypha

TOBIT

In this rather fairy-tale styled story, we learn that piety and faith overcome even blindness and demonology. The hero of the tale is young Tobias, son of Tobit and Anna. The action is placed during the Assyrian captivity, when many Jews lived in or around Nineveh. Tobit, a pious man, is owed a large sum of money by a relative in Media (Persia). He cannot personally collect the money, because he has been accidentally blinded and rendered helpless (2:9–10). Thus it is that young Tobias is entrusted with the task and instructed to journey to Media.

Before embarking on his journey, the young man is visited by a stranger called Azarias, who is really the archangel Raphael in disguise. Azarias offers himself as a guide for Tobias. On the journey, the young man goes to bathe in the Tigris River and is there attacked by a large fish, perhaps a crocodile. Raphael bids Tobias grab hold of his attacker and subdue it, then instructs him to kill the fish for food, first removing its heart, liver and gall bladder (6:4).

Tobias is also told of an unfortunate young woman, a cousin, called Sara in Media (she is the daughter of the man who owes Tobit the money). Every young man Sara marries is mysteriously murdered on his wedding night. Even so, when they meet, Tobias falls in love with Sara and bravely decides to marry her despite the ominous fate of all her previous husbands. Raphael, of course, has a plan concerning this marriage.

Sara, it seems, is admired by a demon called Asmodeus (the Assyrians believed very much in demons), and it is this fiend who murders all rivals on their wedding night. The one thing Asmodeus cannot stand is the smell of certain fumes. Tobias is told by Raphael to burn the heart and liver he has brought with him from his encounter at the Tigris. When the demon inhales these fumes, he flees all the way to Egypt, never to return (8:1–3).

Joyful at his salvation, Tobias leads his new wife back to Nineveh, where the blind Tobit is waiting. Now Raphael tells Tobias how his father's blindness may be cured. "Anoint thou [Tobit's] eyes with the gall, and being pricked therewith, he shall rub, and the whiteness [over his eyes] shall fall away, and he shall see thee" (11:8).

Grateful to Raphael, who is still in disguise, Tobit arranges to pay him a wage from the collected debt. The guide has not only safely conducted Tobias on his journey; he has also rescued Sara and cured Tobit's blindness as well. As the pious old man is about to reward Raphael, the angel appears in his true form as "one of the seven holy angels . . . which go in and out before the glory of the Holy One" (12:15). Everyone is astonished and gratefully offers up blessings of thanksgiving and praise, in which the dream of a rebuilt Jerusalem is emphasized (13:15–18).

Two interesting sidelights of this romantic tale are the references to the prophet Jonah (or Jonas, 14:4), who apparently had recently completed his mission to Nineveh, for Tobit remarks that he is

The Florentine artist Filippino Lippi portrayed this encounter between Tobias and the Angel, in which we see the strange little crocodile held by the boy and the pet dog of Tobias.

The Assyrian demon Pazuzu was, no doubt, a cousin of Asmodeus, the evil spirit that tormented Sara in *Tobit*.

afraid Nineveh shall indeed one day be doomed, as the prophet predicted. Less ominously, this story is also the only one in the Bible that describes the presence of a pet dog (5:16). The animal is mentioned more than once as a companion to both Tobias and the angel (11:4); it is a charming touch in an otherwise mysterious story.

THE STORY OF JUDITH

As is the case with many stories in the Apocrypha, ancient times are recalled in order to disguise current problems. The Book of Tobit, written during Greek subjugation, recalled the prophecies of Jonah about the wickedness of Nineveh and the Assyrian conquerors, a veiled warning about God's vengeance on Israel's foes. The Book of Judith, likely written during the awful days of Syrian persecution—around 150 B.C.—describes alleged events in the days of Nebuchadnezzar, who is erroneously placed on the Assyrian throne in Nineveh (1:1), when in fact he ruled from Babylon, many years after Nineveh fell. This historical error is of no consequence, since the authors of Judith intended to preach a subtle form of revolution against Syria and used vague and distant events to disguise their provocative theme.

In mood, the story of Judith may remind us of Esther and Deborah, for it concerns a heroic woman who dares certain death to save her people. The Hebrews are valiantly defending themselves against Nebuchadnezzar's armies, but the ongoing siege that the fearsome general, Holofernes, mounts against their cities finally threatens to crush all resistance. One day an edict of surrender is presented to the Jews and "then the people fell down and worshipped God, and cried unto God, saying O Lord God of heaven . . . pity the low estate of our nation . . ." (6:18–19). Hoping against hope, the leaders of the people decide to hold out against Holofernes five more days in the belief that God will somehow rescue them.

Judith—her name means woman of Judah—now enters the story (Chapter 8). Though recently widowed, she adorns herself in gorgeous apparel. With only her maid, she plans to venture beyond the fortress of Bethulia—where she lives—into the camp of Holofernes. Once there, she will declare herself a deserter and ingratiate herself, she hopes, into the general's good

graces. The elders of Bethulia agree to Judith's plan, although they are not absolutely certain of what she intends to do. They know her to be a pious and brave young woman—and they trust in God, as does Judith with great fervor (see 9:1–4).

When Judith arrives at Holofernes' camp, she is welcomed as a potential informer. Once Holofernes lays eyes on her, he is smitten by her beauty and invites her to join his ranks. Judith convinces the foreign general of her good intentions toward him, since she pretends to despise her own people as cowards. She makes no pretense, however, about her devotion to God. She is so devout, in fact, that she will not eat the unpurified food of the foreigners but has brought her own victuals in a bag. (This bag is, as we shall see, part of Judith's plan.)

For four days Judith stays in the tent of Holofernes, pretending to betray Judah and allowing the general to believe that she loves him. A banquet is prepared. True to her fashion, Judith eats only her own victuals while Holofernes drinks wine to excess, more than "at any time in one day since he was born" (12:20).

What happens next is described in detail by the authors of this book: "Now when the evening was come . . . Judith was left alone in the tent and Holofernes lying alone upon his bed, for he was filled with wine. Then Judith, standing by his bed, said in her heart, O Lord God, of all power, look at this present upon the works of mine hands for the exaltation of Jerusalem. For now is the time to help thine inheritance,

Restraint pervades Andrea Mantegna's muted, classically posed painting of Judith as she lowers the head of Holofernes into her very functional food bag.

and to execute mine enterprises to the destruction of the enemies which are risen against us.

"Then she came to the pillar of the bed, which was at Holofernes' head, and took down his scimitar from thence, and approached to his bed, and took hold of the hair of his head, and said, Strengthen me, O Lord God of Israel, this day. And she smote him thrice upon his neck with all her might, and she took away his head from him . . ." (13:1–9).

Judith's purpose in accomplishing this bloody act was not solely to avenge her people for the cruelties of Holofernes. She above all wished to inspire courage and resolve in the besieged men of Bethulia and knew that if they could see that Holofernes was dead, they would cast aside fear and defeat the Assyrians.

Judith's problem now was to escape from the enemy camp with Holofernes' head and return safely to Bethulia. For this purpose she had carefully planned each step. She knew, for instance, that Holofernes' guards had grown accustomed to her comings and goings and had even encouraged her to return to Bethulia periodically to spy. They were also quite used to the bag she carried for her special food. Little did they know that on this occasion Judith was returning to Bethulia for good and that her food bag contained their general's severed head.

Once the Jews learned of Judith's great bravery, they responded as she had hoped they would and rose up to smite their oppressors. At the same time, the Assyrians, dumbfounded by the assassination of Holofernes—especially at the hands of a woman—were easy prey to defeat; they even fled in the face of bloody slaughter.

Judith was greatly honored by her people. "They put a garland of olive upon her and her maid . . . and she went before all the people in the dance, leading all the women: and all the men of Israel followed in their armor with garlands, and with songs in their mouths" (15:13).

Susanna

Another woman dominates the next intriguing story of the Apocrypha, this one set in the time of the prophet Daniel. Though cast in the form of a fable, or folk tale, Susanna's story has two important moral lessons: one, the dignity of marriage, and two, the reliability of the Law.

Susanna was the beautiful young wife of Joiakim, a Hebrew living in Babylon, whose house was the center of much legal business. Two elderly judges frequent Joiakim's house, and when they see the lovely Susanna in the garden they lust after her and decide to attempt seduction. One evening, pretending to go their separate ways, each judge returns to the garden to spy upon the young woman as she bathes. When Susanna dismisses her maids and is alone, the two advance. They propose a lecherous plan. Either she will consent to favor them on the spot or they will declare that she had just committed adultery with a young man in their presence. In short, they are saying: It's your word against ours, and since we are two respected judges and you are but a woman, the whole world will believe us.

The virtuous Susanna—aware of her danger but more concerned about the teachings of her religion about marriage—needs no time to decide and declares: "It

The German Altdorfer has erected a fantastic, "biblical" building against a craggy landscape. The elders peer from the trees on the left as Susanna is demurely bathing.

In this shallow Syrian carving, the god Bel, or Baal, holds a lance that seems barbed with lightning.

is better for me to fall into your hands, and not do it [grant their wishes] than to sin in the sight of the Lord" (1:22).

And so the wicked old judges immediately call in the servants and announce their lie that Susanna had committed adultery then and there and that her lover had just escaped by the garden door.

The penalty for adultery in Israel was stoning, and Susanna is thus taken to trial, where the elders, "full of mischievous imagination against Susanna" (1:28), also install themselves. Before the people and the court they recite their deceitful story of how they innocently happened upon the young woman in the garden only to find her in sin with a man. Their story is so convincing—especially considering the fact that they are honored judges themselves—that the court promptly condemns Susanna to death.

But the Lord has not forgotten Susanna or her purity and virtue. Into the court comes Daniel, the prophet. Believing in Susanna's innocence, he demands the right to cross-examine the witnesses, protesting that due process of law had been ignored. Because of his fame, the court complies at once. Now Daniel separates the elders and questions each before the court. "Under what tree [in the garden] sawest thou them companying together?" he asks the first elder. And the old man replies: "Under a mastic tree" (1:54). Then, Daniel asks the very same question to the other man who is brought into the courtroom. But this man replies "under an holm tree." Whereupon the elders snare themselves in their lie by naming different trees.

The court is convinced and immediately condemns the elders as false witnesses, for which they are put to death (see Deuteronomy 19:18 for the basis of this punishment). Susanna is restored to her rightful place as an honorable, virtuous woman, and Daniel has "great reputation in the sight of the people" (1:64).

Bel and the Dragon

This tale of Daniel is in effect a Biblical detective story.

The king of Persia worshiped a huge idol called Bel, which was famous for the vast amount of food and drink it consumed: forty sheep and six vessels of wine a day! The fact that the creature devours this quantity is proof enough to the gullible king that Bel is really a god. But Daniel knows better. "O King, be not deceived," he says, "for this is but clay within and brass without, and did never eat or drink any thing" (1:7). The king is angered and decrees that Daniel shall die unless he can prove his allegations.

For their part, the priests of Bel are delighted with the chance to assert themselves, and so they arrange a test. Huge quantities of meat and drink will be laid before the idol in its temple. Then the priests will leave the area and the king himself will seal the door so that no one many enter undetected. On the morrow, they promise, when the doors are officially opened, all will see that Bel has consumed his daily portion without the aid of the priests. Thus will Daniel be debunked and subject to death.

Sure enough, when the doors are opened before the king, on the following day, all present behold the idol, and nowhere is any food or drink to be seen. The great Daniel has been defeated.

Undaunted, the prophet steps forward and points to the floor, where, unnoticed by the priests, he had strewn ashes before the doors were sealed. There in the ashes are the footprints of the priests, their wives and their children, all of whom had entered by means of a secret door in the temple and consumed the food as they had always previously done.

The king is so enraged at this deception that he orders the priests of Bel executed and turns over the idol and the temple to Daniel. The prophet promptly pulverizes both of them.

Note: Practically the same story is repeated at 1:23. This time another idol, a brass dragon, is destroyed by an explosion arranged by Daniel. For this desecration he is flung into a den of lions (repeating the incident that occurs in Daniel 6:1–24). Happily, here, as before, he is rescued by God and restored to power.

The Maccabees

A casual reading of I and II Maccabees might give the reader the impression that he is studying ancient history and not a religious or sacred document. In most versions of the text of I Maccabees, the name of God does not appear (except where translators have introduced it). This is one of the reasons why it is an Apocryphal book and not part of the Old Testament. However, despite the purely historical value of these stories, there is a tone of sacredness within them, a reverence for the destiny of Israel and the power of faith. The prevalent theme is that those "who show themselves men in behalf of the law [shall] obtain glory" (I Maccabees 2:61–64).

The period covered by I Maccabees is one of persecution, rebellion and eventual triumph for the Jews, the years 166 to 135 B.C. The Seleucid kings ruled Palestine at the time. They were Syrians appointed by

Alexander the Great of Greece. The most oppressive of these kings was Antiochus Epiphanes, who had a particular wrath against Israel. Among the most tyrannical of his actions was the desecration of the temple, which followed a "great massacre" in the land (1:20–24). Antiochus went so far as to prohibit circumcision, the most sacred of Jewish rituals. Those who disobeyed were hanged together with their children, who were to hang suspended from their parents' necks (1:61).

The wickedness of idolatry, the pain of persecution and terror eventually stirred in the Jews the necessity of rebellion. The leaders of the uprising were members of the Apphus family, headed by Mattathias, a virtuous priest of the temple. The most outspoken and courageous of Mattathias' five sons was Judas, called Maccabeus, a word that many believe to mean "the hammerer."

Mattathias was particularly distressed over sacrilegious temple sacrifices instituted by Antiochus. One day, in a rage, he slew one of the king's commissioners who had compelled the Jews to perform pagan rituals. With this act the revolution began, for as Mattathias announced, no man should desecrate God's law, even for a king. "Whosoever is zealous of the law," he cried ". . . let him follow me. So he and his sons fled into the mountains . . ." (2:27–28).

It is Judas Maccabee who carries out the military aspects of the rebellion and succeeds to full political leadership upon Mattathias' death. In a bitter and bloody series of wars, the Maccabeans—as they are now called—though outnumbered and poorly supplied, eventually rout the armies of their enemies. Of greatest moment was the retaking of Jerusalem and the rededication of the temple, which had been sacked and neglected by the Syrians. Judas and his people cleansed the sanctuary and rekindled the sacred fires on the twenty-fifth day of the ninth month, called Kislev. To this day the rededication is celebrated by Jews as the Festival of Chanukah—a festival in which candles are burned for eight successive days.

(A legend, which appears in the Talmud, tells how the Maccabees found a small container of lamp oil in the temple, sufficient to burn for only one day. Miraculously, however, the oil lasted eight full days, until more could be brought; hence the eight candles of the Chanukah celebration.)

The New Kingdom

The wicked king Antiochus, brought low by defeat, soon expired (6:9–13). A new king attempted to repel the Jewish invaders, but all the while the Maccabees were gaining strength. Their success was assured when Judas made a pact with Rome (long antagonistic to the Seleucids).

For five years Judas and his followers held their own. But corruption within the ranks of the Jews led to eventual defeat. In a pitched battle with Greek forces led by Bacchides, Judas was slain (9:18). Amid great honor and mourning, he was buried in Modin.

Jonathan, the brother of Judas, took command of the rebellion. In a long series of campaigns against Bacchides, the Jews finally reorganized their strength and routed the enemy. "Thus the sword ceased from Israel . . . [and] Jonathan . . . began to govern the people; and he destroyed the ungodly men out of Israel" (9:73).

The Greek king Alexander (a descendant of Antiochus) sought peace with Jonathan.

But success was short-lived. A malcontent of the court named Tryphon, in an attempt to usurp the place of Alexander, moved against Judea. And in one of the ensuing battles Jonathan was slain.

Simon, another Maccabee brother, took rule and maintained an uneasy peace. In time, Simon's rule restored prosperity to the Jews. "And Israel rejoiced with great joy: for every man sat under his vine and his fig tree and there was none to fray them . . ." (14:11–12). Upon Simon's death, his son, known as John Hyrcanus, ruled as a king in Israel, and for more than thirty years the Jewish people prospered and were unified.

II Maccabees

II Maccabees is not specifically a sequel to the first book but rather an elaboration of the religious, even miraculous nature of the Maccabean rebellion. It emphasizes the views of the Pharisees, the orthodox party of the day, as opposed to the more secular Saduccean outlook of the previous book. In doing so, it relates many incidents that occurred during the days of Judas Maccabee, and it contains long, rhetorical sections praising the Law and religious piety.

Two stories of martyrdom are famous in this book. The first concerns an old man named Eleazar, a pious Pharisee, who was captured by the forces of Antiochus and ordered to eat swine meat, which was prohibited by Jewish law. At the last minute influential friends of Eleazar substituted kosher meat for the forbidden food, so that it would seem as though the old man was obeying his oppressors when he ate. But Eleazar refused to be a party to such deception, even if it meant losing his life. He reasoned that those who heard of his

Chanukah is the Jewish celebration of national redemption, during which eight candles are successively lit to commemorate the triumph of the Maccabees.

humiliation would lose faith, thinking he had really eaten pork. So Eleazar bravely went to his death, leaving "a notable example to such as be young and die willingly and courageously for the honorable and holy laws" (6:28).

In the same vein, a mother and her seven sons were taken prisoners by the Syrians and again ordered to eat forbidden food.

The pious Jews refused, whereupon Antiochus—that monstrous villain—decreed a hideous death for each son in sight of his mother. Antiochus believed the aged woman would weaken and command her sons to break the holy law. However, as each son was brought before her, prepared for torture, the mother cried out: "Fear not this tormentor . . . take thy death . . ." (7:29).

And so, in obedience to God's law, each son died a martyr, and Antiochus was in a rage. Soon after, the mother also died, no doubt of sorrow. The story ends with these appropriate words: "Let this be enough now to have spoken concerning the idolatrous feasts, and the extreme tortures" (7:41–42).

The Peacable Kingdom, painted in several versions by the colonial American artist Edward Hicks, takes Isaiah's prophecy beyond the time of the Old Testament to the new world (notice William Penn in the distance) when man and beast would settle down peacefully and "a little child" would lead them (see Isaiah, Chapter 11). This is also a major theme of the New Testament.

CHAPTER SEVEN

THE STORY OF JESUS CHRIST AND THE EARLY CHRISTIANS

The Gospels · The Acts · The Epistles · Revelation

The four Gospels, the Acts of the Apostles, the Epistles and the Revelation of St. John the Divine contain the history of the birth, life, death and resurrection of Jesus Christ, plus the story of the early church. Jesus Christ, his teachings and uniqueness are the basis of the Christian religion, and he is, without doubt, the most complex and profound figure in all the Bible. Understanding his role and function is an enormous task that touches on weighty subjects such as theology, mysticism, philosophy and religion itself. The purpose of this book, of course, is to give guidance in understanding the story and not one of investigating the subjects just mentioned.

FACING PAGE: *Christ Feeding the Multitude* (detail) by Jacopo Tintoretto (see pp.292-93).

Therefore, we will continue our exploration, regarding this section of the Bible very much like the Old Testament. Both concern themselves with the Jewish people, their struggles and their love of God. But the New Testament is more than a latter-day addition to the Scriptures. It is, in essence, the source-book of a new religion: Christianity.

Background of the New Testament

St. Paul articulated significant beliefs of the early Christians and inspired the growth and wide acceptance of the new religion. Paul's letters, or epistles, to the newly organized churches of the Middle East, Greece and Rome were the earliest documents of the New Testament. Because Christian leaders of the time felt that their followers also needed to know the life story of Jesus, as well as the message of the epistles, they called for the setting down of the Gospels (probably from godspell: good tidings) as a means of authenticating the message of Paul's texts. Many such gospels had developed in the years immediately following Jesus' death, but none had become official, nor were they widely distributed. Since Paul had not been one of the original disciples of Christ, even his story in the Book of Acts did not reveal much about Jesus himself. Thus the need for the Gospels was self-evident. The choice eventually fell on the four we know.

Because they were probably drawn from firsthand accounts, the Gospels of Matthew, Mark and John bear the names of three of Christ's disciples. Luke was a latter-day Christian, a practicing physician and, being Greek, the only non-Jewish Gospel writer. Many believe that Mark's was the oldest of the written Gospels and that, in another form, it was the primary source of the rest. Such discussions and speculations enter the realm of Biblical exegesis, a realm not necessary for a meaningful reading of the texts themselves.

The question of dating, though equally tangential to the reading, is nevertheless of interest. St. Paul's Epistles, as the earliest part of the New Testament, were written down after A.D. 45 and before 64, around the time Paul probably died in Rome. (Acts was most likely committed to paper after Paul's imprisonment.) The Gospels were set down at different times: Mark around A.D. 70, Matthew and Luke between 70 and 90 and John between 100 and 125. Revelation was written about the same time as John. By the year A.D. 140, the New Testament as we know it was complete.

A very brief summary of each Gospel is given below, followed by an in-depth exploration. Later we will concentrate on the Acts of the Apostles and, in separate sections, the Epistles and the Revelation of St. John the Divine.

The Gospels

Matthew—The first and possibly the best-known of New Testament books, it emphasizes the message that Jesus was the Messiah (Christ) and that he was foreshadowed as such in the Old Testament. Jesus' great sermons—particularly the Sermon on the Mount—are beautifully relayed in this Gospel.

Mark—The wondrous and miraculous nature of Jesus' powers is the focus of this book. Most of the discourses reported in Matthew do not appear here, since the emphasis of Mark seems to be the actions of Jesus as opposed to his words. It is usually believed that the great disciple Peter was a co-author of this Gospel or at least quite influential in its writing.

Luke—This book together with Matthew and Mark form what are known as the Synoptic Gospels, or those most closely related in style. All emphasize the biography or life story of Jesus. Luke, as a Gentile, stresses the universal appeal of Christ's message and his role as the Son of God. Paul may have influenced Luke in this text, since there are so many similarities in viewpoint.

In Luke, the genealogy of Jesus is carried back to Adam, the father of mankind, and in general the scope of this Gospel is the most extensive of all four.

John—Because this book deals with more philosophical and metaphysical questions, it stands apart from the other Gospels. John emphasizes the deity of

Among the gilded bronze panels which Lorenzo Ghiberti designed for Baptistery doors facing the Florence Cathedral are these showing Matthew, Mark, Luke and John, each with his symbol (see Revelation 4:7).

Jesus and stresses what Christ said more than what he did. However, several interesting narrative portions appear in this book and not in the others. The incident of the Samaritan woman at the well is one example (see John, Chapter 4).

The three closely related Gospels will be explored as a unit, along with the narrative parts of John. All will be combined as they are in the Dartmouth Bible so that a clear, comprehensive coverage is offered without unnecessary repetition. The essential ingredients of the Christian faith will be touched on in this guide. Our purpose is, in the words of the Dartmouth scholars, to "do what millions of Christians over the centuries have done, namely, to think of the story of Jesus as one grand, dramatic whole. . . ."

For further clarity, we will subhead the major episodes of the Gospels, and these will in turn be subheaded, so the reader will have a running chart of the key narratives and events. Quotations will be annotated to show from which Gospel they are drawn. Wherever necessary, historical and archaeological explanations will be included, as in previous sections, along with interpretive notes.

EVENTS PRECEDING AND SURROUNDING JESUS' BIRTH

The Gospel of Luke gives us the fullest account of events leading up to the birth of Jesus. Mark and John, in fact, say nothing of these things, nor even of Jesus' birth, whereas Matthew begins with the angel's announcement to Mary. Therefore a reading of Luke 1 to 3 and Matthew 1 and 2 is necessary for all those who wish to span the period known as Advent (the birth of John the Baptist and other events) through Jesus' boyhood visit to Jerusalem.

As we remember from the Apocrypha, the Jewish people, having established their own kingdom under the Maccabees, enjoyed only a brief period of independence. The New Testament takes up their history at a time when the Romans domi-

The Romans, under Titus, fought hard to conquer a Jerusalem that refused to surrender voluntarily. This relief sculpture on the emperor's triumphal arch in Rome shows his laurel-crowned soldiers bearing the Menorah, the silver trumpets and other treasures from the burned and looted temple.

A Sadducean family portrait from Syria during the second century A.D. Such people, though Jews, were assimilated into Roman culture around the time of Christ.

nated the civilized world. Judea was a small and rather insignificant Roman province or outpost administered by a Roman governor, appointed by the emperor (called Caesar) and ruled by a puppet king, also appointed by Caesar. Roman soldiers were everywhere; Roman taxation, persecution and general interference with daily life were oppressive.

Rome had always allowed its provinces a certain independence where local beliefs and customs were concerned in the hopes of keeping order throughout the empire. Consequently, a few Jewish institutions survived, specifically those connected with the religion and, therefore, with the temple, which the puppet king, Herod the Great, had restored about 25 B.C.

One of the surviving institutions was the Sanhedrin, or Supreme Religious Court. It was composed of seventy pious Jews headed by the High Priest of the temple. A strictly religious institution, the Sanhedrin had no legal or judicial power outside religious law. Obedience to the Caesar in civil matters was mandatory, as we shall see from incidents in the Gospels.

Tension and hardship were at a peak in about the year 5 B.C. Various religious and secular groups in Judea were at odds (the Pharisees and Sadducees); Roman oppression was unrelenting and the corruption of Herod, the king, apparent everywhere. The only hope that kept the faithful from despair was the age-old promise of the Redeemer and Saviour of Israel, first

The Roman oppression of the Jews reached one climax under Herod and another about 65 years later, when a Roman army under Vespasian crushed the final desperate uprising at the fortress of Masada. To celebrate his victory, Vespasian issued a "Judea Capta" coin, showing a Jewish man and woman mourning under a palm tree.

were old, it seemed to Zacharias as though a son was one blessing he would never know. But one day, while he officiated in the temple, Zacharias was visited by Gabriel, an angel of God, who told him that his wife would bear a son, to be called John, "and he shall go before him [God] in the spirit and power of Elias, to turn the hearts of the fathers to the children, and the disobedient to the wisdom of the just; to make ready a people prepared for the Lord" (Luke 1:17).

Elias, whom the angel referred to, is

A tablet was set up in the outer court of Herod's temple in Jerusalem to warn Gentiles—in Latin and Greek—against entering the sacred Inner Temple. Here we see a fragment of the original.

prophesied by Isaiah and the other ancient prophets and called Messiah by Daniel. That he would be born to a virgin of King David's family, that he would rise among the people and bring them peace and independence, were thoughts that lingered in every hopeful mind. One might describe this mood as revolutionary in part, the way the American colonists must have felt under English oppression prior to 1776. But in Judea, another emotionally charged idea was prevalent. Not only would the Messiah come to redeem the Chosen People, but God would, at the same time, bring about an end of the world, a Doomsday, in which all men would be judged according to their virtues and sins. Many saw signs of this Doomsday approaching, signs that indicated the great and decisive moment would soon be at hand.

The Announcement of John the Baptist

One of the few truly pious priests of the temple was Zacharias. His wife, Elisabeth, had never borne a child. Now that both another name for Elijah, and it was believed by many that a sign of the coming Messiah would be the symbolic return of the deathless prophet. Now Zacharias was told that he would be the father of Elijah in a new form, in the form of John the Baptist, for the child who was to be born to Elisabeth would "drink neither wine nor strong drink; and he shall be filled with the Holy Ghost, even from his mother's womb" (Luke 1:15). Gabriel further informed Zacharias that he would be unable to speak a single word until his son was born.

The Annunciation to Mary

Shortly after Gabriel visited Zacharias, he appeared to a young woman in Nazareth. Her name was Mary, espoused to Joseph, the local carpenter. Mary was a cousin of Elisabeth, the wife of Zacharias. To Mary would go the singular blessing and honor of being the mother of the Messiah. This Gabriel informs her in stirring words: "Hail, thou that art highly favoured," he says, "the Lord is with thee: blessed art thou among women . . ." (Luke 1:28). Puzzled and alarmed, Mary cannot speak. The angel continues: "Fear not, Mary," he says, ". . . thou shalt conceive in thy womb, and bring forth a son, and shalt call his name Jesus. He shall be great, and shall be called the Son of the Highest: and the Lord God shall give unto him the throne of his father David: And he shall reign over the House of Jacob for ever; and of his kingdom there shall be no end" (Luke 1:30–33).

To prove the miraculous nature of this child, the angel further reveals that Mary shall conceive her baby without a husband; that hers shall be a virgin birth, impossible save for God's own intervention. In addi-

tion, Mary will know the special nature of her child because Elisabeth, thought barren, shall now conceive as a sign of the coming Messiah.

As we see, in his revelation to Mary, Gabriel first utters the name Jesus. In Hebrew, this name is Joshua, or Ye-ho-shu-ah. Jesus is a Greek interpretation. In either case, it means "God (Yahweh) saves." Gabriel also says that God shall give Jesus the "throne of his father David, And he shall reign over the house of Jacob for ever." Tradition had long held that the Messiah would come from a Davidic family, one descended from King David of old. Clearly, Mary's family was of such descent (and probably Joseph's as well). The "house of Jacob" refers to Israel and the Jewish nation. The Gospel writers by and large believed that the Messiah, Jesus, came first to save the Jews and later all mankind. Paul maintained that the "house of Jacob" meant all sincere believers.

The Visit of Mary to Elisabeth

Soon after her miraculous conception, Mary journeyed to a city near Jerusalem where Zacharias and Elisabeth awaited the birth of their son. When the older woman beheld her cousin, now pregnant, she felt her own baby leap, or move, in her womb, as though he were praising the as yet unborn Messiah. Elisabeth as well rejoiced in the news of Mary's special grace. "Blessed is the fruit of thy womb," she cried (Luke 1:42), whereupon Mary responded with a great prayer known in Latin as the *Magnificat*: "My soul doth magnify the Lord

The Italian artist Masolino achieves a subtle poise in his richly patterned Annunciation. The placing of the column and arches in the painting seems both to separate and to unite the angel and the Virgin.

The intimate sympathy between the mothers-to-be, Mary (in red) and her cousin Elizabeth, speaks here through the curved arms linking Giotto's rounded figures and is quietly echoed by his "handmaidens."

. . . for he hath regarded the low estate of his handmaiden: for, behold, from henceforth all generations shall call me blessed" (Luke 1:46–48).

For three months Mary abided with Elisabeth, until just before the birth of John.

John the Baptist

The child born to Elisabeth was eventually known as John the Baptist, his title derived from a Greek word for "immersion." John was to become the leader of an influential Jewish religious group that believed the Kingdom of God would soon overtake the earth. All those who wished to be part of this glorious Paradise had to be cleansed of their sins and rededicated to the Law and to God. Symbolic of this declaration was the act of being plunged, or immersed, into the cold waters of the Jordan River, an act that John performed repeatedly at a bend in the river near Jericho.

John's birth took place just as Gabriel had prophesied, and when Zacharias beheld his son his speech returned and he too prophesied that John would be called "the prophet of the Highest: for thou shalt go before the face of the Lord to prepare his ways . . ." (Luke 1:76).

Because he was to represent Elijah, the forerunner of the Messiah, John lived a solitary rugged life, just as Elijah had. He dressed in animal skins, ate locusts and dwelt for nearly thirty years alone in the wilderness near the lower Jordan.

The Birth of Jesus

The great event, the birth of the Messiah, is now at hand. Mary has been married to Joseph, who was told by an angel of Mary's special status (see Matthew 1:20). The young woman no doubt looks forward to giving birth in her home at Nazareth. But just before her time, word comes from Rome (from the Emperor Augustus Caesar) that a special census is to be taken for the purposes of taxation. This census requires every head of household to return to the city of his birth. Joseph, having been born in Bethlehem near Jerusalem, must now travel some one hundred miles southward, and Mary, "great

THE ROGER WAGNER CHORALE
Magnificat
Three Renaissance and Baroque settings of the Canticle of the Virgin Mary by
MONTEVERDI · VIVALDI · CRISTÓBAL DE MORALES
with orchestra conducted by ROGER WAGNER

The Virgin's hymn (Luke 1:46-55), known as the *Magnificat*, has inspired a great deal of music and art. Botticelli's painting, excerpted on this album cover, shows the Virgin being crowned by heavenly hands.

with child" (Luke 2:5), goes with him.

When the couple finally arrive in Bethlehem, the city is so crowded that there "was no room for them in the inn" (Luke 2:7). Therefore, Mary gave birth to Jesus in a nearby stable. We know this because Luke states that after wrapping the infant in swaddling clothes she "laid him in a manger" (Luke 2:7). Mangers are feeding troughs for stable animals, hence the world-famous Christmas picture of the baby Jesus, born in a stable, laid in a manger, surrounded by barnyard animals.

Note: The actual birthdate of Jesus is unknown. December 25 (Christmas) came to be that day about four hundred years later, associating Jesus' birth with ancient rituals of the winter solstice (when the sun seems to be reborn). The year of Jesus' birth is also in doubt. It was not A.D. 1 as we might assume but more likely 4 B.C. Jesus was thus born four years "before Christ"—which sounds like a paradox. The fact is that the Christian calendar did not come into effect until five centuries after this event, and those who calculated it probably erred by four or five years in trying to make the Christian year called One coincide with the Roman calendar then in use. By that calendar, Jesus was born in the year 753—that is, 753 years after the founding of Rome, or 4 B.C. by our reckoning.

The Adoration of the Shepherds

The birth of this baby was not without notice. Shepherds nearby, "abiding in the field, keeping watch over their flock by night" (Luke 2:8), were astonished to see an angel who greeted them with these famous words: ". . . behold, I bring you good tidings of great joy, which shall be to all people. For unto you is born this day in the city of David a Saviour. . . . Glory to God in the highest, and on earth peace, good will toward men" (Luke 2:10–14). The shepherds eagerly sought out the baby and found him, as the angel had revealed, in a nearby stable.

The adoration of the shepherds was the first earthly homage paid to the heavenly king. A point of touching naturalism is offered in this section. It concerns Mary, the young mother, who is puzzled and amazed, for we read, "But Mary kept all these things, and pondered them in her heart" (Luke 2:19).

The Wise Men

Mary and Joseph eventually took their baby to a house in Bethlehem, where he was circumcised according to Jewish law. Soon after, other visitors came to pay homage, not ordinary shepherds but a group of royal officials, possibly kings, surely "wise men from the East." These travelers had studied the heavens (perhaps they were astrologers) for a sign of the coming Messiah. For some time prior to Jesus' birth, they had seen a brilliant star hovering in the vicinity of Bethlehem. Now, not sure of where the Christ Child might be, the royal entourage went directly to Jerusalem to consult with none other than King Herod.

"Where is he that is born King of the Jews?" they asked (Matthew 2:2). Herod, who feared for his throne, believed they referred to a potential usurper. Rather than let them know his fears, he urged the wise

Present-day Bethlehem, at the coming of twilight, nestles into the peace of a Judean hillside, with a view of the Church of the Nativity (center).

One can almost hear the strummed song of Piero della Francesca's angels as they and the three Kings visit Mary and the Child at the Stable of the Nativity.

men on to Bethlehem, where tradition held such a king would be born.

"Go and search diligently for the young child," he said, "and when ye have found him, bring me word again, that I may come and worship him also" (Matthew 2:8). Of course Herod had no such intention, but this the wise men did not know at the time. Joyously, they set off for Bethlehem.

When they found the house where the holy baby slept—and above which the star shone brightly—they fell on their knees and "presented unto him gifts; gold, and frankincense, and myrrh." The presentation of these three offerings, two of them

The three Kings have each brought along an elaborate retinue so as to make this *Adoration of the Magi* something of a summit meeting, with three castles in the landscape background. The unknown artist has filled the scene with charming animals, including what looks like an organ-grinder's monkey.

Rather more traditional is this circular Florentine treatment of the subject, the work of Fra Angelico and Fra Filippo Lippi. As painted by these two monks, the Adoration becomes an occasion of both grace and joy.

rare spices, implies that three kings led the procession, though the Bible never gives their number. Many believe these wise men, or kings, to have come from Babylon, where stargazing was a holy ritual. Others call them Persians, hence their title Magi, which is an old Persian word for magicians (the Bible, however, never uses this word). In any case, their function was twofold: first to demonstrate the significance of Jesus' birth by their rank and, secondly, indirectly to provide the Holy Family with gold for the soon-to-be-needed flight from Herod's wrath. *Note*: In early tradition, the "three" kings symbolized three races: the white, the black and the yellow—and thus the universality of Christ.

The Slaughter of the Innocents

The wise men did not return to Herod with the news of Jesus' whereabouts, for they were warned away by an angel. Joseph, as well, was told by this angel, in a dream, to "flee into Egypt" (Matthew 2:13) and thus be spared the evil that King Herod was planning. Frustrated that the wise men had not returned and revealed the infant's residence, Herod ordered a general massacre of all newborn male babies in Bethlehem and environs. Like pharaoh slaughtering the Hebrew babes in Moses' time, Herod "slew all the children that were in Bethlehem . . ." (Matthew 2:16), and there was great lamentation and weeping.

The Return

Soon after, Herod the Great, as he was called, died in Jerusalem. Then an angel came to Joseph in Egypt and told him that all was safe and that he should take the child and his mother and return to Judea—but not to Bethlehem; rather to Nazareth, his home.

On the way there, the Holy Family passed through Jerusalem. As was the custom, Mary and Joseph took their baby to the temple to redeem him with an offering (Luke 2:22). In those days, each first-born Hebrew baby boy was symbolically assigned to the priesthood (remember Samuel). But owing to the fact that poor people needed their sons at home to help make a living, the Law allowed the father to "purchase" or redeem back his son by a ritual gift. Joseph, being poor, was able to offer only a pair of turtle doves or pigeons.

While in the temple, Mary and Joseph were approached by a pious old man named Simeon, who perceived the holiness of their child and begged to hold him briefly in his arms. Doing so, he said, "Lord, now lettest thou thy servant depart in peace . . . for mine eyes have seen thy salvation. . ." (Luke 2:29–30). This prayer has become a favorite at Evensong in the Protestant world.

THE CHILDHOOD AND YOUTH OF JESUS

Aside from a few details, the events between Jesus' return to Nazareth with his parents and the onset of his ministry, some thirty years later, are obscure indeed. Except for his appearance at the temple of Jerusalem, when he was twelve years old, we know nothing of his childhood and youth. None of the Gospels says very much, and only Luke tells us of the temple visit.

It was a memorable event, for here the boy Jesus confronted the most learned

Mary and Joseph (right) and the Shepherds (left) are bathed in the light coming from the Christ child in this painting by El Greco.

Gerard David paints a kind of picnic-stop on the Flight into Egypt. Joseph is going after chestnuts; Mary's grapes foreshadow the wine of the Last Supper.

scholars and religious teachers of his day, astonishing them with his command and understanding of the Law (Luke 2:46–48). The episode is important for another fact; here we learn of Jesus' earliest devotion to God and, indeed, we read here the first of his publicly recorded words.

But for Joseph and Mary, the event was problematic. They had come to Jerusalem for the Passover and had lost track of the

Nazareth, the village in Galilee where Jesus learned the carpenter's trade, as it sprawls over the hillside today.

Rembrandt, still in his twenties, spotlights Jesus' presentation in the temple. The artist seizes in one climactic moment old Simeon's fulfillment (Luke 2:29), the priest's blessing and Mary's reverent pride.

Jesus' later visit with "the doctors"—the experts— in the temple also intrigued Rembrandt. This pen-and-brush drawing conveys a remarkable concentration, as well as a rather mature-looking twelve-year-old.

boy in the crowds. After much searching, they found him in the temple with the elders. The mother and father were perturbed; they thought they had lost their son. He in turn was surprised. "How is it that ye sought me?" he asked them. "Wist ye not [did you not know] that I must be about my Father's business?" (Luke 2:49). Jesus, of course, referred to God as his Father. Joseph, the carpenter, was his stepfather; already, at this early age, the boy recognized his holy parentage.

Oddly enough, Mary seemed puzzled at this point. How had one so young as Jesus managed to learn of his miraculous status? This question and many others give us pause when we deal with the so-called lost years of Jesus' biography. Some facts we

may deduce. His health and strength were good and he grew normally (see Luke 2:39–40). He occupied a special place in his parents' home and hearts, hence their eager search for him when they thought him lost. His wisdom and piety were unparalleled, as we infer from his encounter at the temple. In his early teens and twenties, Jesus no doubt learned the carpenter's craft, since it was the custom of the time for a son to be apprenticed to his father. Joseph may have died when Jesus was in his twenties, for we read no more of him after the temple visit, and he is omitted from a listing of Jesus' family given in Mark 6:3. In this verse we learn that Jesus had four brothers and possibly two sisters. No doubt he became the head of household upon Joseph's death, and thus it was necessary for him to hold his peace until the time for his mission was at hand. He led a quiet, hard-working and pious life in the pleasant Galilean hills, where Nazareth nestles. To this day, the small city retains its ancient charm, with narrow streets and open-air shops. Mount Carmel looms over the region; the fields are green, the hills roll northward.

The Baptism and Temptation of Jesus

It was doubtless the reputation of his cousin, John the Baptist, as "the voice of one crying in the wilderness" (Luke 3:4), that first drew Jesus into the public part of his ministry. For years John had preached and warned of doom. For years he had baptized his followers and angered the self-satisfied religious and civic leaders of Judea and Rome, calling them "a generation of vipers" (Matthew 3:7). He spoke constantly of one "mightier than I [who] cometh, the latchet [laces] of whose shoes I am not worthy to unloose . . ." (Luke 3:16).

One day, as John baptized in the Jordan near Jericho, Jesus approached. John seems to have recognized him at once, not only as his cousin from Nazareth but as the Messiah, the "one who cometh." Oddly enough, John forbade him from being baptized on the ground that Jesus was free from sin and had no need of the ritual. But Jesus wished to institute baptism as a mandatory and holy ritual—or sacrament—for all his followers, and so he insisted; "for thus it becometh us to fulfill all righteousness," he said (Matthew 3:15). At the moment of his baptism, the glory of God was made known to those who witnessed the event. As we read in both Matthew (3:17) and Luke (3:21–22), the heavens opened, the Holy Spirit descended in the form of a dove and a voice from heaven was heard saying: "This is my beloved Son, in whom I am well pleased" (see also John 1:32).

There was now no turning back. Jesus, who was about thirty years old, plunged into the work for which he had been born. Into the Judean wilderness he went "to be tempted of the devil" (Matthew 4:1), or, as some scholars believe, to wrestle with all the vanities and doubts that even he, as a man, must have known, for it was necessary that Jesus experience life as any pious man would know it. Despite his exalted mission and miraculous birth, he was not to be spared human anguish and doubt.

The Synoptic Gospels all tell of his encounter with the devil. It lasted forty days and nights, and whether or not we assume that some sort of visible creature called Satan appeared there, or that Jesus faced an inner demon, it nevertheless remains that three grave temptations had to be overcome by this unique young man who slowly but surely was coming to realize his messianic role. First, was he to overwhelm the world with feats of miraculous magic, such as changing stones into bread (Matthew 4:4)? Was he to flaunt the natural order of things by leaping into the air and defying gravity (as Satan proposed—Matthew 4:5–6)? Should he, with a wave of his hand, be master of all the cities of the world and thus, by such trickery, win his followers?

These were the questions that baffled him. He knew that he possessed extraordinary powers and could indeed turn stones

The powerful centrality of Jesus in Piero della Francesca's painting of the Baptism is enhanced by the figure of John the Baptist, in red, and the perfectly immobile dove over Jesus' head.

The story of Jesus enlivens every art form, including films. This picture of the Lord is from Pier Paolo Pasolini's *The Gospel According to St. Matthew*, filmed in southern Italy in 1966.

into bread or into birds for that matter. But drawing upon his vast and faultless knowledge of the Old Testament, he figured out a better way and rejected each temptation.

Because this episode is so critical to what follows in Jesus' ministry, we recommend a careful scrutiny of the triumphant answers Jesus hurled back at his tempter. To the point of making bread by magic, Jesus replied: "Man shall not live by bread alone, but by every word that proceedeth out of the mouth of God" (Matthew 4:4)—a quotation from Deuteronomy 8:3. Scorning magical showmanship as a way to power, Jesus, quoting Deuteronomy 6:16, cried out: "Thou shalt not tempt the Lord thy God." Finally, resisting the glory of kingdoms, for he could have been the mightiest of temporal rulers in all history, Jesus conclusively dismissed Satan, quoting Deuteronomy 6:13: ". . . the Lord thy God, and him only shalt thou serve."

Thus after forty dreadful days and nights of struggle, hunger and doubt, Jesus emerged resolute in his reliance on healing and fulfilling the spiritual truths of the laws of the Old Testament to win his following. This is not to say that Jesus shunned the performance of miracles, as we will see. But these he employed only when it meant helping or satisfying suffering or worthy people. The first such miracle (recorded in John 2:1–11) and the first of his ministry was one undertaken to please his mother. Jesus and Mary were guests at a wedding in Cana, near Nazareth. The supply of wine at the feast soon ran out, threatening to embarrass the hosts, who were close friends of Mary. Though reluctant to resort to his divine powers, Jesus changed ordinary water into wine. Those who witnessed this miracle, including some newfound disciples, henceforth "believed in him" (John 2:11); they were obviously

The tempter, Satan, shows Jesus all the kingdoms of the world, seen in the foreground. But Jesus orders
Satan away, to the joy of the angels on the right, in this gilded miniature by Duccio,
a Sienese artist of the middle ages.

more easily impressed by magic than by ministrations.

The Ministry Begins

Jesus wanted disciples who would be more impressed with his teachings and promise of salvation than with miraculous deeds. Choosing such men demanded great scrutiny and care. Four were called from the fishing stands at the shores of the Galilee: Simon (later called Peter) and his brother, Andrew; James and John, sons of Zebedee. To these fishermen Jesus said: "Follow me, and I will make you fishers of men" (Matthew 4:19).

A tour of preaching and healing followed in the Galilean hills (Jesus wisely stayed away from Jerusalem, where John the Baptist had recently been imprisoned; see Matthew 4:12–13). Although among his own people and despite the fact that he healed incurable lepers and other infirm—including Peter's mother-in-law (Mark 1:30)—Jesus met with indifference, if not scorn, especially in Nazareth. Impious people could not believe that a carpenter's son from their own neighborhood could perfom wondrous deeds or indeed be the long-awaited Messiah. Jesus was philosophical on this as on so many points. "A prophet is not without honor *but* in his own country . . ." he said (Mark 6:4).

After many remarkable incidents of healing, Jesus' fame began to spread, and crowds gathered to be cured and to be saved. The religious leaders of the area, especially the Pharisees, or purists, became alarmed. Often they sent agitators to heckle the young missionary, accusing him of "blasphemies" (Luke 5:21). Jesus patiently explained that the "Son of man hath power upon earth to forgive sins . . ." (Luke 5:24) and to heal. By calling himself the Son of man (and not directly the "Son of God") Jesus displayed his tact and subtlety, for if man is made in the image of God, as Genesis reported, then all men are sons of God who are sons of man. Jesus,

An anonymous 15th-century Spanish painter portrays the moment at the Marriage at Cana when Jesus transforms the water into wine, much to the delight of his mother, by his side.

Jesus' first two disciples, Peter and Andrew, were fishermen, who cast their nets over the waters of Lake Galilee just as nets are still cast today.

however, was *the* Son—with a capital S—and he let this be known only to those who could understand.

More disciples were called during this Galilean ministry: Matthew, an innkeeper and tax collector (Matthew 9:9), and then Philip and Bartholomew; Thomas, James, son of Alpheus and Thaddeus (also called Lebbeus); Simon the Canaanite (or Zealot) and Judas Iscariot, "who also betrayed him" (Matthew 10:3). These, plus the aforementioned, were the twelve disciples (or learners), sometimes called apostles

(from the Greek, *apostolos*: one who is sent out), called to "preach, and to have power to heal sicknesses, and to cast out devils" (Mark 3:15).

With growing fame and a group of worthy followers to aid in his task, Jesus now prepared to deliver what might be called the sum total of his principles and beliefs. He climbed a mount—possibly the one between Magdala and Tiberias near the Sea of Galilee—and there, drawing on Old Testament teachings and on his own exalted insights, he delivered what is called

Tiny squares of colored stone were used in the Byzantine church of Sant'Apollinare Nuovo in Ravenna, Italy, to make up this mosaic of Jesus healing the paralytic, who obediently takes up his bed and walks.

the Sermon on the Mount—a prerequisite reading for all who wish to explore the essence of the New Testament.

The Sermon on the Mount

To begin with, one should read aloud the Beatitudes, or Blessings, best presented in Matthew 5:1–12 (see also Luke 6:20–23). No condensation or paraphrasing suffices for these. They must be read per se. A guide, however, is offered here.

From the Beatitudes we learn that God favors those who strive for personal insight and justification (the poor in spirit, mourners, the meek; those who hunger and thirst for righteousness); those who care about others (the merciful, the pure, the peacemakers, the martyrs). In short, Jesus exalts the lowly, what he calls "the salt of the earth . . ." (Matthew 5:13), those trodden underfoot by life and circumstance, who even so will not be discouraged or lose their God-given light. "Ye are the light of the world" (Matthew

5:14), he announces, the light which many equate with soulful and reverent dignity.

The Sermon on the Mount establishes many powerful points, as we read in Matthew 5, 6 and 7. Here is but a mere outline of them:

Jesus comes not "to destroy the law [Torah], or the prophets . . . but to fulfill [them]" (Matthew 5:17). He urges peacefulness and containment of anger; chastity is exalted; divorce deplored (Matthew 5:32); vain oaths forbidden; the age-old laws of retaliation— "eye for an eye and a tooth for a tooth"—are not abrogated, but a new dimension in forbearance is preached. If you are provoked by someone, says Jesus, and he strikes you across the cheek, "turn to him the other [cheek] also," implying count ten before taking a similar violent course. Be cautious, prudent, above all "love thy neighbor . . . and love your enemies, bless them that curse you, do good to them that hate you . . ." (Matthew 5:43–44). This essential philosophy of Christianity is not offered by Jesus as a "cop-out" or feeble submission to persecution and evil. Carefully understood and read in full, this resounding verse teaches that even our enemies are creatures of God; even evildoers and tyrants are the "children of your Father which is in heaven, for he maketh his sun to rise on the evil and [also] on the good . . ." (Matthew 5:45). We must always and forever resist evildoers, seek to change them, punish them for their proven crimes, but at the same time we must do so lovingly, helpfully, compassionately. A hateful madman like Hitler, who ordered millions of innocents to their deaths in World War II and laid waste most of Europe, cannot be exonerated by men. That is God's task if he chooses it. But even in the throes of our shock and bitterness about such an evildoer, we must see him as part of God's unknowable plan. Loving such an enemy does not mean embracing him, utterly forgiving him or allowing him to run amok. It means comprehending that he is but a man like us, part of our world—for good or ill as God sees fit. It is not our task, according to this Sermon, to be the ultimate judge, but rather to be "perfect, even as your Father which is in heaven is perfect" (Matthew 5:48). Few can be perfect. We must not hate people for this failure but seek always to perfect them (and ourselves). A hard lesson this is, but a challenging one for grownup and child alike.

Jesus further teaches: to give alms without hypocrisy or ulterior motives; not to make a show of religion but to pray sincerely, simply, without "vain repetitions. . . ." Accordingly, Jesus offers a prayer to suffice all needs. It can be found in Matthew 6:9–13. One should go immediately to his Bible and read this section aloud. It is perhaps the central prayer of Christianity and unequaled in poetic beauty and sentiment. It explains itself. No wonder it is known and loved universally as the Lord's Prayer (Paternoster).

The remainder of the Sermon is no less compelling. Jesus warns of greed, hoarding and selfishness. "Judge not, that ye be not judged," he preaches (Matthew 7:1). "Neither cast ye your pearls before swine . . ." meaning, be sensible in preaching, in talk, in what you hope for others. There are false prophets to be sure, those who come like wolves in "sheep's clothing" (Matthew 7:15). They preach vanity which rots like evil fruit, therefore "by their fruits ye shall know them" (Matthew 7:20).

In short, Jesus reiterates what is commonly known as the Golden Rule, the essence, so he says, of the Torah and the prophets: "All things whatsoever ye would that men should do to you, do ye even so to them" (Matthew 7:12; see also Luke 6:31). In the Old Testament we may read: "Love thy neighbor as thyself" (Leviticus 19:18). In the Apocrypha: "Do to no man [that] which thou hatest" (Tobit 4:15). Jesus knew both sources and rendered them conclusively in his immortal Sermon on the Mount. So powerful were his words that when he finished "the people were astonished at his doctrine . . ." (Matthew 7:28).

Miracles and Events in Galilee

After his powerful sermon, Jesus undertook a tour of preaching and curing in the hill country of Galilee. Several significant events occurred that enhanced his growing reputation as a prophet and healer. At Capernaum by the sea, near the site of a famous synagogue, a Roman centurion, or a commander, was converted by Jesus and thus became the first non-Jew (or Gentile) to embrace the ideas of Christ (Luke 7:1–10). At Nain, nearby, Jesus raised the dead son of a poor widow; this is one of three resurrections Jesus performed. The others: the daughter of Jairus (Mark 5:35–43) and Lazarus (John 11:1–46), which we will later explore. Though these resurrections were surely wondrous events, they could not compare to the Resurrection of Jesus himself. Only Jesus, of all those raised, would remain alive forever after. The others were given only a brief respite from death, being mortal as they were.

For all his nobility of spirit and miraculous cures, Jesus was not accepted in Nazareth, his own home village. Possibly certain people there were annoyed by the fact that Jesus mingled so freely with the poor, downtrodden masses, with social outcasts, tax collectors and even merchants of less than noble standing. To these, and to everyone, his message was clear: "Come unto me, all ye that labour and are heavy laden, and I will give you rest" (Matthew 11:28).

One of the most prominent outcasts that Jesus befriended was Mary Magdalene (of Magdala), a woman of easy virtue who may have been the faithless wife referred to in John 8:3, the so-called Woman taken in Adultery. When Jesus first saw this woman, she was at the mercy of a mob who wished to stone her to death in accordance with the laws of the time. Knowing Jesus to be a prominent preacher and an exponent of the Law, they approached him with the woman in hand. Hoping to ensnare him, they asked: "What sayest thou [about her punishment]?" Had Jesus ordered her stoned, the instigators could have pointed to his lack of mercy and strict adherence to the Law (as though he were a Pharisee). Had Jesus suggested that the sinful woman be released, his accusers would have denounced him as a radical and blasphemer. What could Jesus do to avoid either extreme?

He thought for a moment, then said: "He that is without sin among you, let him first cast a stone at her" (John 8:7). Since no man there was haughty enough (or brave enough) to consider himself without sin, no man could cast a stone and each, one by one, conscience-stricken, left the scene. When Jesus was alone with the woman, he exonerated her, exhorting her to "sin no more" (John 8:11).

Some time later, while dining with one of the Pharisees (for Jesus had friends in every quarter), this same sinful woman,

Jesus preached at Capernaum in a synagogue which probably stood on the same site as this later one.

now purified and devout, came to Jesus with perfumes and ointments and, as was the custom of the time, anointed his feet. Many of the guests were shocked that Jesus could allow a fallen woman to act so intimately—despite her obvious humility, for she wept as she held her Master's feet, and when her tears fell on them she then proceeded "to wipe them with the hairs of her head" (Luke 7:38).

Jesus related a short parable—a homespun example—in order to explain his affection for the sinful woman. Two men owed money to a third, he said. The third man generously forgave both debts. Which of the two men was most grateful?

asked Jesus. Naturally, the one who had owed the greater debt. Thus it is that the sinful woman, having much to be forgiven, will be the more pious once her sins are expiated. Jesus always sought out the sinner; what good is it to cure the healthy? he once asked. "For I am not come to call the righteous, but sinners to repentance" (Matthew 9:13).

Some Parables

Telling parables was perhaps Jesus' most persuasive and popular means of preaching and teaching, since parables enabled him to simplify what he called "the mysteries of the kingdom of heaven" (Matthew 13:11). Jesus relates nearly fifty parables, or metaphor lessons, in the four Gospels. The most prominent are these:

The Parable of the Sower (Matthew 13:1–23). A sower flings seeds in all directions. Only those that fall on fertile ground take root. So it is with God's word; some people will miss the point entirely. Others, like the fertile ground, will receive the message and Godliness will grow.

Parables of the Kingdom. (There were seven parables on the theme of the Kingdom of Heaven.) Jesus always referred to a spiritual kingdom, not a political one. Even so, his enemies and even Judas Iscariot, his disciple, chose to believe that he preached political rebellion for the purpose of establishing himself as an earthly king. "The kingdom of heaven," said Jesus, "is like to a grain of mustard seed, which a man took, and sowed in his field: Which

Rembrandt "stages" his *Woman Taken in Adultery* in the foreground, where Jesus dominates. Beyond, the cavernous high altar bustles with ritual.

indeed is the least of all seeds: but when it is grown, it is the greatest [or strongest-tasting] among herbs, and becometh a tree, so that the birds of the air come and lodge in the branches thereof" (Matthew 13:31–32).

The Good Samaritan (Luke 10:25–37). A man "fell among thieves," was beaten, robbed and left to die. Three people passed by—a temple priest, a Levite and a man from Samaria. The first two ignored their brother's agony and "passed by on the other side." But the Samaritan rushed to the victim's aid, brought him to an inn where he might recover and paid his expenses there. Jesus told this story to establish the fact that our neighbors need not be those who live close by but anyone who shows mercy, even if he is a stranger and of another religion or race.

The Foolish Rich Man (Luke 12:13–21). A fortunate farmer was blessed by abundant crops. When he felt that he had laid up enough of them, he decided to take his ease, "eat, drink, and be merry," with no thought of God. But that very night his soul was called and all his wealth availed him nought.

The Pharisee's Table (Luke 14:7–11). Those who seek out prominent places at banquets or in life shall end up the least exalted in heaven. But "he that humbleth himself shall be exalted"—meaning, those who recognize their debts to God will be rewarded.

Three Lost Items. Jesus often reused a given theme to emphasize his point. A shepherd lost one sheep (Luke 15:3–7), a woman lost a single coin (Luke 15:8–10) and a father lost his son to revelry and dishonor (Luke 15:11–32). Each person persevered to regain that which was lost, for as Jesus said, "there is joy in the presence of the angels of God over one sinner that repenteth."

The Lost Son story is better known as the Parable of the Prodigal Son, a touching segment that should be read in its entirety. The son of a wealthy landowner flees to a big city where revelry becomes his occupation. Finally, dissipated and impoverished, the prodigal son returns home. The father is overjoyed and orders a feast. But an elder brother is angered. He who stayed home, tilled the fields and was righteous never was greeted with such joy or festivity. "Is that fair?" he asks. The father answers tenderly: "Son, thou art ever with me, and all that I have is thine. It was meet [appropriate] that we should make merry, and be glad: for this thy brother was dead, and is alive again; and was lost, and is found." Note how many times Jesus repeats this theme: The rescue of one sinner is the greatest joy and achievement.

Rembrandt's almost "impressionistic" drawing captures the pomposity of many Pharisees, such as the one in Luke 18:9-14.

The forbidding landscape between Jericho and Jerusalem (in the distance), the scene of the parable of the Good Samaritan.

The Cunning Steward (Luke 16:1–12). A steward, or household manager, fearing dismissal and poverty, hurriedly and somewhat dishonestly collects his master's debts and skims off a commission from each. This he does to protect his future, and Jesus commends this foresight. A sober attitude toward money is acceptable, since, as Jesus says in this parable, "If therefore ye have not been faithful in the unrighteous mammon, who will commit to your trust the true riches?" Mammon is a word meaning "wealth" or "gain." Thus we may paraphrase the above to say: Those who cannot handle difficult and possibly corruptive things like money cannot be expected to handle the glory of heaven.

Those who allow themselves unnecessarily to be impoverished become a burden to others and have no time for devotion, prayer or the search for salvation. Even so, the love of mammon must never dominate life, as the next parables reveal.

The Rich Man and Lazarus (Luke 16:19–31). A beggar called Lazarus, too ill to work, sought food from a rich man and begged even for "the crumbs which fell from the rich man's table." But he was chased from the premises. Lazarus finally died and was received into "Abraham's bosom" (into the peace of heaven). Soon after, the rich man also died—but his soul lay far from Abraham near the pit of hell.

So intense was the rich man's thirst that he begged Lazarus to but dip his finger in water to "cool my tongue." The gap between the two men, however, was so wide that it could not be bridged. Repentant over his greed in life, the rich man now begged only the chance to warn his brothers, also steeped in mammon, to avoid his fate. Abraham advised him, "They have Moses [the Law] and the prophets; let them hear them." Agonized, the rich man urged that someone be sent from the dead to warn his brothers. Abraham still refused and spoke prophetically (or rather Jesus spoke prophetically in relating this story). "If they hear not Moses and the prophets, neither will they be persuaded, though one rose from the dead." In short, even Christ Risen cannot persuade those who have no faith in the Law of God.

The Pharisee and the Publican (Luke 18:9–14). The same theme is offered by contrasting the artificial piety of a rich and haughty Pharisee, who thanks God that "I am not as other men," and a commonplace publican, or bureaucrat, who cries, "God be merciful to me a sinner." Jesus is far more impressed with the publican's humility than with the Pharisee's false show of pride.

The Wedding Feast (Matthew 22:1–14). An elaborate wedding feast was arranged by a king for his son, and servants were sent to gather the guests. But none would come. Dire results followed, including many deaths. Finally, the king sent his ser-

vants beyond the town to gather all those who were available, "both bad and good." A large number of people responded, some properly dressed, others improperly dressed. The latter were expelled from the feast with much "weeping and gnashing of teeth." Jesus relates the feast to heaven; to it "many are called, but few are chosen."

The Wise and Foolish Virgins (Matthew 25:1–13). Another wedding feast is used as the focus of a similar parable about spiritual responsibilities. In this one, a group of virgins, or bridesmaids, bored at waiting for the bridal procession, nod off to sleep and are not ready to light their lamps when the bridegroom arrives. Another group of maidens is fully prepared and joins the party, leaving the others behind. Jesus compares himself to the bridegroom (as he often does). When he arrives, all must be ready, alert, their lamps trimmed and blazing.

GROWING ANTAGONISM TO JESUS

It is one of the more poignant and puzzling parts of Jesus' story that his reverent and uplifting message was greeted in part by hatred and scorn. The Pharisees, temple priests, many merchants and those he called a "generation of vipers" (Matthew 12:34) resisted his words and spread malicious statements about him, even accusing him of being an ally of Satan (Matthew 12:25). "How can Satan cast out Satan?" Jesus asked as he cured a blind and dumb man in Galilee. "And if a house be divided against itself, that house cannot stand" (Mark 3:25).

Wherever Jesus went, wherever he healed and preached, antagonists rose up to heckle him. But he always responded logically and effectively. For example, hoping to ensnare Jesus on a charge of disloyalty to

With unsurpassed eloquence Rembrandt pictures the Prodigal Son's instant of homecoming (notice the slipped sandal). He is in rags, with head shaven, in strong contrast to his prosperous brother at the right.

The parable of the unforgiving servant (see Matthew 18:23-35) has just floored its actors in the original off-Broadway company of *Godspell*. Adapted from Matthew's gospel by John Tebelak, with songs by Stephen Schwartz, *Godspell* was a modern-day mystery play with a rock beat.

the Roman government, some of the Pharisees approached him in public and asked, "Is it lawful to give tribute to Caesar, or not?" (Mark 12:14). Jesus knew their hypocrisy and asked to be shown a coin. On this coin were the face and motto of Caesar, the emperor. Jesus was not worried. "Render to Caesar the things that are Caesar's, and to God the things that are God's," he said (Mark 12:17), meaning, since taxes or tribute are an earthly requirement ordered by an earthly govern-

ment, men must obey. But this in no way conflicts with obedience to God.

Among the miracles Jesus performed at this time were the healing of the Gadarene demoniac (Mark 5:1–20), a hopelessly bedeviled man who lived like an animal in the mountains. Jesus calmed him by exorcising the demons who possessed him and sending them to their deaths in the bodies of swine. He also raised the daughter of Jairus, a high temple official (beginning Mark 5:21), stilled a violent storm at sea and then walked upon the waters (Luke 8:22 and Matthew 14:25).

Blind and dumb people were given sight and speech by his hand, and before long thousands sought him and mobbed him in the streets, seeking help and cure. Of these poor, unhappy people Jesus could only say they were "as sheep having no shepherd" (Matthew 9:36). Because this fact concerned him deeply, he began to organize his disciples so that they might become shepherds (the Latin is *pastors*) and guide those who sought salvation. Even the disciples were to be as sheep. "I send you forth as sheep in the midst of wolves," he said (Matthew 10:16). "Heal the sick, cleanse the lepers, raise the dead, cast out devils: freely ye have received, freely give . . ." (Matthew 10:8). To all corners of the Holy Land the disciples went preaching his message. Jesus knew well in advance why he needed these disciples. He knew his own mission would soon be cut short. This ominous truth was brought home with shocking force when the news came that John the Baptist had been beheaded on the orders of King Herod Antipas, son of the former Herod (Mark 6:21–29).

"Thou Art the Christ"

Cautiously, but yet bold in their mission, the disciples continued to preach.

We seem to be standing with Jesus (left) in Tintoretto's view of him walking lightly on Lake Galilee, while Peter starts toward him from the boat.

Five thousand people gathered one day to hear the master, and when he had spoken he saw that the people were hungry, since they were far from home and their tables. Jesus knew that he had to feed them bodily as well as spiritually. Taking five loaves of barley bread and two small fishes, Jesus, before the multitude, multiplied the bread and the fishes so that every one of the five thousand followers could be fed. So impressed were the people with this astounding event that they clamored to make Jesus their king (John 6:15). This dangerous idea unnecessarily gave a political flavor to Jesus' spiritual mission.

The Pharisees and other enemies of Jesus hit upon this political factor as a sword with which to strike Jesus. Furthermore, they continuously disputed him on petty matters of law. Jesus always answered his foes and unflinchingly continued to heal and preach all along the coast of the land and toward Jerusalem, where his destiny drew him. Everywhere he warned of the "signs of the times" (Matthew 16:3), the coming kingdom and the messianic age. Astonishing miracles, such as the cure of the blind man of Bethsaida (Mark 8:22–26), increased his fame with those that loved him but deepened the antagonism of his enemies.

Did Jesus begin to wonder if men knew who he was? One day, in this vein, he asked his disciples "Whom do men say that

293

I the Son of man, am?" (Matthew 16:13). Only Peter was bold enough to announce: "Thou art the Christ, the Son of the living God" (Matthew 16:16).

So moved was Jesus by Peter's understanding that he laid upon Peter the leadership of the disciples when the time would come for his own departure. "Upon this rock [Peter in Latin is a derivative of "rock"], I will build my church; and the gates of hell shall not prevail against it" (Matthew 16:18). Thus it is that all the Roman Catholic popes consider themselves descendants of Peter, and indeed all Christian clergymen regard themselves as spiritual heirs of Peter and the other apostles, fulfilling Jesus' plan to build a church—or rather a community of believers—based not on Peter's authority as a person but upon the truth that he announced: "Thou art the Christ."

Jesus Prepares for His Passion (Transfiguration)

Keeping to himself the facts of his impending death, Jesus moved on toward Jerusalem with his followers. Everywhere, he urged the faithful to "take up [the] cross, and follow me . . ." meaning, take upon yourself the burden of personal salvation, "for what shall it profit a man, if he shall gain the whole world, and lose his own soul?" (Mark 8:36).

One night Jesus went up to the mountains to pray, leaving Peter, James and John on guard to watch, for by now the enemies of Jesus sought to catch him and arrest him at every turn. They feared a public uprising should they do so while he preached, therefore they watched him cautiously.

While the three disciples waited, Jesus prayed, and in the midst of his contempla-

tion there appeared to him Moses and Elias (or Elijah), warning him of his coming death. At the same time, the two great Hebrew sages of the past welcomed Jesus to their company, and he was transfigured with glory so that his followers were awed. Once again, at this epochal moment the voice of God was heard exclaiming: "This is my beloved Son, in whom I am well pleased; hear ye him" (Matthew 17:5).

Though transfigured and now touched by immortality, Jesus still wished that his divine nature be undisclosed. "Tell the vision to no man, until the Son of man be risen again from the dead," he told his disciples (Matthew 17:9). Then he spoke of forthcoming passion and glorious suffering.

Undaunted by what was to come, Jesus went on healing and preaching. He cured an epileptic boy; he blessed the little children; he warned of temptation and preached about forgiveness and the great value of mercy. Then he continued toward his last days in Jerusalem. Instructions to his disciples were given wherever possible, and to them he confided more and more of his divine and special nature. "All things are delivered to me of my Father," he said, "and no man knoweth who the Son is, but the Father; and who the Father is, but the Son, and he to whom the Son will reveal him" (Luke 10:22).

While preaching of mercy and goodness, Jesus never ceased to warn against hypocrisy and vice. "Woe unto you, Lawyers!" (Luke 11:52), he cried to the insensitive officials of the cities. "Except ye repent, ye shall all likewise perish" (Luke 13:5). He was especially angered when the Pharisees and others tried to interfere with his healing missions by haggling over fine points of law. They feared his growing

This is the upper half of Raphael's last painting, in which the disciples, roused from sleep, shade their eyes against the brightness as Jesus talks with Moses (left) and Elijah.

reputation and greatness. When a well-known blind man—a man born blind—was miraculously given sight by Jesus, they grew more anxious and fearful (see John 9:1–41). Then at Bethany, Jesus astonished the world. There he came to visit his dear friend Lazarus. But Lazarus had died (this Jesus knew). Martha and Mary, the sisters of Lazarus and devout followers of Jesus, were in deep mourning. They agonized that Jesus had not come earlier and saved their brother from death. Now it was too late; Lazarus was dead already four days—and buried.

Jesus had purposely waited for these things to happen. Standing at the tomb of Lazarus with Martha and Mary, plus many other neighbors and friends, Jesus called forth Lazarus and the dead man rose up, alive again at Jesus' behest. The news of this resurrection quickly spread to Jerusalem and further intensified plots to

capture Jesus and destroy him. Also known was the promise Jesus had spoken at Lazarus' tomb, the promise that forms the very basis of Christianity, for Jesus said as he prepared to raise Lazarus: "I am the resurrection, and the life: he that believeth in me, though he were dead, yet shall he live: And whosoever liveth and believeth in me shall never die" (John 11:25–26).

By these words, and his subsequent deed, Jesus gave hope that even death—the relentless enemy of man—would one day be conquered by faith in God and by decent conduct in life, such as faith inspires.

Bethany was but a short journey from the great and bustling city of Jerusalem where Jesus knew he would die. Fearlessly he moved onward; his death was part of God's great plan for human salvation, and though the idea of death disturbed him as a man, the knowledge of his divine role inspired his actions. He knew that in "the

third day [after death] he shall rise again" (Mark 10:34) as incontrovertible proof of his divinity and God's plan.

Jesus in Jerusalem

Jesus' initial entry into Jerusalem was on a Sunday (subsequently called Palm Sunday), during the week of the Passover celebration. His fame by now was so great that "the whole multitude of the disciples began to rejoice and praise God . . ." (Luke 19:37) when he appeared riding a simple white colt. So deep-felt were the people's emotions that they clamored to demonstrate their love of God. Tearing palms from the trees and spreading their garments on the path, they exulted with cries of "Hosanna to the Son of David . . . Hosanna in the highest" (Matthew 21:9). Hosanna means "God Most High!"

Though glad for this outpouring of the people's love, Jesus also lamented in his heart because he knew that one day Jerusalem, the great city of the Jews, would fall to heathen conquest. Even as he rode triumphantly through the streets his anguish was apparent; the Pharisees shouted at him to restrain his followers in their exuberance. He answered as always, in kind: "I tell you that if these [people] should hold their peace, the stones [of the street] would immediately cry out" (Luke 19:40).

From his glorious procession, Jesus went directly to the temple. There he found a situation that deeply angered him. Merchants had set up their stalls within the temple grounds on the pretense of changing money. As noted, it was the custom in

In this painting by Benozzo Gozzoli, Lazarus' winding sheet has not yet been removed as Jesus and his disciples call him forth. Lazarus' sisters kneel at lower left.

Jesus triumphantly enters Jerusalem as the citizens wave their palms and spread their cloaks before him in Albrecht Dürer's sharp and contrast-filled woodcut.

those days to offer doves or pigeons as sacrifice at the altar. In order to buy these birds, one had to use special "temple coins" free of the pagan image of Caesar, who was, after all, considered a god by his followers. These imperial coins, which were the legal tender of Judea, were exchanged for others, and the moneychangers handled the transaction. Apparently, by now, owing to the corruption of the times, the moneychangers were charging a fee for their service. Those who sold the doves

In a rare burst of anger, Jesus drives the moneychangers from the temple, using a knotted rope. While the disciples watch with others in El Greco's painting, the vendors shrink back and flee.

This coin, struck around 135 A.D., was probably used as temple currency. It depicts the four-columned façade of Herod's temple.

were also probably turning a profit. Jesus wanted them all excluded from the sacred place. "My house," he cried, "shall be called the house of prayer; but ye have made it a den of thieves" (Matthew 21:13).

So great was Jesus' anger that he forcibly overturned the moneychangers' booths and set upon them with a whip of cords. This the priests and power brokers watched with bitterness, and their plans to capture the radical missionary were intensified.

The final week of Jesus' life was crowded with incident and with preaching. One night, returning to Bethany, as he did after each day's visit to the holy city, Jesus saw a fig tree that was bare. He pointed to this tree as an example of those who are unprepared for the Lord when he comes, and he cursed it so that it withered. By this act Jesus wanted to show how a man may wither without faith. Faith is all; "what things soever ye desire, when ye pray, believe that ye receive them, and ye shall have them . . ." he stated (Mark 11:24).

Jerusalem teemed with pilgrims and worshipers come for the Passover. Roman soldiers were on guard everywhere. The common people thronged the streets. At every turn Jesus preached his message, and at every turn the Pharisees and religious officials dogged his heels, hoping to ensnare him. Yet they were ever fearful of arresting him in public and causing a riot among his followers.

Tension mounted as Jesus, full well knowing his fate, scorned his enemies publicly: "Woe unto you, ye blind guides," he cried (Matthew 23:16), and they answered with threats of death—"For Herod will kill thee" (Luke 13:31).

Patiently to his followers Jesus described the coming kingdom of God as a fulfillment of the Hebrew prophets. He warned of false messiahs and urged the faithful to "watch and pray" (Mark 13:33). A time will come, he told them, when Jesus, at the right hand of God, shall take in all who hunger and thirst for righteousness and those who seek salvation. His message was clear: "Come, ye blessed of my Father, inherit the kingdom prepared for you . . ." (Matthew 25:34).

The Final Hours

There now follows a guide to the last earthly hours of Jesus the man. Nothing, of course, parallels reading the Gospels for the drama and power of this story. A guide can only direct; it cannot replace the original. The events that followed Jesus' sermon in the temple, which we quoted above, are these:

The Plot—The enemies of Jesus, seeking a way to capture him in seclusion, enlisted the services of Judas Iscariot, a misguided disciple who had counted on Jesus to lead a political rebellion against Rome. When he realized that Jesus spoke only of heavenly thrones and not of earthly power, Judas turned traitor. For thirty pieces of silver (about fifty dollars) he agreed to lead the authorities to Jesus' secret place of prayer (Matthew 26:1–16).

The Last Supper—The first Seder, or feast of Passover, at this time took place on a Thursday night. Jesus gathered his disciples in a humble room on Mount Zion for what was to be their last supper together. (According to the Gospel of John, this meal took place on the night before the Seder.)

Judas Iscariot was at this feast. Jesus knew what was to come but said nothing directly. First, as a sign of his humility, he bathed the feet of each disciple—for this was a custom before a feast. Then seated at the table, he announced: "One of you shall betray me" (John 13:21). The disciples were horrified, but only Judas Iscariot shrunk in fear. Unfortunately, his fear did not hold him back from his crime, and when he saw a chance he slipped away from the table on the pretense of buying provisions (for Judas was the treasurer of the group). Jesus allowed him to leave. When he was gone, the master rose and with great simplicity instituted the ritual known throughout Christianity as the Lord's Supper, the Communion, a symbolic feast that would enable every faithful Christian to share in the final hours of Christ by partaking of bread (or a wafer), of which Jesus said: "This is my body" and of wine, of which he said: "This is my blood of the New Testament, which is shed for many" in the remission of sins— (Mark 14:22–25).

Jesus then uttered what he called a new commandment, "that ye love one another,

as I have loved you." He added prophetically: "Greater love hath no man than this, that a man lay down his life for his friends" (John 15:12–13).

After the feast and the Communion ceremony, the disciples sang a hymn and retired with Jesus to the Mount of Olives, his favorite place of prayer. Peter, who went with them, was deeply troubled because Jesus had predicted that three times before the cock crowed at sunrise Peter would deny knowing Jesus.

The Agony in the Garden—At a small garden enclave on the mount, a place called Gethsemane, Jesus secluded himself to pray, hoping his disciples would watch against danger (but instead they slept, for it was night). Jesus prayed so intently that a great agony came over him. As a man he suffered the fears of all men. If death could

Jesus presided over a Passover supper in a house located on the site where the Cenacle Church stands today, with its own vaulted upper room. "Cenacle" means a sort of supper.

Leonardo da Vinci's masterpiece has been ravaged not only by time and exposure but also by the artist's own experimentation with materials. It depicts the moment immediately after Jesus has announced, "One

of you shall betray me.'' Each disciple is distraught and confused by these words. But Judas, in blue with his elbow on the table (left center), knows well what Jesus means.

El Greco's kneeling form of Jesus looks sadly at the Cup of Sorrow offered by the Angel. On the road at the right, the soldiers are coming. Three disciples sleep in a cave, oblivious to the dramatic scene.

pass him by, he would wish it so. But if God chose otherwise, he would obey. It is not "what I will, but what thou wilt," he said (Mark 14:36). Twice he prayed in this fashion, so profoundly that bloodlike sweat dropped from his brow.

While still in prayer he was approached by Judas Iscariot, stealthily leading a band of soldiers. The signal Judas had arranged was ironic. He would kiss the man he was to betray. Unashamedly, he went up to Jesus and kissed him. ". . . Betrayest thou the Son of man with a kiss?" said Jesus knowingly (Luke 22:48). Before a minute

more had passed, the guards, alerted by this signal, had swooped down on him.

Hearing the tumult, the disciples rushed to Jesus' side, one of them with a sword drawn. Jesus was appalled: "Put up again thy sword into his place," he cried, "for all they that take the sword shall perish with the sword" (Matthew 26:52). His captors, of course, heeded him not and moved in with spears and staves. A violent fracas followed and, true to Jesus' fears, many of the disciples "forsook him, and fled" (Matthew 26:56).

Before the High Priest—Jesus was now

brought, bound, to the high priest of the temple, Caiaphas, a powerful arbiter of religious law. This man heard Jesus and concluded that he was a blasphemer, deserving death. Meanwhile, outside in the early dawn, Peter waited for news. Someone caught sight of him and asked if he were not a friend and disciple of the captured Jesus. "I do not know the man," Peter replied (Matthew 26:72). Three times he made this timid denial and then the cock crowed. Peter remembered Jesus' prediction, and he went out "and wept bitterly" (Luke 22:62). Even Peter, the Rock, was frightened to the point of cowardice.

Judas, the betrayer, fearful when he realized that he had put Jesus in the way of death, hurriedly returned the thirty pieces of silver to the priests, who scorned it and set the money aside to buy a graveyard for the poor—a so-called "potter's field" (see Matthew 27:6–9). Judas in his turn rushed away and hanged himself (Matthew 27:5).

Before Pontius Pilate—Because the religious court in Judea had no power to execute those it had condemned, it was now necessary for Caiaphas and his group to turn Jesus over to a civil authority—in this case to the court of Pontius Pilate, the Roman governor of Judea and the most powerful man in the land. Pilate was only concerned with infringements of political

Another modern version of the Last Supper is this scene from the film *The Gospel According to St. Matthew*, directed by Pier Paolo Pasolini.

Jesus is almost smothered in Judas' signaling embrace, as a disciple (left) slashes a soldier's ear. Giotto's account of the taking of Christ is one of the earliest paintings to show such dramatic force.

or legal ordinances and was scornful of Jewish religious law. But by convincing Pilate that Jesus wished to make himself an actual king, by actual rebellion, the priests finally excited Pilate's interest. When he bluntly asked Jesus: "Art thou the King of the Jews?" Jesus responded in effect by saying "Yes"—meaning: Yes, as a heavenly king, for "my kingdom is not of this world

. . ." (John 18:36; see also Mark 15:2–5).

Before King Herod—Pilate was at first confused. But believing Jesus to be a mere religious fanatic, he dismissed the case. The religious leaders, however, pressed the issue until Pilate decided to pass the captive over to Herod Antipas, who was the puppet king of Judea with jurisdiction in Galilee, where Jesus had lived as a boy.

Herod was in Jerusalem at the time and was deeply flattered by Pilate's deference to him. His questioning of Jesus consisted of mockery and banalities. Nothing came of it at all, except that Jesus was returned to Pilate dressed in a tattered regal robe, which Herod placed on him in order to ridicule his claims of kingship (Luke 23:5–11).

The Final Trial and Sentencing—Now follows a tense and difficult part of the story in which various forces contend and argue regarding Jesus' fate. Who precisely was to blame for his death is often obscured by the infighting that the Gospels varyingly depict. Ultimately, Pilate, as supreme governor of Judea, had to authorize the death sentence. At the same time, the high priest and certain other religious leaders clearly clamored for Jesus' death, since they feared his popularity with the people. The people themselves, the everyday Jews of Judea, had formed the multitudes that had greeted him with palms and Hosannas only a few days before. It was not the people but rather a clique of antagonists—the religious establishment—that called for Jesus' death and urged Pilate to release a common murderer named Barabbas in accordance with an amnesty custom of the time (Mark 15:6–9). Pilate indicated that he was innocent of Jesus' blood, though he is earlier accused of bloody actions by Luke (13:1). He even washed his hands in public as a symbolic act of this innocence. Nevertheless, hoping to satisfy the priests, Pilate ordered Jesus whipped, spat upon and in mockery crowned with a wreath of thorns (Mark 15:17–19).

According to the Gospels, Pilate seemed earnestly unwilling to take the prisoner's life. Was it because his wife, fearful of an

The olive trees growing on these lower slopes of the Mount of Olives, not far from the Garden of Gethsemane, are probably offshoots of those which Jesus may have known.

ominous dream, had appealed to him for mercy? (Matthew 27:19) Was Pilate's wavering the result of his confusion about religious law? Only when Jesus' enemies threatened to report his indecision to Caesar did he relent. They warned: "If thou let this man go, thou art not Caesar's friend: Whosoever maketh himself a king speaketh against Caesar" (John 19:12). This argument convinced Pilate at last to authorize the execution.

Why Jesus Died—The "people" referred to as those clamoring for Jesus' death and instigating Pilate clearly represent not the entire population of Judea but rather a mob of malcontents assembled by the priests.

For their part, the priests believed Jesus to be a false Messiah, despite the reports of his miracles and integrity. And they apparently acted out of fear more than hatred. Herod could not have cared less, and the Romans, Galileans and even the henchmen of the priests who whipped, taunted, spat upon and mocked the captive Jesus were acting as any unruly mob whose passions have been inflamed.

Jesus himself forgave them all (Luke 23:34). But more to the point, the crucifixion of Christ was inevitable and necessary for the truly central event of Christian theology: the Resurrection that was to follow. Jesus himself announced this fact clearly in Mark 10:33–34. "Behold, we go up to Jerusalem," he said, "and the Son of man shall be delivered unto the chief priests, and unto the scribes; and they shall condemn him to death, and shall deliver him to the gentiles [Romans]: and they shall mock him, and shall scourge him: and shall spit upon him, and shall kill him; and the third day he shall rise again" (see also Matthew 16:21, Mark 9:31–32, Luke 18:31–33 and John 13:21 for similar ideas).

Thus we must conclude that the manner, cause and responsibility for Jesus' death, no matter how tragic and shameful, are incidental to his own prediction that he would inevitably suffer and die in order to rise again and thus verify his role as Saviour and Lord.

The Crucifixion—The dark hour is at hand. Bound, bleeding and abused, Jesus of Nazareth is led by Roman soldiers through the narrow streets of Jerusalem to a hill called Golgotha: "the place of a skull" (Mark 15:22). Upon his back, as was the custom, he bears the upper beam of the T-shaped cross upon which he is to hang. Crucifixion, the agonizingly slow and painful mode of execution employed for centuries by the Romans, was a cruel means of death in which the victim was nailed through the palms of his hands and through the arches of his feet to the cross so that the weight of his own body eventually caused heart congestion and, after many hours, death.

When Jesus was nailed to the cross, he uttered: "Father forgive them; for they know not what they do . . ." (Luke 23:34). The cross was then raised. Upon it was placed a sign reading, in mockery, *Jesus of Nazareth, Rex Judea* [King of the Jews]. (In Latin, the letter J becomes I, hence the famous abbreviation INRI.) Jesus' garment was taken from him and the Roman soldiers cast lots for it by playing dice. Many mocked Jesus on the cross there on the hill of skulls overlooking Jerusalem. "If thou be the son of God, . . . the King of Israel, . . . come down from the cross," they jeered (Matthew 27:40, 42).

The 19th-century Frenchman Honoré Daumier paints a realistic mob scene, known as *Ecce Homo* ("Here is the Man"). A father's face reflects his child's amazement at the dignity of Jesus.

Two differently eloquent paintings of Christ carrying the Cross: Simone Martini's (left) is a vividly decorative, late medieval crowd scene in which Mary Magdalene, with arms upturned, is almost as important as Jesus. El Greco's (right) uses flickering baroque highlights to intensify the awesome sacrifice.

On Jesus' right and left there hung on crosses two convicts also condemned to die. One of them believed in Jesus' divinity and begged for his comfort. Jesus, though suffering in pain, answered: "Today shalt thou be with me in paradise" (Luke 23:43).

At the foot of the cross some of the disciples watched in anguish. Mary, the mother of Jesus, and her sister and Mary Magdalene mourned and wept. Jesus looked upon his mother for the last time on earth and consigned her to the care of John, the Evangel.

The sixth hour struck (three o'clock in the afternoon by most reckonings). An ominous darkness lowercd over the land. For three more hours Jesus suffered on the cross, and then in the ninth hour (six o'clock) he cried out: "My God, my God, why hast thou forsaken me?" (Mark 15:34), a quotation from Psalm 22 that bespeaks a momentary fear and anxiety in Jesus' heart, for he was also a man and he suffered as a man. A moment later, however, he had regained his composure. "Father," he said in radiant calm, "into thy hands I commend my spirit: and having said thus, he gave up the ghost" (Luke 23:46).

Now at this moment of Jesus' death, great and awesome natural disturbances are reported in the Gospels. An earthquake occurs; graves open and the wandering of spirits is observed. In the holy temple, the sacred veil of the inner sanctum "was rent [torn] in twain from the top to the bottom" (Matthew 27:51). Such terrible events cause one of the Roman centurions to de-

The North Italian painter Andrea Mantegna portrays the story of the Crucifixion under a clear blue sky. To either side of Jesus' cross are two contrasting groups: his mother and the other women (left) and the soldiers gambling for his robe (right).

Rembrandt's etching known as *The Three Crosses* shows Jesus between the thieves in a downpour of light, which illuminates the main figures, including the Virgin Mary (right), while the rest of the world pulls away into darkness.

clare, as he looked upon Jesus' body, "Truly this was the Son of God" (Matthew 27:54).

The Burial—Every single event of this tragic day (Good Friday in church tradition) is of meaning and concern to devout Christians all over the world, from the arrest in Gethsemane to the trial to the painful procession through the narrow streets of Jerusalem to Golgotha. Jesus' Passion, as it is known, represents the whole sorrow and despair of human suffering in any form. It is a dark, foreboding story. Even the burial is fraught with details of meaning: the rush to prepare and

bury the body in advance of the coming Sabbath (Saturday) during which no burials were allowed; the piercing of Jesus' body with a spear (the *coup de grâce*, or death blow); the search for a suitable nearby grave—all are vividly depicted.

A wealthy Jew of kindly feelings, Joseph of Arimathea, offered the disciples an empty grave in his family tomb. This grave was not dug underground but carved into the living rock of a hillside garden. Pontius Pilate, hearing that Jesus was dead and being warned of his promise to reappear after death, ordered a huge rock rolled in front of this grave and set a

A modern reenactment of Christ's Passion takes place on Easter in the Holy Land. The faithful carry
a heavy cross along the path trod by Jesus nearly 2,000 years ago.

315

watch of Roman soldiers before it lest the disciples come and steal Jesus' body so they can say he was risen from the dead.

The death and burial of Jesus are soon events of the past. The Sabbath evening comes; the city returns to normal. The story is ended—or is it?

The Resurrection—All that has preceded this moment, all the sorrow, tragedy and pain, were simply a prelude to the central event of the Christian faith (see I Corinthians 15:14), the Resurrection and reappearance of Jesus, not as a man but as Christ, the Risen Lord; God in earthly form. This astonishing moment, predicted by Jesus while he preached, is of course the essence of the Easter celebration and triumphantly overcomes the gloom and despair of Holy Thursday (the arrest and trial) and Good Friday (the crucifixion and death).

The first Easter Sunday begins as several women, including Mary Magdalene, come to the gravesite in order properly to entomb the body, for on Friday they were hurried by the oncoming Sabbath and could not finish their sacred labors. They find to their amazement that the huge rock which Pilate ordered rolled before the grave is now some distance away. The grave itself is empty, the guards have fled and Jesus is gone!

Each of the four Gospels relates in powerful and dramatic detail what happened next; each should be read separately: Matthew 28:2–15; Mark 16:5–11; Luke 24:3–12 and John 20:11–18.

In sum, an angel appears and reports the

In *The Descent From the Cross*, Rembrandt shows himself as a young man up against Jesus' abdomen. The saintly Joseph of Arimathea waits at the right to help with the burial as night rapidly descends.

At the entrance to this Jewish grave close to Jerusalem, a wheellike stone, seen on the left, can easily be rolled down an inclined track to seal the entrance, as was done to Jesus' tomb. To reopen the tomb, however, several men must push the stone back up the slope and wedge it into place.

Rising or Resurrection of Jesus. "He is not here," cries the angel, "for he is risen, as he said" (Matthew 28:6). "Go your way, tell his disciples . . ." (Mark 16:7). Only Mary Magdalene, confused and tearful, remains behind. A man approaches her whom she takes to be a gardener.

"Woman, why weepest thou?" he asks.

She tells him: "Because they have taken away my Lord . . ." Then the man reveals himself: Jesus, risen. "Go to my brethren," he tells Mary, "and say unto them, I ascended unto my Father, unto your Father; and to my God, and your God" (John 20:17).

Thus it was that Mary Magdalene, a humble, once sinful woman, was the first person to see Jesus as Christ.

The Ascension—Events follow rapidly for the next forty days. The Risen Lord appears to many disciples and followers. Two of the faithful dine with him at a town called Emmaus, but they do not know it is Jesus until he vanishes from their sight while blessing the bread (Luke 24:13–35).

Both in Jerusalem and in Galilee, Jesus appears. Even so, one of his disciples, Thomas, called Didymus, is doubtful that the stories of the Resurrection are true. Then one day Jesus shows himself to Thomas ("doubting Thomas"), points to the wounds in his palms where he was nailed to the cross and convinces the disciple. The lesson of this incident is of major importance. As Jesus says: "Thomas, because thou hast seen me, thou hast believed: blessed are they that have *not* seen, and yet have believed" (John 20:29).

He met again with the disciples at the Sea of Galilee and brought them good fishing as of old and he talked with them, as of old, and preached of the kingdom.

Then, forty days after his death, Jesus led his disciples to the Mount of Olives near Jerusalem and in sight of them and his mother, "he was received up into heaven," where he "sat on the right hand of God" (Mark 16:19).

It is John who has the final, most appropriate word of all the Gospels (which end with the story of the Ascension).

"And there are also many other things which Jesus did," he writes, "the which, if they should be written every one, I suppose that even the world itself could not contain the books that should be written. Amen" (John 21:25).

THE ARCHAEOLOGY OF JESUS' PASSION

The Gospels are filled with references to actual places in the Holy Land which today form an integral part of every Christian's faith. These are called the holy places. Especially important are those associated with the trial, crucifixion and resurrection of Jesus. To these sites millions of devout Christians have made pilgrimages over the centuries since the first Easter.

The major sites are not always agreed upon by archaeologists and religious scholars. Since Jesus' time much has happened in and around Jerusalem to alter what might have been. Even so, certain places are established, whether by tradition or archaeological proof, and these we will briefly note.

The Pavement (in Hebrew, "Gabbatha"): A ledge where prisoners were tried near the Antonia Tower within the walls of Old Jerusalem (see John 19:13). Here Pontius Pilate probably held court and interrogated Jesus.

Herod's Palace: Opposite the Antonia Tower, near the outer wall, was the Jerusalem palace where Jesus was questioned by the foolish Judean king (Luke 23:7).

The Via Dolorosa (Street of Sorrows): A narrow winding series of streets in the old city of Jerusalem that passes from the Pavement up to Golgotha (now believed to

Rembrandt painted the angel of the Resurrection lifting away the slab over Jesus' grave in a shower of light that sends the Roman soldiers scattering. Serenely, Jesus comes to life at the extreme right.

and an institution. The man was Saul of Tarsus, better known as St. Paul, and the institution the Christian Church. Many scholars attribute to Paul the spread of Christianity in the civilized world and the clarification of Christian theology and doctrine. Jesus Christ was the source and essence of the faith, Paul its organizer and chief spokesman. Without Paul, Christianity might have remained a special but insignificant segment of Judaism. Remember that all the original Christians, including the Apostle Paul, were devout and faithful Jews. Without Paul's letters (see the Epistles), sermons, theories and pronouncements, the religion of Jesus might have eventually disappeared amid the confusion of religious sects, cults and clans of the time.

Instead, within four centuries of the crucifixion of Jesus by the Romans, Christianity had become the official religion of the Roman Empire and the crucified Christ, hanging on the cross, the religious symbol for countless millions. In large measure, this was due to the tireless, inspired work of Paul.

The Acts tell how this man, who at first violently opposed the teachings of Christ, worked and suffered to become the chief apostle of the faith. It also chronicles the events following Jesus' ascension, events fraught with conflict and drama.

Though Paul is the key figure of this book, other major leaders of the faith are presented in its pages in vivid detail: Peter, the head of the Jerusalem group; Luke, the physician and evangel; the disciples Mark and Timothy, as well as antagonists such as

Above Jerusalem's Garden of Gethsemane, with its Church of All Nations, rises the wooded slope of the Mount of Olives and the Russian Orthodox Church of Mary Magdalene.

Felix and Festus, governors of Palestine after Pilate; Agrippa, son of King Herod, and other prominent figures. In part, the book of Acts is a biography (of Paul), in part an adventure story (with a memorable ship's diary by Luke included), in part a discussion of religion and belief. Perhaps the best way to explore this important and detailed section of the New Testament is to examine separately these three aspects: the story of Paul; the story of the other apostles —their adventures, so to speak—and the themes or religious messages of the book.

A MAN NAMED PAUL

As Saul of Tarsus, Paul first appears in the text in Chapter 7, Verse 58. It is a dramatic appearance, for Saul is part of a gang that has kidnapped a young Christian preacher named Stephen and then stoned him to death. Paul (or Saul, before his conversion) did not actually take part in the stoning of Stephen, but he guarded the coats of those who did. Indeed, it was Saul's profession to persecute Christians, and he "made havoc of the church, entering into every house, and haling [arresting] men and women [he then] committed them to prison" (8:3).

One day as Paul headed toward Damascus to continue his brutal activities, a monumental thing happened to him. "Suddenly there shined round about him a light from heaven: And he fell to the earth, and heard a voice saying to him, Saul, Saul, why persecutest me? And [Saul] said, Who art thou, Lord? And the Lord said, I am Jesus whom thou persecutest . . ." (9:3–5). Astonished and frightened, Paul fell into a sort of trance; his sight went from him. He only knew that Christ was now wholly and powerfully within him.

Blind and bewildered, Paul continued

gropingly toward Damascus, where Jesus had told him to await further word. In Damascus, Paul was visited by some faithful Christians who had been informed by the Lord that this man, once an enemy of the church, was to become its greatest advocate.

Paul is baptized and accepts the calling of Christ. His sight returns; so does his strength. With unprecedented zeal, he begins the first of his many missions on behalf of Christianity. At first, the Jews who had once trusted him think that he is mad. The Christians who had feared him think him a deceiver. But he persists in the company of a disciple named Barnabas. He visits the group headed by Peter in Jerusalem, and when they hear him preach on behalf of the Risen Christ, they realize that he is "in the comfort of the Holy Ghost" (9:31) and worthy to be a Christian apostle.

In this youthful, energetic painting of the Stoning of St. Stephen, Rembrandt pictures himself just above the kneeling martyr's head.

"I could not see for the glory of that light" (Acts 22:11), says Paul, describing his conversion on the road to Damascus. He is bathed in that glory (lower left) in one of Michelangelo's last paintings.

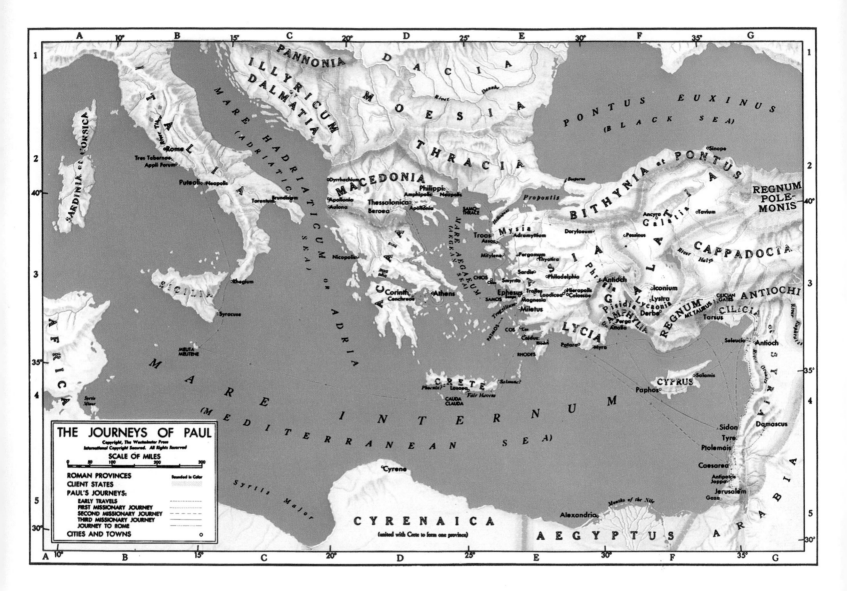

The Journeys of Paul

The Missions

Paul's first extensive mission was to the flourishing city of Antioch in northern Syria, where there was a poor but faithful community of Christians. There he not only preached of the Risen Christ but offered money to help establish the church. It was ever Paul's practice to combine preaching with practical actions.

For a while Antioch became a base for Paul from which he traveled to places as far away as Galatia (modern Turkey), heading toward Greece and another city called Antioch. Throughout his missions, Paul experienced relentless difficulties not only from non-Christians, who objected to the competition of a new faith, but also from Christians themselves, who resisted Paul's revolutionary notion of preaching the word of Christ to the Gentiles, the non-Jews, of the world. Until this period, the majority of early Christians had been at the same time practicing members of the Jewish faith, either by birth or conversion. They had no basic theological conflict, since Judaism had long preached the coming of a Messiah as Redeemer. The Christian-Jews, as they might be called, simply asserted that Jesus of Nazareth was that Messiah. The other Jews believed that he was not, that the Messiah was yet to come and with him the end of all time. If Jesus were truly Christ, they asked, how was it that Judgment Day and the Messianic Age had not followed upon his arrival? To this Christians answered that Christ himself had decided to postpone the end of time to allow mankind a full chance to repent; Jesus Christ was nonetheless the true Messiah. This controversy was significant but not violent, and Jews of both persuasions (Christian-Jews and non-Christian Jews) lived in relative harmony. One thing Christian-Jews accepted without question was the ritual of circumcision instituted by God through Abraham centuries before. Every Jewish male was circumcised soon after birth and obeyed the laws of Judaism, including the kosher rules of proper diet, the observance of Sabbath on Saturday and other practices.

The Gentile Question

Paul was faced with a weighty problem. He believed Christianity could flourish only if it was taken up by the millions and millions of Gentiles, most of whom now worshiped idols. Yet he knew that these Gentiles would not first become Jews, thereby undergoing circumcision. The Jews he preached to—although they accepted Jesus as an exalted prophet—were, by and large, not persuaded to accept the Risen Christ. What alternative did he have?

A long and apparently heated debate ensued between Paul and the Peter group over this "Gentile question" (see 15:1–21). Finally, a compromise was reached, mainly through the good offices of Peter. "God,

which knoweth the hearts [of Gentiles], bare them witness," he said, "giving them the Holy Ghost, even as he did unto us . . . now therefore why tempt ye God, to put a yoke upon the neck of the disciples . . ." (15:8–10). In other words, if men are pure and filled with love for Jesus, how can we—mere disciples of God—risk not bringing them to Christ? Don't we have enough trouble with unbelievers? If people come to us who want to believe, shall we burden ourselves with details and arguments? Later, Paul further explained that since Jesus had been circumcised as a baby, he symbolically took upon himself the circumcision ritual for all those who accepted him.

With the agreement to allow Paul to preach to and convert Gentiles, Christianity took a giant step forward.

The European Journey

Successful in this conflict, Paul now began preaching far and wide, into Greece, an act that brought Christianity to Europe. He went as well to the borders of Turkey and from there back to Jerusalem. Wherever he spoke, Paul and his associates were greeted warmly by the people and angrily by local religious leaders. At times he was reviled in public, at other times stoned or jailed. But his faith and fortitude were unswerving. Few men have been so wholly dedicated to a mission as the apostle Paul. He preached in the greatest cities of the area, even in Athens, where he said: "God that made the world and all things therein, seeing that he is Lord of heaven and earth, dwelleth not in temples made with hands . . ." (17:24–25). You can imagine how unpopular was this idea in the city of the Parthenon, that great and beautiful temple to the goddess Athena.

In the Greek city of Ephesus, Paul challenged the idol makers and threatened their business. A great riot broke out in which the apostle was nearly mobbed, saved only by the intercession of a kindly official named Alexander (19:23–41).

In a period of about thirty years Paul managed to write the epistles and documents that established the tenets of the Christian faith and preach the sermons which helped cement the foundations of the new religion.

On the Way to Rome

Then in about the year A.D. 60, Paul was arrested on this way to Jerusalem by the Roman governor Felix. This time it was not because of his message that he was arrested but because everywhere Paul went trouble and dissension followed. Felix wanted to keep the apostle in protective custody and out of action. For two years he was detained at the port of Caesarea, where Paul no doubt consolidated his writings. As a citizen of Rome, which he was because of his birth at Tarsus, a Roman province, Paul was spared being held and tried by his Jewish enemies. Yet the Romans were not great friends of his. Felix's successor, Festus, wanted to get rid of him and on Paul's own urging decided to send him for trial to Rome itself. This Paul eagerly anticipated since he knew that once he brought the Christian religion to Rome, the center of the world, its impact would be enormous.

While awaiting his transport to Rome for trial, Paul was brought before the Judean king Herod Agrippa. For hours, Paul spoke of Christ, the new faith, the promise of salvation, resurrection and eternal life (25:13 passim). Festus, hearing this lengthy discourse, mocked: "Paul, thou art beside thyself," he said. "Much learning doth make thee mad" (26:24). But Agrippa was less cynical. In fact he was almost persuaded to become a Christian and even wished to acquit Paul then and there of any alleged wrongdoings. But the machinery for sending Paul to Rome had been set in motion and nothing could interfere.

Paul's Fate

A stormy, adventurous journey by sea brings Paul to several ports on his way to Rome. He is accompanied by Luke, who writes of the crossing in great detail (see 27:9–44). Finally, the ship arrives in the seaport of Puteoli, near Rome. Paul is delivered to the prison there, awaiting trial. Time passes. Eventually he is transported to a Roman house, where he lives in custody for two years. It almost seems as though the Roman officials have forgotten about his trial. Suddenly, the narrative stops. We never learn of the great apostle's fate. Some say that Paul survived his trial and went on to preach in Spain and elsewhere (as he hints in Romans 15:24 and 28). A more tragic tradition holds that Paul, like Peter, was among those Christians put to death by the mad emperor, Nero, in A.D. 64. In any case, Paul's influence and energy stamped themselves forever on Christianity, as his letters reveal. He was tireless, unassuming and fervent. After his conversion on the Damascus Road, he traveled several thousand miles as a missionary, was persecuted to the point of death at the hands of enemies and suffered a "thorn in the flesh"—an illness that plagued him all his life.

In this painting by Rembrandt, Paul at his desk seems held back from writing by the very depth of his thoughts. Paul said in II Timothy 4:7 : "I have fought a good fight . . . I have kept the faith."

Throughout, he never lost pride in his Jewish faith or faith in Christ the Redeemer. His life's work may be summed up in these, his own words: "Having therefore obtained help of God, I continue unto this day, witnessing both to small and great, saying none other things than those which the prophets and Moses did say should come: that Christ should suffer, and that he should be first that should rise from the dead, and should show light unto the people [the Jews] and to the gentiles" (26:22–23).

The Adventures of the Apostles

When Jesus ascended to God, he left his disciples, now numbering eleven (Judas Iscariot having killed himself) to the leadership of Peter, the "rock." The followers of Christ began to pick up the pieces of their lives and launch the preaching and missionary work that Christ had ordained. A man named Matthias was chosen to replace Judas, bringing the number back to twelve.

Then on the Day of Pentecost, the Jewish holiday celebrating Moses' descent from Sinai with the Law, the faithful went to pray in Jerusalem, "and suddenly there came a sound from heaven as of a rushing mighty wind, and it filled all the house where they were sitting. And there appeared unto them cloven tongues like as of fire, and it sat upon each of them. And they were all filled with the Holy Ghost, and began to speak with other tongues as the Spirit gave them utterance" (2:2–4).

It was a miraculous event, signifying the ultimate dedication of the disciples to Christ. Flickering fires appeared over each head and each man, though educated only in Hebrew and possibly Greek, spoke in foreign languages or in words of unusual sounds so that Libyans, Romans, Arabians and Mesopotamians in the crowd could understand their sacred message. Beholding such a miracle, in the name of Jesus Christ, three thousand souls were converted on the spot (2:41). Of course, antagonists toward the new faith, seeing such popularity, became anxious and conspiratorial as never before.

Undaunted, the disciples continued their work of healing and preaching—and arousing suspicions. As more and more people converted to the new faith, Peter, John and the others became more and more entangled with the religious leaders of the temple. To these officials Peter and John made a simple reply when questioned about their activities. "Whether it be right in the sight of God to hearken unto you more than unto God, judge ye. For we cannot but speak the things which we have seen and heard" (4:19–20).

Though many converted, giving over their wealth and belongings to the cause, trouble plagued Peter. He was jailed for his preaching and miraculously set free from prison. One of his judges, a pious Jew named Gamaliel, impressed by this miracle, urged his associates to "refrain from these men, and let them alone . . . if [their work] be of God, ye cannot overthrow it . . ." (5:38–39).

Healing and Converting

With the stoning of the disciple named Stephen—the outrage in which Saul of Tarsus participated—the early Christians

The dove represents the Holy Ghost descending in this 16th-century manuscript painting of the excitement of Pentecost. Giulio Clovio's illumination includes the inscription "Lord open my lips" (Acts 2:4).

DOMINE LABIA
MEA APERIES

On a Vatican fresco, Raphael's angel appears in a burst of light, about to unchain the imprisoned Peter.

become more bold. Now they had a martyr to inspire them, for Stephen in death had called upon Jesus Christ to forgive his murderers (7:59–60). No doubt this unusual martyrdom inspired Saul as well and lay behind his remarkable conversion on the Damascus Road.

Among the most significant conversions that Peter accomplished was that of a Roman centurion named Cornelius. He was a sensitive man who sought God but knew nothing of Christ. In a vision, he was told to seek out Peter in Joppa, a seaport not far from Jerusalem. This was to be no ordinary conversion, for Cornelius was not only a Gentile but a high-ranking Roman official. Peter had been prepared for this conversion by a vision from God in which he saw an image of many beasts and birds mixed together and was told that the old dietary laws of Moses no longer applied. From this Peter drew the lesson that "God is no respecter of persons: But in every nation he that feareth him, and worketh righteousness, is accepted with him" (10:34–35). This lesson he later applied to the "Gentile question" that Paul had raised.

The Fate of Peter

Soon after the conversion of Cornelius —which probably caused much talk in Judea—and in the wake of many more conversions and the raising of a dead woman by Peter (9:36–43), the Judean authorities decided to take drastic steps. James, the brother of John, one of the original disciples, was assassinated by orders of Herod Agrippa and Peter was arrested. Once again, though bound by chains and guarded, the leader was freed from bondage by the intervention of an angel (12:6–10). Not long after, possibly shocked by

The apostles' world was under close imperial watch. Here, on the arch of Constantine, the Emperor inspects prisoners.

Peter's escape, Herod Agrippa died suddenly while seated on his throne.

From this point to the end of Acts, Peter and the Jerusalem group are of lesser importance compared to the work of Paul and his associates. Whenever the great apostle comes to Jerusalem, he, of course, meets with Peter and the disciples. But we learn no more of Peter from Acts and must surmise his fate from the letters he wrote (I and II Peter) while imprisoned in Rome during the persecutions ordered by Nero. Tradition tells how this humble fisherman, who rose to become the "rock" of the Christian Church and its chief disciple along with Paul, died in Rome, A.D. 64, crucified upside down so that he might be lower than his Lord even in death.

In a companion piece to the Conversion of Paul (see p. 325), Michelangelo shows Peter being crucified upside down, so that he would be lower than his Lord even in death.

The Message of Acts

Though busy with dramatic detail and biography, the Acts of the Apostles reveals a striking message concerning faith and fortitude. Basically from its pages we learn of the miraculous nature of Christianity and the strength it inspires, through the Holy Ghost, in its followers. The universality of Christ's message is also emphasized in the conversion of Gentiles and the far-reaching mission of Paul and his associates. Jesus' own words reappear in many cases, and we even learn of a famous saying never quoted in the Gospels, for Paul reports the "words of the Lord Jesus, how he said, It is more blessed to give than to receive" (20:35).

An image of struggle, suffering and persecution for the new faith dominates this book and sets the tone for much of Christian history in the next few centuries. The tireless, self-sacrificing efforts of countless men and women (indeed, many female leaders emerge in this text: Dorcas, Lydia, Priscilla) is consistent, reminding us of the essential missionary theme in all Christian work.

Above all, the abiding message of God's love through Christ dominates the coming and going, the "acts," of the apostles. The book ends anticlimatically with Paul's confinement in Rome (28:30–31). But we may find significance in this ending, for indeed we may say that the Acts of the Apostles continue from that time to this—and forevermore.

The Epistles

Romans—All the epistles are named either for the author or the recipient of the letter. In this case, the Romans represent those early Christians who attempted to organize a church in the Imperial City of the Caesars. Paul wrote to them that he would come to Rome, if possible (it took three years to accomplish this). The theme of this epistle is that the mercy of Christ is exalted even above the Law of Moses; man as a sinful creature can be saved only by God's intercession through Christ and not by mechanical dependence on the Law. One of Paul's purposes in this document is to convince his fellow Jews of Christ's mission (Chapters 9–11). He also stresses obedience to civil law and calls again on all Christians to unite in brotherly love. He speaks of many personal matters (Chapter 16), greeting various colleagues and friends. Perhaps it is Chapter 8 that best summarizes Romans: "For the law of the Spirit of life in Christ Jesus hath made me free from the law of sin and death" (8:2). "If God be for us, who can be against us?" (8:31) "He that spared not his own Son, but delivered him up for us all, how shall he not with him also freely give us all things?" (8:32)

I Corinthians— This is the first of two extant epistles by Paul to the Christians of Corinth, a city near Athens in Greece. In it, Paul expresses great concern for various disorders occurring in the church, especially in the form of rivalries, factions, abuses of ritual (such as the Communion), problems about marriage (on which Paul felt strongly) and the role of women in the church. Questions of the Resurrection, its validity and function in the faith are emphatically discussed in Chapter 15; apparently many early Christians were wavering on this issue.

Perhaps the most memorable and deepfelt moment in this letter is Chapter 13, which is not only a hymn to human love but an exalted work of poetry which should be read in its entirety. It begins:

The last two of a procession of columnlike martyrs—those who suffer for the Lord—approaching the throne of Christ, done in mosaic from Sant'Apollinare Nuovo in 6th-century Ravenna.

"Though I speak with the tongues of men and of angels, and have not charity [or love], I am become as sounding brass, or a tinkling cymbal." By this Paul means: Though I know all manner of knowledge, earthly and divine, and have no capacity for brotherly love, then my sentiments, my sermons and such are like a superficial noise. The apostle goes on to say: "Charity suffereth long, and is kind; charity envieth not . . . beareth all things, believeth all things, hopeth all things, endureth all things . . ." (13:4 and 7). Paul's astonishing poetic gift is evident not only in this paean

to charity but also in world-famous expressions that come from this epistle, such as "O Death, where is thy sting?" (15:55), meaning Death, you cannot hurt me now since I have faith in Christ, and "There is a natural body and there is a spiritual body . . . and as we have borne the image of the earthly, we shall also bear the image of the heavenly" (15:44 and 49).

II Corinthians—After spending quite some time in Corinth, Paul summed up his mission in this letter addressed to the Christians of the city. In this very personal document, the apostle tells of his sufferings and difficulties in spreading the message of Christ, all of which is as nothing when he thinks of the comfort that faithful Christians afford him by their loyalty and love. Though he has been close to death and abused—even by some of his followers—Paul rejoices in Christ and in his hope for the future.

Many profound subjects are touched in this letter, including questions of the afterlife (Chapter 5). This life, says Paul, is but a preparation for the glory of heaven. Christ has taken away the finality of death for those who follow him. II Corinthians also gives us a view of Paul's personality and even of his appearance. Apparently he suffered from some constant pain or ailment, which he describes as "a thorn in the flesh" (12:7); perhaps it was epilepsy. He also insists that though he may appear to some as weak and foolish in person, he is "bold" when "I am present with that confidence [in Christ]" (10:2).

It is important to note that Paul refers in this epistle to the ritual of Communion and the concept of the Trinity: God, the Father; Christ, the Son; and the Holy Ghost, or Spirit (see Chapter 13:14). Centuries later, this concept of three divine persons in one (in Jesus Christ) became the official doctrine of the Roman Catholic Church and a fundamental belief of most Christians everywhere.

Note: A footnote to this epistle informs us that it was "written . . . by Titus and Lucas," two followers of Paul who acted as his scribes, or secretaries.

Galatians—Galatia is a region in Asia Minor that included the ancient cities of Iconium, Antioch, Lystra and Derbe (all of which are now part of Turkey). Conversion of the Galatians to Christianity was widespread as a result of Paul's influence. But the Galatians were not Jews, and many early Christians insisted that followers of Jesus had to be born in the Jewish faith and therefore had to be circumcised according to the ancient ritual established in Abraham's time. In this epistle, Paul does much to declare independence for Christianity from the Jewish religion, insisting that circumcision is not necessary for salvation, since Christ, as a circumcised Jew, stands for all faithful men. The rift between the Jewish sect of Christians (of which St. Peter was the leader) and the Gentile Christians (which Paul represented, although he himself was a Jew) was of considerable impact in the early church, as we have seen in exploring the Acts of the Apostles.

In Galatians, Paul clarified the eligibility of Christians by asserting his authority. "The Gospel that was preached of me," he declares, "is not after man. For I neither received it of man, neither was I taught it, but by the revelation of Jesus Christ" (1:11–12). In other words, Paul's message comes directly from God.

After much persuasive argument on behalf of Christian universality, Paul repeats one of his most constant themes: "There is neither Jew nor Greek, there is neither bond nor free, there is neither male nor female: for ye are all one in Christ Jesus" (3:28). He then utters what some have called the essence of the New Testament. "But the fruit of the Spirit is love, joy, peace, long-suffering [patience], gentleness, goodness, faith, meekness, temperance: against such there is no law. . . . If we live in the Spirit, let us also walk in the Spirit. Let us not be desirous of vain glory . . ." (5:22–26).

Ephesians—Ephesus was a large and beautiful Greek city devoted to worship of pagan gods, especially Diana. Largely through Paul's efforts, a significant Christian church arose in this place. But it was mainly made up of Jewish Christians, and here again, as in Galatia, conflicts occurred between the Gentile, or non-Jewish, group and the original followers of Christ.

A shepherd in the rocky uplands of present-day Yalvac, Turkey, which was the Galatian Antioch visited by Paul on his third journey.

Typical of Ephesian statues of their patron goddess Diana was this one in bronze and gold; it leaves no doubt in the mind that she is the goddess of fertility.

One of Paul's most far-reaching and dynamic ideas was the conversion of non-Jews to Christ, for in this way he opened the doors to a worldwide Christian religion. The Epistle to the Ephesians asserts this "universal church" and the belief that only through Jesus Christ (sometimes referred to as Christ Jesus) can man come to God, the Father (2:18). As in the other epistles, notable phrases jump out at us: "Put on the whole armor of God," cries Paul (6:11) and "the breastplate of righteousness" (6:14), quotations that indicate Paul's knowledge of the Apocrypha, where the same expressions are used (see Wisdom of Solomon 5:18).

The port city of Ephesus—and its temple—drew many worshipers of Diana, and Paul's influence was resented as discouraging tourism. Yet the Christian church flourished there, as the Epistle to the Ephesians proves.

Philippians—Near Macedonia in Greece was a small Roman enclave called Philippi, and here Paul founded the first Christian church on European soil (St. Luke was its first pastor, or leader). Paul was particularly fond of this church, and many believe this epistle was among the last he ever wrote. It is filled with affectionate phrases and deep thanks for an offering of money made by the Philippians to Paul. Though he usually earned his living weaving tent cloth (the trade he learned as a boy; see Acts 18:3), the apostle occasionally needed outside support. Doubtless at the end of his life, broken by years in prison and much persecution, Paul could not earn his living in the usual way. Thus did he gratefully accept the generous dole.

In style, this epistle is the most casual and conversational. However, several references to doctrine may be found in it, including a call to rejoice in the Lord, for "the peace of God, which passeth all understanding, shall keep your hearts and minds through Christ Jesus" (4:7). Paul also relates his most precise theological view of Jesus; that he is "in the form of God . . . [who] took upon him the form of a servant, and was made in the likeness of men: and being found in fashion as a man, he humbled himself, and became obedient unto death, even the death of the cross. Wherefore God also hath highly exalted him, and given him a name which is above every name . . ." (2:6–9). Put in another way, Paul is saying: God took the form of a man called Jesus (the Incarnation), but Jesus the man temporarily gave up his divine nature so that he could live fully as a man, even to the point of a cruel and painful death. That death, which he overcame—being divine—by resurrection, will act as a penance before God for all men if they accept it as such and follow Christ's teachings and example.

Colossians—Colossae was another city in Asia Minor (Turkey). While in prison in Rome, Paul learned of disruption and heresies among the early Christians in that place. The heresies involved the paganlike worship of angels. Like the letter to the Ephesians, probably written around the same time, this one stresses discipline of religion, the deity of Christ and reliance upon Faith, Love and Hope. "Set your affection on things above, not on things on earth" (3:2), the apostle writes. He further speaks of a "mystery" (1:27) in which Christ functions through men as "the hope of glory." Mystery in this case implies a *sense* of God as opposed to a knowledge of the same. Mysticism is derived from this idea—mystics arrive at truth through feelings, through the unconscious.

I Thessalonians—The great Greek city of Thessaly (modern Salonica) had a small but growing church that frequently underwent persecution by local pagans. Paul comforted the faithful by advising them that Christ would remember their suffering at the end of time. It is believed by many that I and II Thessalonians were among the earliest of Paul's epistles. Thus they may be the original documents of Christianity. They establish the style of all the other letters, part doctrinal, part pastoral—or instructive—about matters of theology and religion, and partly concerned with church organization and daily routines.

Several major themes emerge in I Thessalonians: The church will take care of her own "as a nurse cherisheth her children" (2:7) so long as the children are faithful, frugal and deserving; those who suffer for Christ and his church will find glory when

Jesus comes again (2:13–19). The Second Coming of Christ is indeed one of the most significant and influential ideas conveyed by this letter. "For the Lord himself shall descend from heaven with a shout . . . and the dead in Christ shall rise first . . ." (4:16–18). The living and the dead on equal terms will then join God "in the air."

Lest this vision of the end of time too greatly excite the faithful, Paul cautiously advises them to "watch and be sober." The dead only sleep until the coming, he says. But the living must not sleep in self-satisfaction of their salvation. Rather they must "ever follow that which is good . . . pray without ceasing . . . prove all things; hold fast that which is good. Abstain from all appearance of evil" (5:15, 17, 21–22).

II Thessalonians—A second, short message to the church of Thessalonica repeats the vision of Christ's Second Coming, "the Day of the Lord," which shall be a terrible time for sinners and disbelievers (1:9). The faithful must thus guard against being "shaken in mind"—wavering in belief. Much disbelief, or apostasy, called "the working of Satan," will occur before God's coming and the faithful will be sorely tested. Paul ends his letter with the hope that his friends and followers will pray for him and his companions, for he was, at that time, oppressed by enemies in Corinth, where he lived.

I Timothy—In Ephesus there dwelled two devoted disciples of Paul; they were Timothy and Titus, leaders of the early church. Timothy was part Jewish and one of the first Gentiles to accept Christianity at the hands of Paul. He often acted as a courier and secretary to the apostle (as did Titus) and was particularly close to him.

The two letters to Timothy and the one to Titus are known as "pastoral letters," concerned with organizational matters in the church. Some scholars believe they were not written by Paul but by later-day apostles who felt a need to purify church procedures and therefore used the authority of Paul's name. Whatever the case, these pastoral letters have served for centuries as guidance for all church leaders and laymen.

To begin with, Paul warns Timothy about false teachers and lazy Christians who expect charity but give no work or prayer. In a striking revelation, Paul even goes so far as to call himself a blasphemer and a persecutor of the faithful before his conversion (which we have explored in the Acts of the Apostles). Thus it is possible, he implies, that others may be unworthy unless they, like a true convert, are totally devoted to Christ. The apostle also concerns himself with the role of women in the church. Paul is somewhat ambivalent about women. Sin came into the world through Eve, he reports, but at the same time salvation came through Mary, the mother of Jesus. He exhorts women to dress prudently and generally to take a background role in church affairs "in silence" (2:11–12).

Other pastoral topics touched on in this letter include the role of bishops and deacons, proper treatment of widows and the aged and questions of slavery and wealth (there shall be neither in heaven). The famous remark "the love of money is the root of all evil" appears in this text (6:10).

II Timothy—In this letter, the apostle sums up his hard but glorious mission and he urges the faithful to "hold fast . . . in faith and love . . ." (1:13). Retracing the course of his many sojourns and persecutions, the humble tent weaver, who—in essence—created the form of the Christian religion, awaits martyrdom at the hands of the bloated and fanatic Nero, emperor of Rome. Paul is unafraid: "For now I am ready to be offered, and the time of my departure is at hand. I have fought the good fight, I have finished my course, I have kept the faith: henceforth there is laid up for me a crown of righteousness which the Lord, the righteous judge, shall give me at that day: and not to me only, but unto all them also that love his appearing" (4:6–8). After this heartfelt and courageous statement, Paul goes on to reveal his underlying humbleness and humanity. As a footnote, he exhorts Timothy to hurry to Rome and bring "the cloke that I left at Troas . . . and the books, but especially the parchments" (4:13). Apparently it was cold in Rome, and the apostle needed his coat.

Titus—Greek-born and a Gentile, Titus was converted early in Paul's career and sent to the island of Crete to establish Christianity there. Like the letters to Timothy, this one deals with church matters as well as doctrine. The topics include respect for the elders of the church, suspicion of false teachers and the value of good works (2:14). A code of decent conduct is laid down here by Paul acceptable to all civilized men, and it is "to obey magistrates, to be ready to every good work, to speak evil of no man, to be no brawlers, but gentle, showing all meekness unto all men . . ." (3:1–2).

Philemon—This brief epistle (it contains one chapter) was written by Paul to a friend named Philemon of Colossae. It concerns a slave, Onesimus, who robbed Philemon and fled to Rome. There the

The man in this Hellenistic statuette is wearing a warm cloak like the one Paul wanted (see II Timothy 4:13).

A wall painting in Herculaneum, a Roman city partly preserved under volcanic ash, shows a pair of elegant women being dressed and anointed with a vanity criticized by Paul in I Timothy.

A Roman tomb carving showing a huge, slave-powered crane. Its operators, like its owners, were welcomed into the Church, which offered a future-world reward for all believers after their toils of earthly life.

slave was converted to Christianity by Paul. By law Onesimus had to be returned to his master, and this Paul advocated. His letter is an appeal to Philemon to forgive the now penitent Onesimus and welcome him as a "brother beloved" (1:16). We do not know if Philemon acted according to Paul's request, even though the apostle offered to reimburse him for the stolen money. But some thirty or forty years later a bishop arose at Ephesus, near Colossae, and his name was Onesimus—possibly the slave of Philemon—now grown to full freedom and grace.

Paul's subtle plea for brotherhood, his tactful appeal to Philemon that he receive Onesimus "as myself" (1:17), makes this letter a paragon of compassion.

Hebrews—In this general epistle, Paul—or possibly another apostle—appeals to the Jews of the day to accept Christ as the Son of God. By associating Jesus with the Old Testament and with the priesthood of the Levis (the tribe of Moses), the author of this letter hoped to bolster the faith of those Jews already converted and prepare for further conversions. It is believed by some that impending Roman persecution of Jews and Christians—especially around Jerusalem—inspired this call to steadfast faith and courage. Another element clearly evident in Hebrews is the argument against elaborate temple rituals and sacrifice. Jesus is "the great high priest, that is passed into the heavens," says Paul (4:14), and there is no longer a need for the priestly caste and its rituals. Jesus is also extolled as God's instrument in the creation of heaven and earth (1:2), both of which are "the works of thine hands" (1:10); Jesus is better than the angels (1:4), yet by his own choice was made "a little lower than the angels for the suffering of death . . . for every man" (2:9). He is "worthy of more glory than Moses" (3:3); he is a king and priest all in one like the ancient Melchizedek of Genesis (see Genesis 14:18–20).

This epistle further speaks of a new covenant (8:8) based on the Jewish law, but a "better covenant, which was established upon better promises" (8:6). In Chapter 9, Paul actually uses the expression "the new testament" (9:15) for the first time. The essential concepts of Christianity are repeated: Sin shall be removed by faith in Christ (10:1–25); Christ's sacrifice has replaced the earlier sacrificial traditions;

apostasy—or disbelief—threatens us all.

In Chapter 11 a chronicle of Old Testament heroes is presented, beginning with Abel, the murdered son of Adam. These faithful foreshadowed Jesus Christ. A call to courage and diligence in faith rounds out this epistle and seems to imply dread events soon to come for all concerned. The fall of Jerusalem to the Romans, A.D. 70, is indirectly predicted.

James—Subtitled a General Epistle, this is the first letter we so far encounter that is clearly written by somone other than Paul. James, in this case, is traditionally believed to be the brother of Jesus (or, in Catholic belief, his cousin). Surnamed "the Just," he spent much of his life proselytizing for the new faith among Gentiles as well as Jews. According to some reports, James was martyred by a mob in the temple at Jerusalem.

His letter outlines the values of Christianity as a new religion, stressing the numerous trials that a faithful Christian will have to endure. Patience, wisdom and faith will overcome all bitterness, he says. In proverblike sentences James warns of temptation, riches, false witness, ill temper and vainglory. "If ye have respect to persons, ye commit sin" (2:9), he writes, meaning: When you allow yourself to be led by earthly leaders, you fall into error and corruption. Charity to the poor, good works and prayers are emphasized, for "as the body without the spirit is dead, so faith without works is dead also" (2:26). The institution of confession is presented in this epistle (5:16), but the dominant theme is that man must guard his tongue against falsehood and vain oaths, since "the tongue is a little member, and boasteth great things" (3:5).

I Peter—The most prominent leader in early Christianity, along with Paul, was Peter, the fisherman-disciple of Christ, upon whose faith the Christian Church was founded (see Matthew 16:18). Peter was the head of the Christian-Jews in Jerusalem. But it is believed that he eventually went to Rome, inspired by a vision of Christ, and there died a martyr's death, crucified upside down, for he felt unworthy of imitating his Lord even in death. While in Rome, living under the corruption of Nero's imperium, Peter dictated this epistle (and at least one other recorded though no longer extant). In it he urges obedience to law, sobriety and courage, even amid cruel and pagan persecution. Everywhere the great disciple warns against hatred and vengeance. "The trial of your faith," he writes, "[is] much more precious than of gold that perisheth, though it be tried with fire . . ." (1:7). ". . . Be sober, and hope to the end for the grace that is to be brought unto you at the revelation of Jesus Christ . . ." (1:13). ". . . See that ye love one another with a pure heart fervently: Being born again, not of corruptible seed, but of incorruptibility, by the word of God, which liveth and abideth for ever" (1:23). Following these statements, there is an exquisite verse, well worth committing to memory:

"For all flesh is as grass, and all the glory of man as the flower of grass. The grass withereth, and the flower thereof falleth away: But the word of the Lord endureth for ever" (1:24–25).

Repeated references to the painful trials and suffering of the faithful and of the great rewards hereafter make this letter a sort of first-aid kit to all oppressed believers. Peter also touches on questions of morality, marriage, charity (warning against the power of "filthy lucre"—5:2) and pastoral affairs,

Roman sculpture dwelt upon the power and authority of earthly rulers. This one shows Nero, who persecuted the early Christians and burned the city of Rome.

urging younger members of the church to submit to their elders and "humble yourselves therefore under the mighty hand of God . . ." (5:6).

II Peter—This epistle was among the last accepted into the New Testament, since many church fathers believed it to be the work of someone other than Peter himself. Whoever the author may have been, the letter seems to continue the message of I Peter (and parallels that of Jude, which follows later). Apostasy is of great concern to the writer. He fears the Christians will waver in the face of persecution. For steadfastness, seven divine qualities are outlined in Chapter 1 (Verses 5–11): virtue, knowledge, self-control, patience, Godliness,

brotherly kindness, love—"for if these things be in you, and abound, they make you that ye shall be neither barren nor unfruitful in the knowledge of our Lord Jesus Christ" (1:8).

Peter reaffirms the truth of the Gospels. They are not "cunningly devised fables," he declares, but were witnessed by many, including himself. Even so, there shall be many false teachers, even in the church, and they will lead others to disbelief and doubt. These persons will be punished as were the sinners of the Old Testament (the people of Noah's generation, for instance—2:5). Such apostasy will anger and grieve the Lord, who will therefore delay his return to earth, for to God "one day is . . . as a thousand years, and a thousand years as one day" (3:8).

I John—According to tradition this powerful document—a mini-course in Christian theology—was written by John the Beloved Disciple of Christ, who was also the author of the fourth Gospel. He is likewise thought to have been the author of the Apocalypse. Whether it was the Gospel writer John or another John, the individual who wrote this and the following two epistles was one of the most brilliant philosophers of the new faith and a bulwark against heresy and confusion.

It is very likely that John's epistles were provoked by a growing heretical movement in the church, generally known as Gnosticism. In it, spiritual matters were distinct from material matters. Thus, Gnostics usually insisted that Christ was a phantom, or spirit, unrelated to the man Jesus. The idea that God could take on human form repelled the Gnostics, and so they denied the Incarnation. Jesus only *seemed* to be human, they said, and therefore was not really the Son of God but some sort of magical illusion. (This heresy is known in Christianity as *docetism*, from the Greek work "to seem.")

Our exploration need not go too deeply into the philosophical and theological questions behind this letter, since the words themselves have meaning on many levels—as wise advice for the faithful and as counteraction for apostasy.

John begins this letter with the same theme that opens his Gospel: "That which was from the beginning . . . the Word of life . . . that which we have seen and heard . . . and truly our fellowship is with the Father, and with his Son Jesus Christ" (1:1–3). In short, Jesus is the incarnation of God. Twenty times or more John repeats the phrase "Son of God" referring to Jesus; his argument against docetism is clear. In a similar vein, John in his Gospel calls Jesus "the light of the world" (John 8:12), and here in the epistle he repeats this theme (1:5–6). For the first and only time in the Bible John uses the expression "anti-Christ" (2:18 and 22 and later in II John 7), one person, or several, who will rise up repeatedly to deny, defame and disgrace Jesus Christ. Sin must therefore be carefully avoided lest man pave the way for the anti-Christ. "He that committeth sin is of the devil" (3:8), he warns. Love and faith will restore the spirit and save the world. "Let us love one another: for love is of God . . . for God is love," he exults (4:7–8).

The epistle ends with a ringing declaration of eternal life and the rewards of faith in Christ. "God hath given to us eternal life, and this life is in his Son" (5:11).

II John—This and the following epistle have a more personalized tone than the powerful letter just presented. The second, written to a woman pastor, called the "elect lady," touches on familiar themes:

Peter and a delivering angel, from an earthenware sculpture by Luca della Robbia, the best-known of a famous family of artists. Besides being the first Pope of Christianity, Peter also wrote two epistles.

apostasy, the value of truth, and then briefly turns to specific pastoral matters, urging brotherly love and vigilance against the anti-Christ.

III John—Similarly brief, this epistle is addressed to one Gaius, possibly a church leader in Corinth and a recent convert. Faith, truth and love are again emphasized. John then turns to the problem of a man named Diotrephes, who seems to have been one of the false teachers referred to in I John. "He that doeth evil," the disciple points out, "hath not seen God" (1:11).

Jude—The last of the epistles was written by Jude (or Judas), a brother of Jesus (hardly to be confused with Judas Iscariot, the betrayer). Jude's concern is with the same "false teachers" that worried Paul, James and John. He minces no words about their apostasy: "These filthy dreamers defile the flesh . . . and speak evil of dignities" (1:8), he cries. "Woe unto them!" (1:11). The author goes on to describe a prophecy of Enoch, father of Noah—a section that reveals Jude's familiarity with the Apocrypha. Enoch, he writes, prophesied the coming of the Lord "with ten thousands of his saints" (1:14).

Jude's brief epistle ends with one of the most beautiful blessings in all the Bible: "Now unto him that is able to keep you from falling, and to present you faultless before the presence of his glory with exceeding joy, To the only wise God our Saviour, be glory and majesty, dominion and power, both now and ever. Amen" (1:24–25).

The Apocalypse
The Revelation of St. John the Divine

Perhaps the most complicated and difficult book in the entire Bible is this extraordinary revelation attributed to the Evangel John and presumably written by him in old age as he sat in exile on the Greek island of Patmos. The book teems with fantastic allusions and images describing the end of time, the return of Christ to judge the world, the fall of Satan and the New Heaven that will arise in glory. Because of its apocalyptic (end-of-time) message, its stirring phrases and vivid pictures, and perhaps because of its obscurities, Revelation has become a favorite of visionaries and a fundamental document for religious interpretations of the future and of heaven and hell. As such, this one book has served to inspire numerous literary works, preeminent among them Dante's *Divine Comedy* and Milton's *Paradise Lost*, and in many ways it is like the Books of Daniel and Ezekiel in the Old Testament; both similarly deal in sacred visions and dreams.

Devout Christians regard every word and passage of Revelation to be factual and significant. Scholars—no less devout but far more literal—see the work as typical of a literature popular in former times, a literature that disguised religious sentiment with symbol and fantasy, thereby protecting the religious message from the scrutiny of enemies. Because this particular apocalypse was written during a period of terrible persecution against Christians at the hands of the Romans (ca. A.D. 96), it naturally employed subtle wording and codes in true apocalyptic style. The Romans at that time worshiped their emperors as gods and detested both Jews and Christians who defied their beliefs. Christians could await the Second Coming of Christ as their only hope in such peril. Revelation intensified their faith in this coming and made it seem imminent. Besides, this book served to denounce the evils of Roman paganism, to justify suffering and predict eventual triumph for the faithful.

All these sentiments were couched in mysterious words so that only the enlightened could decipher the message. The Romans hardly ever associated the Great Beast and Satan, mentioned in Revelation, with their own godly emperor. Nor would they know that the Lamb of God referred to was Jesus Christ—the alpha and omega, the beginning and end, of all things.

There follows a brief exploration of this intricate book, with emphasis on its more famous images and ideas.

JOHN'S VISION

Revelation begins with Christ himself announcing his presence to John in order "to show unto his servants things which must shortly come to pass . . ." (1:1). Seven churches are greeted. They are represented in various coded ways, as seven stars (2:1), seven golden candlesticks,

Titian pictures John nearly blown off the Greek island of Patmos by the wonder of what he sees and hears in Revelation. Note his symbol, the eagle.

seven spirits and so forth. Indeed, many numbers are used in this book in mystic ways, but seven as the number of Creation is predominant. The most famous reference is "the seven seals" of a wondrous book that is opened in John's vision. In this book, man's fate is sealed and recorded.

The Lamb of God

Chapter 4 launches the central action of Revelation as God throws open a door in heaven and reveals his glorious golden throne. Hosts of angels crowd around him, crying, "Holy, holy, holy, Lord God Almighty . . . ." (4:8)

The sealed book is presented. Only Christ as the Lamb of God (the ultimate sacrifice) is fit and "worthy to open the book, and to loose the seals thereof" (5:2). Christ breaks the first seal and a roar of thunder is heard. Celestial creatures cry out, "Come and see . . ." (6:1), and John beholds the famous four horsemen of the Apocalypse, frightening figures that represent the Conqueror, who brings war; the Bowman, who brings civil strife; the Judge, who brings famine; and finally there comes a "pale horse: and his name that sat on him was Death, and Hell followed with him" (6:8).

These four horsemen are given power over the world to punish the sinner. The Lamb loosens the other seals. At the sixth, a shattering earthquake arises, "and the sun became black . . . and the moon became as blood; And the stars of heaven fell unto the earth . . ." (6:12). It is the "great day of wrath" descended on mankind.

The promise of God's intercession gladdens the author in the face of wrathful tidings. When the seventh seal is cut, a deep "silence" overtakes heaven, and even the angels who crowd the scene cry, "Woe, woe, woe, to the inhabiters of the earth . . ." (8:13).

The Heavenly Woman

Is there no hope for mankind in the Day of Wrath which shall befall the earth? Crushing images of bottomless pits, swarms of locusts, scorpions, darkness and despair fill the text. Chapter 12, however, brings at last a vision of hope: "a woman clothed with the sun, and the moon under her feet . . ." appears. Many scholars accept her as Mary, mother of Jesus. She unites with the archangels to war upon Satan, the archfiend. "And they overcame him by the blood of the Lamb . . ." (12:11). The war between the diabolic hordes of Satan, which include fearsome dragons and horned beasts, and the angelic forces of Christ form the main narrative portion of Revelation, culminating in the ferocious Battle of Armageddon (16:12–16).

The Lamb urges mankind to be steadfast throughout. Evil will be destroyed, he announces. Even the abominable Babylon will fall (in this case, Babylon represents all corrupt and wicked places). The war finally goes in favor of the angels, and the devil is "bound . . . a thousand years, and cast . . . into the bottomless pit" (20:2–3). His enchainment, however, we are warned, is temporary.

Doomsday

In the final judgment, which John details in Chapter 20, Satan will be utterly destroyed and burn forever in "a lake of fire and brimstone" (20:10). Out of all this ter-

Dürer's woodcut of the four Horsemen of the Apocalypse (Revelation 6:1-8) bristles with the symbols of devastation that they represent.

ror and despair "a new heaven and a new earth" (21:1) will emerge. John describes this paradise in glowing terms, equating it with the holy city of Jerusalem. Only this city shall be a "new Jerusalem coming down from God out of heaven, prepared as a bride adorned for her husband . . ." (21:2). In a description of unparalleled beauty and hope, the writer tells how "God himself shall be with them" (those who survive Doomsday and dwell in heaven) "and God shall wipe away all tears from their eyes; and there shall be no more death, neither sorrow, nor crying, neither shall there be any more pain: for the former things are passed away" (21:3–4). Further descriptions of Paradise include its twelve gates of pearl—hence the pearly gates— trees of succulent fruit, waters "clear as crystal" and a celestial sphere of light, wherein "there shall be no night."

Revelation is the final entry in the New Testament, a fitting conclusion to the stirring stories and thoughts related.

We have now explored, as best we could, that epochal work called the Bible. No amount of exploration, of course, can equal reading the original along the lines recommended in the previous pages. Even then a profound and comprehensive appreciation of the Bible, its style, message and thousands of details can take a lifetime of scholarly and devoted work to achieve. But a good beginning is half the journey.

Late in life, Michelangelo returned to the Sistine Chapel in Rome, where he had painted the ceiling with Biblical scenes. Now, he illustrated the Bible's prophecy of Final Judgment on the rounded wall behind the altar. A thundering Christ, shown in detail, commands the whole momentous event, recalling Revelation 22.

A Basic Bible Bibliography

Should you and your family wish further material to study,
the following books are recommended.

Chase, Mary Ellen, *The Bible and the Common Reader.* New York: Macmillan, 1944. An appealing account of the origins, style and characters of the Bible.

Cornfeld, Gaalyah, ed., *Adam to Daniel* and *Daniel to Paul.* New York: The Macmillan Co., 1961. An illustrated guide to the Old and New Testaments in two volumes.

Gottwald, Norman K., *Light to the Nations.* New York: Harper & Row, 1959. An illustrated, basic guide to the Old Testament.

Kee, Howard D., and Young, Franklin W., *Understanding the New Testament.* Englewood Cliffs, N.J.: Prentice-Hall, 1960. A traditional introductory account.

Keller, Werner, *The Bible as History.* New York: Morrow and Co., 1956. A confirmation of the Book of Books.

Neil, William, ed., *The Bible Companion.* New York: McGraw-Hill, 1960. A reference work, illustrated, with contributions by clergymen and scholars.

Nelson Bible Concordance. Nelson, 1900. A basic, alphabetical guide to principal words and names in the Bible, citing passages in which they occur.

Rachleff, Owen S., *Great Bible Stories.* New York: Abradale, 1971. An illustrated treasury of Bible stories.

The Westminster Dictionary of the Bible. London: Westminster, 1944. A time-honored, modern alphabetical guide.

Also, *Harper's Bible Dictionary.* New York: Harper & Bros., 1952.

List of Illustrations

Index

NOTE: Text references are indicated by regular numerals; illustrations are indicated by *italic* numerals. Paintings are indexed by subject, and are also listed by title under the name of the artist. A complete list of illustrations will be found on pages 353–356.

Bethsaida, blind man of, 293. *See also* miracles of Jesus
Beth-shan temple, 135
Bez, *224*
Bible: American Revised Edition (ARE), 19; Apocalyptic books, 241; Apocrypha, 12, 19, 118, 168, 176, 237, 239-53, 258, 284, 338, 346; Authorized Version, *see* King James; chronology in, 14, 144; Coptic, *17*; Coverdale, *18*; cultural importance of, 7-8; English translation, 18; as geological map, 11; King James, *18*, 19, 189; as literature, 26, 34, 39, 75, 107, 131, 175, 177-78, 193, 194, 197, 198, 203, 216; origins of, 12-19; psychology in, 65; repeated stories, *see* in, 48-49; Revised Standard Version (RSV), 19, 166; themes of, 25, 26, 32, 121, 177, 181-83; Tyndale, 18; Vulgate, 14-16; the "writings," 14. *See also* Apocrypha; New Testament; Old Testament
Biblical marriage customs, *see* marriage and marriage customs
Biblical universe, 37, *39*
Bildad, 179
Blake, William (1757-1827): *Creation of Adam, 27*; *Job, 181*
blind man of Bethsaida, 293. *See also* miracles of Jesus
Bloch, Ernest, 203
Boaz, 124-25
Bohun, Humphrey de, 194-*95*
Botticelli, Sandro (c. 1444-1510): *Magnificat, 265*
Brill, Paul (1554-1626): *God Creates the Animals, 24-25*
British Museum, 183
Bruegel, Pieter, the Elder (c. 1525-1569): *The Triumph of Death, 32-33*
burning bush, 83-85, 120; in art, *84, 101*
Byzantine art, *130*

C

Caesar, 292, 298
Caesarea, 328
Caiaphas, 304-5
Cain Slaying Abel (Bertram), 34-*35*
Cairo Museum, 90
Caleb, 100
calendar: Christian, 265-66; Mesopotamian, 36. *See also* time
Calvary, 320. *See also* Crucifixion; Golgotha
Cana, wedding at, 278-*80*. *See also* miracles of Jesus
Canaan and Canaanites, 56, 60, *66, 110, 118*; conquest of, 109-16; crossing into, 100; drought, 70-72; God's promise on, 46-47, 55, 88, 95, *110*; pagan gods in, 54, 117. *See also* Israel; Judea
Capernaum, 284; synagogue, *82, 128, 176, 226, 285*
Carchemich, *111*
Carlyle, Thomas, 176, 177
Castagno, Andrea del (c. 1423-1457): *The Youthful David, 133*
Chaldeans, 228-29, 230. *See also* Babylon and Babylonians
Chamberlain, R. B., 198
Chanukah, 250

charity, 336
Christ, 204, 239; as unicorn, *24, 25. See also* Jesus; Messiah
Christ Feeding the Multitude (Tintoretto), *254-55*
Christianity and Christian Church, 97, 204, 226, 229; basis of, 255, 295; central event of, 317; early history, 321-49; essential philosophy of, 283, 321, 342; Paul's effect on, 323; Roman persecution of, 352, 346. See also *Acts of the Apostles*; Epistles; Jesus; Judeo-Christian heritage; Protestants; Roman Catholic Church
Christmas, 194. *See also* Jesus
Chronicles, 14, 147, 150, 152, 161, 240
Church of All Nations, 320, *322-23*
circumcision, 50, 250, 327, 337; of Jesus, 266, 327
Cleopatra, 240
Clovio, Giulio, 330-*31*
Codex Sinaiticus, 17
Colossians, 339
Commandments, 26, 92, 97
Communion, 301, 335, 336
Connelly, Marc: *Green Pastures*, 39-42
Constantine the Great, 320; arch of, *333*
Constitution of the United States, 97
Copley, John Singleton (1738-1815): *Samuel and Eli, 126-27*
Coptic Bible, *17*
Corinth, 340, 345
Corinthians, 317, 335
Cornelius, 333
Corot, Jean Baptiste Camille (1796-1875): *Destruction of Sodom, 52*
Covenant, *see* Abraham; Ark of the Covenant; God
Coverdale, Miles, 19
Coverdale's Bible, *18*
Cranach, Lucas, the Elder (1472-1553): *The Garden of Eden, 28-29*
Creation, 19, 26-27; in art, *22-23, 24-25, 27*; of human beings, 27-28, 36, 48-49; number of, 348
Crete, 341
Crucifixion, 308-14; in art, *312-13, 315, 316*; site of, 308, 319-20. *See also* Jesus
cunning steward parable, 289
Cyrus (Persia), 162, 163, 213, 233

D

Dagon, 11
Daly, James, *182-83*
Damascus, 213, 323-24
Daniel, 161, 162, 206, 209, 216, 227-37, 239; handwriting on the wall, 232-33; interprets Nebuchadnezzar's dreams, 228-29; late dreams and visions, 235-36; in lions' den, 233-35, *237*, 249; Messianic prophecies, 235, 236, 261; and Susanna, 247, 248-49; under the Persians, 233-36. See also *Daniel, Book of*
Daniel, Book of, 17, 227-37, 345; fiery furnace, *230-31, 234. See also* Daniel
Dante: *Divine Comedy*, 346
Darius the Great (Persia), 162, 163, 164, 228; Daniel and, 233-35
Dartmouth Bible, 198, 257-58

Dartmouth College, 198
daughter of Jairus, 284, 292. *See also* miracles of Jesus
Daumier, Honoré (1808-1879): *Ecce Homo, 308-9*
David, 123, 130-45, 147, 240; Absalom and, *142*, 143-44; ancestor of Jesus, 136-37, 261, 262; anointing of, *129, 130*; in art, *132, 133, 137, 141, 142, 188*; as author of *Psalms*, 141, 143, 144, 190-91, 193; and Bathsheba, 143, 144, 145, 193; death, 145-46; empire of, 141; in Ezekiel's prophecy, 226; friendship with Jonathan, 132-34, 136, 139; God's curse on, 143; as king, 136-41; lament for Saul and Jonathan, 136; marries Abigail, 134; marries Michal, 132, 136; rise of, 132-34; and Saul, 130-31, *132-39*; slays Goliath, 131-32, *133. See also Psalms*
David, Gerard (c. 1460-1523): *The Rest on the Flight into Egypt, 272*
da Vinci, Leonardo (1452-1519), 8; *Last Supper, 302-3*
Day of Atonement, 98
Dead Sea, 47, 51 123, 193
Dead Sea Scrolls, *16*, 17, 214
death, 31-32, 295, 335, 336
Deborah, 117, 118-19, 244
Declaration of Independence, 8
Delacroix, Eugène (1798-1863): *Jacob Wrestling with the Angel, 64*
Delilah, 121, 122
della Francesca, Piero, *see* Piero della Francesca
demons, 243
Derbe, 337
Destruction of Sodom (Corot), 52
Deuteronomy, 79, 102, 103, 104-7, 109, 154, 248-49; image of God in, 26, 104; quoted by Jesus, 278; *Sh'ma*, 107
Diana, 337, *338*
Dinah, 63
Diotrephes, 345
disciples of Jesus, 280, 281; after Jesus' death, 330-35; at Ascension, 318, *320*; at Gethsemane, 301, *304*; on Jesus' identity, 293-94; receive Holy Ghost, 330, *331*; and risen Christ, 318; as shepherds, 292; at Transfiguration, 294, *295*
Divine Comedy (Dante), 346
docetism, 345
Doomsday, 261, 348-50
Dorcas, 335
dove, 38, *39*
dreams: Daniel's, 235-36; Jacob's, 62; Joseph's, 66; Laban's, 65; Nebuchadnezzar's, 228-29, 231; pharoah's, 68-69; Pilate's wife's, 308
Duccio (c. 1255-1318): *The Temptation of Jesus, 279*
Dürer, Albrecht (1491-1528): *Four Horsemen of the Apocalypse*, 348-49; *Jesus' Entry Into Jerusalem, 298*
Dutch art, *61, 101, 148-49, 175, 228. See also* Rembrandt; Rubens; Steen; Uytewael

E

Easter, 317, 321. *See also* Resurrection
Ecce Homo (Daumier), 308-9

Joseph in Egypt (Mann), 75
Joseph and His Brothers (Mann), 75
Joseph Thrown Into the Pit (Murillo), *67*
Joshua, 92, 100, 108-17; in art, *112*; battle of Jericho, 110-13; farewell and death, 116-17; stops sun and moon, 114-*15*; tomb of, *116*; conquest of Canaan, 113-16; crossing the Jordan, 109-10
Josiah, 150, 154
Jotham, 209
Judah, 64, 67, 68, 75; tribe of, 136
Judah, kingdom of, *134*, 150, 225; Babylonian Captivity of, 161; in Isaiah's time, 209-14; in Jeremiah's time, 214-20; restoration, 225. *See also* Hebrew nation; Israel; Jews
Judas Iscariot, 281, 287, 300-301, *302-3*, 304, 305, *306*, 330
Judas Maccabeus, 235, *238-39*, 250
Jude (apostle), 344; Epistle of, 345-46
Judea, 50; as Roman province, 260; Syrian occupation, 235-36. *See also* Canaan; Israel; Judah
Judeo-Christian heritage, 7, 189
Judgment Day, 236, 350-*51*. See also *Revelation*
Judges, 117-23, 125; Deborah, 117, 118-19; Gideon, 117, *119*-21; Jephthah, 117, *121*; list of, 117; Samson, 117, 118, *120*, 121-23, 125; themes, 117, 121
Judith, 118, 243-47; in art, *245*

K

Kadesh, 100, 118
kashruth, 98
Kenyon, Kathleen, 113
Khayyam, Omar, 203
Khirbet Timna, *116*
King James Bible, *18*, *19*, 189
Kingdom of God, 265, 300
Kingdom of Heaven parables, 287
Kings, Book of, 145-50, 152, 158, 183-84, 222; story of Elijah, 150, 154-58; Temple of Solomon, 147-48
Korah, 101-2
kosher, 98

L

Laban, 56, 60, 62-63, 64-65
Lachish, *218*, *219*
Lamb of God, 346, 348
Lamentations, 14, 206, 214, 216, 220; psalms at, 194
Last Supper, 301, *302-3*, *305*; psalms at, 194
Law of Moses, 14, 335, 342; health regulations, 98; the priesthood, 97; retaliation, 97, 283; the tabernacle, 95-97; Ten Commandments, 26, 92, 97
Lazarus (beggar), 289-91
Lazarus (brother of Martha and Mary): raised from the dead, 284, 295, *296-97*, 321. *See also* miracles of Jesus
Leah, 62-63
Lemuel, 198
Leonardo da Vinci, *see* da Vinci, Leonardo
Levi, 64, 65-66, 98, 116; tribe, 81, 342
Leviathan, 180
Leviticus, 79, 98-100, 107, 284
Lippi, Filippino (c. 1457-1504): *Tobias and the Angel*, 242-43

Lippi, Fra Filippo (1406-1469): *Adoration of the Magi*, 269
Lord's Prayer (Paternoster), 283
lost coin parable, 287-88. *See also* parables of Jesus
lost sheep parable, 287-88. *See also* parables of Jesus
Lot, 46, 47, 51, 52-53; wife of, *52*, *53*
Lucas, 337
Luini, Bernardino (1490-1532): *Deliverance of the Israelites*, 90-91
Luke (evangelist), 159, 256, 323, 339; Paul and, 256, 328; Gospel of, 256, 258, 261-66, 270-75
Luther, Martin, 189
Lydia, 335
Lystra, 337

M

Maccabees, 239, 240, 249-53, 258; Jonathan, 250-51; Judas, 250; period of, 249-50; Simon, 251
MacGimsey, Robert, *234*
Machpelah, 55, 57, 60, *75*
MacLeish, Archibald: *J.B.*, *182-83*
Magdalen, the, *see* Mary Magdalene
Magnificat, 262-64, *265*
Malachi, 206, 209
Manasseh, 154, 241
Manasseh-Ephraim, tribe of, 116
Mann, Thomas: *Joseph and His Brothers*, 75
manna, 100
Mantegna, Andrea (1431-1506): *The Ascension*, 320; *The Crucifixion*, 312-13; *Judith and Holofernes*, 244-45
Marcus Aurelius, 203
Marduk, 43, 232
Mark (evangelist), 193, 194, 323; Gospel of, 256, 275
marriage at Cana, 278-80. *See also* miracles of Jesus
marriage and marriage customs, 11, *48*, 56, 62-63, 98, 134, 166; dignity of, 247; in Song of Solomon, 204-5; Paul on, 335
Martha, 295
Martini, Simone (1284-1344): *Christ Carrying the Cross*, 310
martyrs, *336*
Mary (mother of Jesus), *137*, 264, 273, 340, 348; Annunciation to, 262, *263*; at Ascension, *320*; birth of Jesus, 265, 266, *267*, *271*; at Crucifixion, 312-13, *315*; *Magnificat* of, 262-64, *265*; at marriage of Cana, 278-*80*; presentation of Jesus, 270, *274*; visits Elisabeth, 262-64
Mary (sister of Lazarus), 295
Mary Magdalene, 284-87; in art, *286*; church of, 320, *322-23*; at Crucifixion, *310*, 313; and risen Christ, 317-18
Masada, 261
Masolino da Panicale (1383-1447): *The Annunciation*, 262-63
Massey, Raymond, *182-83*
Mattathias, 250
Matthew (evangelist), 187, 193; becomes disciple, 281
Matthew, Gospel according to: date and

focus, 256; in drama and film, *278*, *292*, *305*; Lord's Prayer, 283; material unique to, 258, 266-70; Sermon on the Mount, 281-84
Matthias, 330
Medes, 229, 233, 235. *See also* Persians
medieval art, *188*, *212*, *230*, *279*; Biblical picture book, *44-45*, *119*, *141*; Cain and Abel, *34-35*; Psalters, *12*, *136-37*, *194-95*; Tyndale's Bible, *18*. *See also* names of artists
Meditations (Marcus Aurelius), 203
Megiddo, *118*, *145*, *146*, *147*
Melchizedek, 47, 342
Mendelssohn, Felix, 8; *Elijah* oratorio, 159
Mephibosheth, 139
Merneptah (pharaoh), *80*, 85-90
Merneptah's stele, *81*
Meshach, *228*, 230-31, 233
Mesopotamia and Mesopotamians, 10, 11, 56; art and artifacts, *11*, *37*; calendar, 36; Code of Hammurabi, 11; defined, 42; and the Flood, 37, 38; religion and gods, *11*, 45. *See also* Babylon and Babylonians
Messiah, 207, 226; prophecies, 210, 211, 213, 235, 236, 261. *See also* Jesus
Messiah (Handel), 197, *211*
Methuselah, 36, 115
Micah, 183, 207-8, 209
Michal, 132, 136
Michelangelo (1475-1564), 9; *Conversion of St. Paul*, *325*; *Creation of the Sun, Moon, and Plants*, *22-23*; *Crucifixion of St. Peter*, *334*; *The Flood*, *40-41*; *Isaiah*, *208*; *Jeremiah*, *221*; *Last Judgment*, 350-*51*; *Temptation and Expulsion*, *30-31*; *Zechariah*, *206*
Midian and Midianites, 67-68, 83, *119-20*
Milton, John: *Paradise Lost*, 75, 346
Minor Prophets, 183, 206, 207-9
miracles of Jesus: calms storm, 292; casts out demons, 291, 292; cures blind and dumb, 292, 293; heals epileptic, 294; heals paralytic, *282*; loaves and fishes, 293; Peter's mother-in-law, 280; raises daughter of Jairus, 284, 292; raises Lazarus, 284, 295, *296-97*; raises widow's son, 284; walks on water, 292, *293*
Miriam, 81-83, 90, 100
Moab and Moabites, 102, 123, 213, 220
Mohammed, 12
monotheism, 213
Mordecai, 170-75
Morocco, 86
Moses, 11, 12, 26, 79-107, 113, 116, 147, 191, 240, 291, 330, 333, 342; appears to Jesus, 294, *295*; in art, *90-91*, *96-97*, *98*, *102*, *103*; as author of *Job*, 177; blessing on Israel, 107; and burning bush, 83-85; childhood, 80-83; contest with Egyptian magicians, 85-87; death of, *103*; forty years in the desert, 100-104; Gideon compared to, 120; Law of, 14, 92, 95-97, 98, 205, 283, 335, 342; on Mount Sinai, 92-95, *96-97*; offends God, 102-3; psalm of, 194; tribe of, 98
Moses and Monotheism (Freud), 80-81
Moslems, 49, 57, 321. *See also* Islam
Mount Carmel, *156*, 276
Mount Ebal, 114
Mount Gilboa, 135
Mount Moriah, 55, 150-*51*
Mount Nebo, *103*

Mount of Olives, *138, 301, 306,* 318, 320-21, *322-23*

Mount Sinai (Horeb), 17, *90-93*

Mount Sodom, 51, *52-53*

Mount Zion, 301

Murillo, Bartolomé (1618-1682): *Joseph Thrown Into the Pit, 67*

music and musicians, *132, 159, 190, 191, 202, 240;* based on *Ecclesiastes,* 203; *Magnificat,* 265. *See also* names of composers

mustard seed parable, 287. *See also* parables of Jesus

N

Naboth, 157

Nahor, 56

Nahum, 206, 208-9, 216

Nain, widow of, 284

Naomi, 123-5

Nathan, 143

Nativity, *267. See also* Jesus

Nazareth, 262, 265, 270, 276; Jesus in, 280, 284; modern, *273*

Nebuchadnezzar, 161-62, 163, 167, 217, 220, 222, 244; conquest of Jerusalem, 154, 161, *228;* conversion to God, 231-32; Daniel and, 228-33; dreams, 228-29, 231

Nehemiah, 14, 162, 166-68, 174, 226, 240

Nero, 328, *344*

New Testament, 12, 187, 239, 255-350; *Acts of the Apostles,* 321-35; background of, 255-56; beginning of, 16; dates for, 256; earliest known texts, 17, 255; Epistles, 255-56, 335-49; Gospels, 255-321; *Revelation,* 346-50; Uncial Codices, 17. *See also* Bible; Gospels; Jesus

New York City Ballet, *9*

Nimrod, 42

Nineveh, 206, 207; Jonah and, 183-87; Tobias story, 241-43, 244

Ningal, *45*

Noah, 12, 36-42, 49, 115, 241, 344, 345; ark, 37; character of, 36; children of, 50; symbols of, 38-39

Numbers, 79, 88, 100-104, 107, 109; Balaam's ass, *104-5;* brazen serpent, 104

Nunza, 48

O

Obadiah, 183, 206, 209, 216

"O God Our Help in Ages Past" (Watts), 194

Old Testament, 12, 14-17, 25-237, 342, 343, 344; *Chronicles,* 14, 147, 150, 152, 161, 240; chronology ends, 168; Codex Sinaiticus, 17; *Daniel,* 17, 227-37, 346; *Deuteronomy,* 26, 79, 102, 103, 104-7, 109, 154, 248-49, 278; *Ecclesiastes,* 146, 189, *201,* 202-3, 240; *Exodus,* 11, 79-98, 100, 107, 110, 167, 177; *Ezekiel,* 220-27, 346; *Ezra,* 14, 17, 161, 162, 240; *Genesis,* 19, 25-77, 79, 88, 141, 280, 342; *Isaiah,* 16, 17, 162, 208, 209-14; *Jeremiah,* 17, 162, 214-20; Jesus' knowledge of, 281, 283, 284; *Job,* 14, 162, 176-83, 192, 197; *Jonah,* 183-87; *Joshua,* 108-17; *Judges,* 117-23, 125; *Kings,* 145-50, 152, 158, 183-84, 222; *Lamentations,* 14, 206, 214, 216, 220; *Leviticus, 79,* 98-100, 107, 284; *Numbers, 79,*

88, 100-104, 107, 109; Pentateuch, 14, 97; Prophets, 205-37; *Proverbs,* 189, 197-202, 240; *Psalms, 188,* 189-97, 202; *Ruth,* 123-25; *Samuel,* 125-45; *Scroll of Esther,* 168-76; Septuagint, 14-16, 17, 241; the *Sh'ma,* 104; Song of Solomon, 189, 202, 203-5; written versions, 16-17

Onesimus, 341-42

oral tradition, 14

Original Sin, 31

Orpah, 123

Othniel, 117

P

Palestine, 241, 323. *See also* Israel

Palm Sunday, 297, *298*

parables of Jesus, 285-91; cunning steward, 289; fig tree, 300; foolish rich man, 287; Good Samaritan, 287, 289; of the Kingdom, 287; mustard seed, 287; Pharisee and the publican, 291; Pharisee's table, 287; Prodigal Son, 288, *290;* rich man and Lazarus, 289-91; sower, 287; three lost items, 287-88; wedding feast, 291; wise and foolish virgins, 291

Paradise Lost (Milton), 75, 346

Paradise with Christ (anon.), *12*

Pascal, Blaise, 19

Pasolini, Pier Paolo: *The Gospel According to St. Matthew, 278, 305*

Passover, 164; Elijah's cup, 159; first, 87-88; first in Promised Land, 110; *Haggadah,* 194; Jesus' passion and death on, 297, 300-314; psalms, 194-97

Patmos, 346, *347*

Patriarchs, *see* Abraham; Isaac; Jacob; Moses

Paul, 255, 262, 321-30, 335, 345; arrested, 328, 335; in art, *329;* conversion of, 323-24, *325;* Epistles of, 16, 328, 335-43; European journey, 327-28; on Gentile question, 327; influence on Luke, 256; personality and appearance, 336; role in development of Christianity, 323; as Saul of Tarsus, 323, 330

Pazuzu, 243

Peaceable Kingdom, The (Hicks), *252-53*

Penn, William, 252-53

Pentateuch, 14, 97. See also *Genesis; Exodus; Leviticus; Numbers; Deuteronomy*

Pentecost, 330, *331*

Persepolis, 163, *164-65, 173*

Persia and Persians, 233, 235, 240, 241, 270; Ahasuerus (Xerxes I), 163, 164, 169-76, 240; art and artifacts, 52, *164-65, 169, 173, 187, 222;* Artaxerxes I, 166-67, 169; conquered by Greece, 162; conquest of Babylon, 162, 163, 211, 228, 229; Cyrus, 162, 163, 213, 233; Darius, 162, 163, 164, 228, 233-35; law, 233; rise of, 213

Peter (apostle), 280, *293,* 323, 324; after Jesus' death, 330; converts Cornelius, 333; death, 328, 333-34, 343; denies Jesus, 301, 305; Epistles, 343-44; as first pope, 294; on Gentile question, 327, 331; imprisoned, *332,* 333; mother-in-law, 280; at Transfiguration, 294

Petrarch, 115

Petrie, Flinders, 70, 80

Pharisees, 239, 251, 260, 284, *288;* antagonism to Jesus, 280, 291-92, 293, 294-95, 297; parables about, 287, 291

Philemon, 341-42

Philip (apostle), 281

Philippians, 339

Philistia, 220

Philistines, 11, 116, 128, 131-32, 135, 139-40, 141, 144; capture the Ark, 126; Samson and, 121, 122-23

Piazzetta, Giovanni (1682-1754): *Elijah Taken Up in a Chariot, 158-59*

Piero della Francesca (c. 1420-1492): *Baptism of Christ,* 277; *The Nativity,* 267

Pithom, 80

Plummer, Christopher, *182-83*

Pontius Pilate, 305-6, 307-8, 314-17, 318

Potiphar's wife, 68

Poussin, Nicolas, *147*

Prayer of Manasses, 241

Priscilla, 335

Prodigal Son, *9,* 288, *290*

Promised Land, *see* Canaan; Israel

prophets and prophecy, 150-52, 158-59, 205-37, 283, 300; Amos, 150-52, 206, 207; Daniel, 206, 209, 227-37; dominant messages, 207; Elijah, 8, 150, 154-59, 205, 209, 261-62, 265, 294, *295;* Elisha, 157-58; Ezekiel, 206, 209, 220-27; Ezra, 14, 17, 161, 162, 240; Habakkuk, 209; Haggai, 206, 209; Hosea, 207, 209; Isaiah, 162, 206, 207, 209-14, 227; Jeremiah, 206, 209, 214-20; Joel, 207, 209; Jonah, 186-87, 206, 207; major, 206; Malachi, 206, 209; Micah, 207-8, 209; minor, 183, 206, 207-9; Nahum, 206, 208-9; Obadiah, 206, 209; word, 206; Zechariah, 206, 209; Zephaniah, 209

Protestants, 194, 270

Proverbs, 14, 189, 197-202, 240; authorship of, 198; thematic groupings, 197, 198-202

Psalms, 8, 14, 25, 141, 143, 144, 189-97, 202; angels in, 52; in art, *188, 190, 191, 192, 194-95;* authorship of, 190-91, 193; groupings, 191; individual, 192-97; Jesus foreshadowed in, 192; Jesus quotes, 313; of Moses, 194; as music, 189-90; Shepherd's Song, 193, 194; Praise (Hallel), 194; of Solomon, 241; Song of the Exiles, 162-63, 197; themes of, 191-92

Psalter, *see* Psalms

Ptolemy Philadelphus (Egypt), 14-16

Purim, 168-76

Pyramids of Gizeh, *69, 78*

R

Rachel, 62-63, 64, 65, 118; Tomb of, *66*

Rahab, 110, 111, *118*

rainbow, 38-39

Ramesses II, *80-81,* 83, 90

ram's horn, *111, 129*

Raphael (archangel), 241-43

Raphael (painter) (1483-1520), 8; *Jacob's Dream, 63; The Liberation of St. Peter, 332; The Transfiguration, 295; The Vision of Ezekiel, 223*

Ravenna, Italy: Church of Sant'Apollinare Nuovo, *282, 336;* San Vitale, *84-85*

Rawlinson, Henry, 232

Picture Credits